PRAISE FOR

Agrarian Spirit:
Cultivating Faith, Community, and the Land

"This is an inspiring synthesis of current ecological thought and spiritual reflection in the Christian tradition. . . . Wirzba acknowledges the difficulties in constructing this vision alongside the spotty record of ecological care in Christianity's past, yet he still finds possibilities within the tradition to create a framework that draws on religious meaning and energy to advocate a holistic, responsively ecological way of living."
—*Library Journal*

"There are multiple books on the philosophy and history of American agrarianism, but Norman Wirzba provides—for the first time—a comprehensive 'spirituality' of agrarian consciousness. . . . Wirzba's book comes at the right moment, pointing us to the shared vulnerability—the deep interconnectedness—that is at the same time our plight and our salvation."
—*Current*

"This is an outstanding place to start for both personal and communal work in the redemption of our earthly call to live fully within God's creation and live wholly in our creaturely selves. . . . Wirzba offers this gift to the church as a way for all of us to cast aside an ideology we may not have known we have, one that puts humans in a singular relationship with God and leaves all the rest of His good creation as merely a backdrop."
—*Christian Scholar's Review*

T0339163

"I knew this would be a good book, and it is. In his typical clear style, Norman Wirzba takes complex philosophical arguments, agrarian practical insights, and solid theological teaching and mixes them together in accessible prose to encourage and challenge readers."

—*The Christian Century*

"At its heart, this book is an attempt to prompt readers to think more deeply about themselves as but one creature among many in God's creation and to live more lovingly and gently in creation as a result. . . . Readers will find this a source of inspiration for pursuing a more bountiful way of life among God's other creatures."

—*Reading Religion*

"Our current economic habits reveal a vision of the world in which people and creation are disposable capital, to be caught up in the machinery of production and profit. In *Agrarian Spirit*, Wirzba offers a balm—a restorative perspective that undermines the values of disposability and exploitation."

—*Englewood Review of Books*

"Genuine, theologically nuanced and inviting. . . . Embodying the very dispositions he advocates in the book, Wirzba demonstrates in word and spirit how loving neighbour and place brings one closer to God's loving power, at work in the depths of the world."

—*Scottish Theological Journal*

AGRARIAN SPIRIT

AGRARIAN SPIRIT

CULTIVATING FAITH, COMMUNITY, AND THE LAND

NORMAN WIRZBA

University of Notre Dame Press
Notre Dame, Indiana

Published by the University of Notre Dame Press

Paperback edition published in 2024

Library of Congress Control Number: 2022935746

ISBN: 978-0-268-20309-2 (Hardback)
ISBN: 978-0-268-20310-8 (Paperback)
ISBN: 978-0-268-20311-5 (WebPDF)
ISBN: 978-0-268-20308-5 (Epub)

For Wendell Berry, Wes Jackson, Fred Kirschenmann,

Vandana Shiva, Gene Logsdon (‡), and Ellen Davis

CONTENTS

The God of scripture is an agrarian God. This does not mean that God hates cities or shuns wilderness. Instead, it means that God's reality is constantly revealed in the divine power that creates, sustains, nurtures, liberates, empowers, and heals the world. These are each agrarian ways of being that have as their goal the flourishing of all creaturely life, for it is precisely in each creature realizing its unique potential that God is glorified. What we do not see in scripture is a God who mines, clear-cuts, commodifies, abuses, or abandons creatures. Put another way, the God at work in Israel's history, become incarnate in Jesus, and made abidingly present in the Holy Spirit manifests ways of being that are strikingly at odds with the economic policies and political priorities that define our modern world.

Throughout scripture God is often characterized as a gardener, farmer, shepherd, and carpenter. Of course, none of these characterizations exhaust the depth of God's ways with the world, but what they communicate is that in God's estimation nothing is more fundamental or important than to nurture the life that nurtures us. The knowledge and the skills of nurture, however, which we might also describe as the patient attention that inspires the care of each other, are not easily obtained. They have been eroding for some time as people increasingly, and not through any personal fault of their own, shop and purchase their way through life. The speed and inattention with which many people now move through their days—it is no accident that social scientists refer to our time as the "Great Acceleration"—indicate that it will take considerable intentional effort and communal support to grow the courtesy and cultivate the kindness that genuine nurture requires.

I believe that agrarian traditions have a great deal to teach us about how to live in this world in ways that honor God's desire that creatures flourish and flower. Right from the start, scripture invites human beings to participate in God's gardening ways with the world so as to appreciate life's fragility and splendor, and its vulnerability and virility. This would be a genuinely grounded spirituality in which the work of one's hands joins with the life-creating power of God that is always and already at work in forests and fields and active in bees and sheep. It would be our earthy and embodied participation in God's agrarian Spirit.

There is no shortage of books dealing with spiritual themes and spiritual practices. As I have written *Agrarian Spirit*, my aim has been to highlight the difference that agrarian ways of thinking, feeling, and working make for how several aspects of a spiritual life are conceived and realized. The chapter on prayer, for instance, does not attempt anything like a thorough examination of this central practice. Instead, it reconsiders the action of praying and its goals in light of agrarian sensibilities. Similarly, the chapter on humility shows how agrarian ways of living with plants and animals can help us understand what humility is about and why it matters. The chapter on descent asks how our thinking about mysticism is transformed when our focus is "down and among" rather than "up and away." My hope is that *Agrarian Spirit* will help readers think about spiritual practices in a fresh manner.

Agrarian ways of life have been the norm for most people around the world for at least ten thousand years. This means that people made sense of their lives and calibrated their expectations for what life should be in terms of creaturely realities like birth, germination, photosynthesis, fertility, digestion, illness, and death. At their best, agrarian traditions gave people the instruction and the skills they needed to nurture the land and communities that nurtured them. Moreover, we cannot make sense of Jewish and Christian scriptures if we do not attend to and appreciate the embodied entanglements with soils, waters, plants, animals, and weather that shaped how Jews and Christians thought about themselves and about God. The entanglements are fundamental, and they abide. It cannot be stressed enough that there is no human life apart from them, which is why scripture speaks repeatedly of the human need to care for each other, fellow creatures, and the land.

I believe that an agrarian development of spiritual practices is crucial in this Anthropocene epoch when the dominant economic and political policies of our time are rendering so much of this planet uninhabitable and so many of its (human and nonhuman) creatures expendable. The definitive marker of an agrarian is not being a farmer but being committed to the flourishing of people, fellow creatures, and the land *altogether*. As such, agrarians are also committed to spiritual practices that are at once embodied, social, and economic and are focused on the healing of the earth that God has only and always loved.

ACKNOWLEDGMENTS

This book would not have happened without the support of Stephen Wrinn, director at the University of Notre Dame Press. Steve has been a friend and trusted colleague for nearly twenty years. Over that time he has encouraged good writing and thinking about agrarian themes and has made it his mission to promote excellent books that address the pressing needs of our time. The publishing world is a better place because of his influence. I should also say that this book would have been inconceivable to me apart from the friendship, first of Wendell Berry, and then of the many agrarian writers he introduced me to, most notably Wes Jackson, Vandana Shiva, Fred Kirschenmann, and Gene Logsdon. Ellen Davis became an invaluable companion and colleague shortly thereafter, and I am grateful for her insights and continuing support along the way. Together they have taught me more than I can say. I am grateful for their friendship and wisdom. And special thanks to Nathaniel Lo for preparing the index.

I was raised on a farm in southern Alberta, even made plans to become a farmer myself. Though I was immersed in farm work from an early age, it took my agrarian friends to show me, several years later, that something like agrarian philosophy or agrarian theology is even possible. They have helped me understand why and how agricultural life can be a powerful lens through which to frame and assess life's most important questions. Agrarianism is not a niche topic or occupation that is of concern only to the ever-dwindling number of farmers that remain. It is a *culture* in the full sense of the term because it holds up a comprehensive vision for how people might live responsibly and beautifully in their places and with each other.

PART I

Agrarian Fundamentals

CHAPTER ONE

On Not Losing Creation

Every existing thing is equally upheld in its existence by God's creative love. The friends of God should love him to the point of merging their love into his with regard to all things here below.

—Simone Weil

An agrarian-informed faith hinges on the assumption that this world and its life are sacred gifts of God that are meant to be cherished and celebrated. This sounds straightforward enough until one realizes how many spiritualities have been, and continue to be, premised on the exact opposite assumption. These spiritualities, though sometimes waxing eloquent about the beauties of this world, are fundamentally dualistic or gnostic. What I mean is that they assume materiality and embodiment to be deficient, and thus a lower order of reality that must ultimately be left behind, if not destroyed altogether. It's as if God made a mistake in creating creatures that are finite, fallible, and marked by need. The focus of these spiritualities is the ethereal human soul, and the point of their prescribed spiritual practices is to liberate the soul from places and bodies that are variously described as fleeting, frustrating, or foul. Heavenly bliss can't be here or in this life. It is somewhere else, waiting to be entered after we die.

I believe all of this to be a massive mistake, a catastrophe really, because it despises what should be the unending source of our care, devotion, and delight. To understand why I believe this, it is important to lay out in clear and succinct terms what it means to affirm this world and its life as created by God. Again, one might suppose that all sorts of people affirm a divinely created world. Ask people what they think of when they think of God and they will often say that God is the Creator, the Supreme Being who made it all a long, long time ago. But if you ask what their affirmation means for their thinking about their bodies, neighborhoods, and watersheds, or how this thinking translates into specific economic and political policies, the responses either trail off or become so vague as to be useless. In other words, the idea of creation may have something to say about when or how it all began, but not very much about the practices and policies that order this life here and now. How else should we explain the contradiction in which people affirm God as the Creator while consenting to the destruction of what God creates and daily sustains?

What difference does it make to affirm this world as created by God?

The idea that the places of this life are created by God rests on the conviction that every created thing—ranging from soils, waters, and clouds to earthworms, fish, and people—is loved by God. There isn't a single creature that has to exist or is the source of its own being. That anything exists at all is because God wants it to be. If God did not love for something other than God to be, and then make room for it and nurture it, nothing would exist. As the opening poem on creation in scripture (Genesis 1–2:4) sees it, God loves creatures so much that God, while in the midst of creating them, regularly pauses to note how good and fitting their being is. This is a divine love so arresting and profound that it prompts God to observe the first Sabbath, which is the hallowed time to relish and delight in the beauty, fertility, and fecundity of everything around. On that first Sabbath sunrise, when God looks out onto a freshly made world, what God perceives is God's own love variously made visible, tactile, auditory, fragrant, and nutritious. God's creative activity, we might say, comes to its fulfillment in the Sabbath rest that is so deeply affirmative and joy-inducing that there simply is no other place that God wants to be.

If what I have said of creation is true, then it is crucial that we appreciate that created beings and places are not simply the *focus* or *object* of God's love and attention. They are also, and in ways we do not fully understand, the *material means* and the *embodied expressions* of divine love. In scripture God is often named Emmanuel, God-with-us. Now we can appreciate why. God is forever wanting to be with creatures because they are the embodied sites through which God's love is always already at work in the world. It may be more accurate to say that God is with *and* within us, since that does a better job communicating the intimacy of God's presence in creaturely life. No creature is a random or pointless fluke. No creature has ever been devoid of God's affirming presence. Instead, every creature is precious, a sacred and gracious gift worthy of our respect and cherishing.

This means that material reality is never to be despised or rejected because in doing so one would also be despising the divine love that is constantly animating and circulating through it. Any and all desires that end with this world being destroyed and left behind are fundamentally confused (at best) or dangerously sick (at worst). Any and all hopes that people might finally escape from this created world to be with God somewhere else are misguided because they forget that this created universe is where God is present and where God's love is active. If you want to be with God, don't look up and away to some destination far beyond the blue. Look down and around, because that is where God is at work and where God wants to be. God does not ever flee from creatures. God *abides* with them as a gardener attends to her garden, preparing the conditions for fruitful life and then staying close in the modes of nurture, protection, and celebration. This is why Simone Weil is right to say that the fundamental human task is to train and join our love with the divine love that daily sustains the life of all the creatures of this earth.

It isn't hard to sympathize with the yearning to be with God somewhere else. For too many people, life either is or has been made to be difficult, if not unbearable, by innumerable injustices and forms of abandonment. When this earthly life has been made so miserable, the desire to flee from it makes a lot of sense. Even so, this yearning should be resisted because if God is the Source and Sustenance of *every* place and creature, then God cannot be confined to any circumscribed place, no matter how wonderful or far away. To want to flee from this earth is also to want to flee from where God always, already is. To locate God somewhere else would be to "separate" God from the very realities that God loves and where God is at work. The truly radical theological claim is that the Creator is constantly present to every creature as its animating power, and that what God most wants for each creature is that it realize whatever potential is uniquely its to achieve. As the great Orthodox theologian Maximus the Confessor once put it, "God wills always and in all things to accomplish the mystery of his embodiment."[1] In other words, the eternal desire of God is that each kind of creature realize to the full all the capacities within it that are made possible by God's love. The presence of God, we might say, is not ever somewhere else but is, instead, to be found here and now in the material and spiritual realization of life's abundance.[2]

What I have been describing will come as a huge disappointment to many people committed to a spiritual life. This is because the idea of the soul's escape to a disembodied, ethereal elsewhere is so attractive and compelling. But the idea needs to be resisted. Why? Because embodiment is not the problem. If it were, then the eternal, creating Word of God could not have become flesh and dwelt among us (John 1:14). If every place and every distinct body is the material medium of God's love, and if our bodies are temples of God's animating spirit (1 Corinthians 6:19)—sites through which the love of God can be highlighted and spread—then people should, like God, only ever care for, cherish, and celebrate them. One of the clearest indications that embodiment is not the problem can be found in the Christian affirmation (in Colossians 1:15–20) that "the fullness of God dwelled bodily" in Jesus of Nazareth. Not some fragment or limited degree of God, but the fullness (*pleroma* as the Greek has it) of God. In this pronouncement we discover that there is nothing about embodiment or the materiality of creation that is in itself an obstacle to God's presence. Those who claim that embodiment must be overcome and left behind are guilty of what I call a failure of incarnational nerve.

God's frustration and grief are not with the creaturely condition itself, since, as we have already seen, creatureliness is precisely what God loves and where God's love is made real. Instead, God's anger and sorrow are directed at the forces and ways of being that cause creatures to suffer, hunger, or be violated. Injustice, abuse, and neglect are condemned by God precisely because they represent assaults on the integrity and sanctity of the created bodies God loves. As Jesus's own resurrected life and his bodily ascension reveal, life with God—what often goes under the name of life in heaven—is not closed to embodiment. It is closed only to the destructive ways of being that do bodies harm. In other words, heaven is closed to sin, but it is not closed to embodiment.

This is why it makes little sense to think that heaven is attained by getting to a location somewhere far away. To be in heaven is to be in the places that God loves and to experience God's love as the only power inspiring and animating the bodies that are there. The aim of a spiritual life, therefore, must always be on refining and making real *in this world* the divine love that creates, nurtures, and beautifies embodied life. In a stunning passage that should put a stop to all versions of otherworldly flight, scripture ends with God *descending* to be with creatures in their healed habitats and communities. God's desire is not to be apart from creatures but to be *with* them and to make a divine home *among* mortals (Revelation 21:3). People are fooling themselves (and others) if they think they can enter heaven apart from the exercise of love, because apart from spiritual transformation they will simply take to a new location the destructive habits and practices that do so much harm here. Put another way, heaven is not about one's *transportation* to another realm. It is, instead, about the *transformation* of this life so that God's love is everywhere incarnate and active. Love alone assures that a place created as paradise is not turned into another hell on earth.

The divine love that creates, sustains, and heals creaturely life is not sentimental or naive. In large part this is because God's love is not coercive or constraining. From the start, God gives to creatures the freedom to become themselves. No creature is simply the passive recipient of its life: it also plays an active role in the furtherance of its own life and the life all around it. As the Genesis creation poem puts it, God creates a vibrant world in which creatures bring forth new life and explore possibilities that have not yet been realized. In this dynamic world, fertility and fecundity are clear results and are evidenced in the beauty of the diversity of life forms that populate Earth. But so too are suffering and pain, as creaturely freedoms and finitudes collide. Being with others, even in the best of circumstances, often results in frustration and harm. This is why love's work is work that calls for the disciplines of attention, patience, repentance, gentleness, humility, and mercy. The crucial effort is the sympathetic one that comes alongside fellow creatures and is committed to places in modalities of respect and care. Knowing how often the intention to care brings about harm, confession of wrongdoing is love's steadfast accompaniment.

We live in a world much abused and deeply wounded by us. It has, to use the words of the apostle Paul (in Romans 8), been subjected to futility owing to human waywardness and the refusal by people to live into their creaturely condition. As a result, the whole of creation is waiting for the true followers of God to come forth and live in ways that promote creaturely freedom and flourishing. This is what agrarian faith is fundamentally about. The "spirituality" that I develop in this book is not ethereal, otherworldly, or disembodied. Instead, it is fully incarnate and deeply rooted in the being of soils and neighborhoods, and the lives of chickens and children. It focuses on and develops the embodied, communal, and economic practices that draw us more intimately into life with others and, in doing that, also more practically into life with God.

As I develop what agrarian faith looks like, it is important to note that theologians have traditionally distinguished between two expressions of faith: *fides qua* and *fides quae*. The former refers to the habits and practices—what some writers refer to as "spiritual exercises"—that cultivate trust in and love of God: the *ways* of faith.[3] The latter refers to the beliefs and doctrines that help people organize their thinking about God: the *teachings* of the faith. These two should be viewed as mutually illuminating, rather than as in conflict with each other. Even so, in this book my focus will be primarily on the practices and dispositions that people should cultivate to participate in God's gardening and farming ways with the world. My hope is that, as I foreground several spiritual exercises and then develop them in an agrarian way, fresh insight into the life of God and this world may emerge, and people will be better positioned to witness to and participate in the love of God circulating through all of it.

If God is the primordial and essential Agrarian—the One who creates and sustains the world by planting, gardening, farming, and shepherding life—and if a spiritual practice refers to a person's growing (yet always imperfect) participation in God's ways of being with creatures, then the cultivation of distinctly agrarian spiritual exercises becomes a matter of the greatest social, practical, and theological significance.

CHAPTER TWO

Why Agrarian?

The demographic trends of the last several decades suggest that a book *Agrarian Spirit* is out of step with the times. Urbanization is now a global phenomenon, with the dawn of the twenty-first century marking the first time when more people live in cities than live in rural or "wild" places. The pace and extent of urban development have grown dramatically as farmers and peasants, many of them facing hostile economic and political forces, leave climate-stressed and violence-stricken lands in search of shelter, employment, and subsistence. The cities that receive them often lack the infrastructure—the housing, education, medical, and support services—necessary to provide for their needs. By the year 2050 it is expected that more than two-thirds of all people will live in cities, with several of these residing in high-density megacities with populations in the tens of millions. Of these residents, one in three will live in slums. By contrast, in the year 1800 less than 10 percent of people across the globe lived in urban centers.[1]

There is considerable debate about how best to contrast an urban versus a rural environment, with scholars contesting the definitions and characteristics of each. What is clear, however, is that the movement from country to city entails much more than a change in location. More fundamental are the changes in sensibilities and responsibilities that often accompany relocation and that affect how people think and feel about their world and their place within it. Never before have so many people lived in ways that require little or no understanding of their embodied dependence on the land, its waters and weather, and all the diverse microbial, plant, and animal life they support. Can people care for and protect what they know little about?

For millennia, hunters, fishers, foragers, peasants, and farmers have worked out their lives in terms of what soils, watersheds, plants, animals, and weather made possible. To survive, let alone to live well, the vast majority of people needed to hone their sympathies and calibrate their desires to the habits and fertility cycles of animals, the germination, growth, and maturation of plants, the seasons of the year, and the movements of water. To do that, they needed to study what their places and fellow creatures allowed and then develop the practical skills to work within ecologically determined limits and possibilities. They didn't always do it well, but sometimes they succeeded in developing the economies that did not violate or compromise the ecological contexts on which every economy depends.

By contrast, today's urban dwellers are mostly insulated from these considerations as increasingly vast infrastructures composed of warehouses, distribution centers, stores, pipelines, electricity grids, transportation networks, service providers, and the World Wide Web deliver the materials, food, and energy they need to live. In the most developed countries, the majority of people spend roughly 90 percent of their time indoors, working, sleeping, playing, eating, exercising, and learning in climate- and light-controlled buildings. For a growing number of people, dependence on the land has been eclipsed by dependence on the Internet, while the skills of tracking, growing, harvesting, building, and repairing have been replaced by shopping. To appreciate the nature of our changed circumstances, consider that in the past people spent the bulk of their working days sourcing and storing up food and energy for their community's needs, whereas in today's fast-food economies people can feed themselves in a matter of minutes and with little more effort than it takes to swipe a credit card or turn on a microwave oven.

My point is not to condemn urban life or shopping as inherently or necessarily harmful. It is, instead, to highlight that as a species we have embarked on an unprecedented experiment in which the future flourishing of multispecies life is at stake. The experiment, framed as a question, is this: Given the tremendous life- and earth-altering powers now at our disposal, will people deploy these powers to enhance the shared vitality of lands and creatures if they have lost sympathetic and practical touch with the ecological realities (and limits) that make their living possible? The question is especially urgent when we recognize that we now live in an Anthropocene world where the future of earth and life systems will be determined by the technological reach and economic priorities that citizens choose or condone. The track record of the past several decades of industrial development is not encouraging.

If it is fair to assume that people tend to care *for* what they care *about*, then it becomes all the more important that we attend to the conditions that foster honest awareness and genuine insight regarding the requirements of a decent and sustainable life. Information isn't enough. What is needed is a felt, sympathetic, and practical connection with the liveliness of a place—what we might also describe as the birthing and nurturing potential of a place—a connection intimate enough that one becomes attuned to its vitality and possibilities, but also its fragility and limits. What would it take for people to be so in touch with their places that they feel in their bodies the struggle and suffering, but also the strength and vitality, of the creatures they are with? As people understand the factors that promote soil fertility, for instance, things like cover-cropping and the application of plant and animal manures, they can become advocates for regenerative forms of agriculture that heal eroded or denuded lands and that produce nutritious food at the same time. As people see the social and ecological effects of mountaintop removal (MTR) mining, and also understand why this has become the preferred method of coal extraction, they can then put themselves in a position to support renewable, community-building forms of electricity production. As people appreciate how vital, vulnerable, and precious fresh water is, they can become defenders of glaciers, streams, and aquifers, and advocates for clean, available, and affordable water in rural and urban communities alike.

From an agrarian point of view, there is clearly an aesthetic dimension to deeper and more intimate connections with the places and creatures that nurture us. If people aim to reverse the degrading and destroying trajectories of the past, then it will be important for them to develop hospitable ways of being that create the time and space for the goodness and beauty of this world to appear. This is a slow and patience-requiring process. The future of a healthy and vibrant world depends on people seeing, hearing, smelling, touching, and tasting fields, forests, waterways, and fellow creatures *as gracious gifts* and not merely as units of production or consumption. This possibility rests, for instance, on people coming into the presence of soil and discerning its mysterious and miraculous generative powers, listening to birdsong and hearing invitations to relationship, catching the fragrance of a forest and sensing the myriad forms of relationships and life pulsing through it, feeling the flow of fresh water over one's hand and delighting in its cleansing, slaking, cooling, playful, and restorative possibilities, and savoring a bowl of vanilla custard and fresh raspberries on a summer afternoon and finding there one of the most satisfying expressions of God's desire that creatures be happy (and not merely fed).

An adequate aesthetic, however, is rooted in kinesthetic experience as people work to satisfy their needs for energy, shelter, beauty, food, and building materials. Embodied engagement, along with the training and skill development such engagement entails, is crucial because it is through sustained working and living with creatures that one's perceptive capacities are corrected and sharpened, one's sympathies inspired, and one's responsibilities better directed. To grow a thriving neighborhood, for instance, one has to understand its history, know its infrastructure and how it works (or doesn't), listen to its residents, participate in its life, discern why some policy recommendations might work, and then commit to sticking around so that mistakes can be corrected and successes celebrated. A great way to do that is to come alongside neighbors and share in the physical labor of building homes, parks, and business opportunities. To prepare a delicious meal you need quality ingredients and thus also an understanding of the many elements—healthy soil, clean water, contented animals, good agricultural work and food processing, and appropriate distribution networks—that facilitate quality all along the way. A great way to do that is to grow and cook some of your own food or participate in community gardening projects.

By foregrounding the importance of a working relationship with a place I do not mean to recommend yet one more back-to-the-land movement. To argue for an agrarian position is not to argue for a reverse migration from cities to the countryside, nor is it to long for a bygone age in which the majority of people were farmers. For a variety of reasons, such recommendations are ill advised and practically unworkable because (a) there isn't enough land for every person to farm; (b) not enough people possess the intelligence, skill, and sympathy to farm in ways that honor the land and the creatures that live from it; and (c) the history of agricultural communities is saturated with abuse, slavery, racism, xenophobia, sexism, and neglect. An authentic agrarian position cannot be rooted in "nostalgia."[2] There is too much bad farming and too much injustice in that past. It must instead look to the past as a source of instruction and insight as people work to correct the mistakes and abuses it contains and then join with current scientists, ecologists, and practitioners to develop regenerative farming and energy systems that can be viable for millennia to come. The realization of an authentic agrarianism is a prospect that lies before us rather than behind us.

Given agriculture's often beleaguered history, and given the destructive effects of many of today's conventional agricultural methods, it is also important that we not equate agrarianism with farming. To advocate for an agrarian position one does not need to be a full-time farmer. What is necessary is that one be committed to the practices and policies that promote the health and vitality of lands, creatures, and people *altogether*. Practically speaking, that means supporting—financially with one's shopping priorities, and politically with one's voice and votes—the farming communities that do good work.

For too much of human history people have pursued paths of Development, Progress, and Glory that were at the expense of soil fertility, clean water, species diversity, animal contentment, worker protections, and community vitality. Economies have been devised that not only *occlude* the ecological contexts upon which they depend but work *against* them, and thereby have facilitated the creation of a planet that in many of its regions is becoming uninhabitable for people and fellow creatures alike. Political priorities that *exploit* and then *abandon* the communities that sustain (potentially) convivial life have dominated too many of our societies. If our hope is to live long and beneficially in the land, then our highest priority must be to cultivate the personal sympathies, foster the practical skills, and commit to the economic and political policies that nurture the world that nurtures us.

Given today's global social and ecological realities, the pertinent marker of whether a person is an agrarian is not whether he or she lives in the country or the city. This is because plenty of people living in rural regions cannot grow a tomato or fix their own homes, while many others living in cities grow a great variety of fruits and vegetables, are engaged in energy infrastructure projects, and are dedicated to building just workplaces and thriving neighborhoods. Agrarians are distinguished by their commitment to work for the well-being of their places and communities, and they do this by developing the practical skills that cultivate the material and social goods—things like fertile soil, clean water, abundant green spaces, nutritious food, genuine health care, safe neighborhoods, beautiful homes, child and family support, youth empowerment, inclusion and honoring of the elderly, and worthwhile work—that promote a thriving world. To be an agrarian is to do the work that nourishes life in its many material, physiological, environmental, social, and cultural dimensions. It is to know and act upon the fundamental truth that people are *landed* beings and so cannot possibly thrive apart from the thriving of the land and its many creatures.

CULTIVATING MATERIAL INTELLIGENCE

Agrarian ways of thinking grow out of agrarian ways of being. In other words, something like an agrarian philosophy is rooted in the cultivation of the practical skills—like animal husbandry, home construction and repair, education and empowerment of people, plant production, and neighborly support—that generate the insights and sympathies that make an agrarian position compelling, even indispensable. Agrarian work is primary because it inspires, directs, and disciplines whatever thinking accompanies it. Agrarian work is fundamental because it puts people in touch with what we might call the matter-of-fact nature of geo-biological realities—most basically, the dietary and health requirements of plant and animal bodies, but also the many ecosystem processes that support both—that people simply need to know and respect if they are to live well wherever they are. In the performances of growing, making, gathering, and repairing, people acquire what Glenn Adamson has called the "material intelligence" that agrarians find crucial to their position. By *material intelligence* Adamson means "a deep understanding of the material world around us, an ability to read that environment, and the know-how required to give it new form."[3] This form of intelligence has been eroded as people are increasingly encouraged to *view* their world on screens and shelves and so are in danger of losing a tactile, fully sensuous, and practiced connection with the world that makes their living possible.

To appreciate what material intelligence is, consider a slice of apple pie. What is it? A delicious and nutritious item of food, to be sure. But it is also so much more if you are a baker or grow an apple orchard. As a baker you know that a pie crust is a work of art in which butter, flour, and water, when folded together properly (keeping the butter cold), create the flakiness eaters love. Too much hand manipulation ruins the crust, making it doughy and tough. You also know that not all apples are the same. Which variety should you use, and how should you slice, spice, and prepare them? Of course, multiple excellent pie recipes will yield a delicious dessert (or main course!), but what an expert pie maker is able to do is work with the ingredients at hand, sense what is possible in them, and then craft accordingly. Good bakers know that they must make themselves the students of the ingredients and baking processes they use because apart from this complex intelligence they will not succeed.

If we turn to the apples themselves, we discover that there are endless varieties of apples to choose from (though grocery stores have consistently promoted only a small fraction of these). These apples don't just grow anywhere or automatically. Some are adapted to specific regions and weather patterns, whereas others are the result of selective breeding that encourages specific qualities of fleshy texture or taste.

Orchardists know there is no guarantee that there will be an apple crop each year. A late frost or some form of blight can easily doom a year's harvest. This is why they are constantly alert and responsive to changing ecological and meteorological systems. They *understand* that apples are ultimately gifts to be received rather than products to be controlled. They *know* that their most important work is to cooperate with geo-bio-chemical processes going on around them. Like bakers who appreciate the potential of the ingredients they use, orchardists understand the potential of a place and its trees and, through an effort that is best described as an improvisational dance, grow the apples that define a delicious pie.

Of course, eaters of the pie do not have to know all these things to still enjoy it. But their enjoyment and their understanding are undoubtedly deepened by the work of baking and growing. Moreover, their sympathies (for bakers and baking processes, for growers and growing processes) are enlarged because they appreciate the vulnerability and noninevitability of a piece of pie. By having a more complex and nuanced understanding of what an apple pie is and how it comes to be, they might come to the stunning realization that the world has the potential to taste really good when the potential latent within human skill is applied to the flavor potential embedded within plants. The crucial insight, however, is that without the skills of baking and growing, the delectable character of this world remains hidden.

Using Adamson's definition, we can now see how practical skill makes it possible for people to "read" their world in fresh ways. To read is much more than to register that there are marks on a page. It is to understand that the marks are words that communicate meaning and significance. When people lose material intelligence, they move through the world oblivious to where they are and who they are with. Places, creatures, and objects are clearly present, but they remain mute and indecipherable, carrying only surface significance because people have not engaged with them so as to discover their potential and limits. Imagine encountering an apple tree but not knowing that you can eat its apples or give them new forms by making applesauce, apple juice, and hard cider, or baking apple pies, cakes, squares, and strudels. How many of the world's flavors, beauties, and uses remain hidden because people have not developed the sympathies and skills that open its potential?[4] Reading the world with understanding, much like reading words on a page, is a skill that has to be learned. It takes instruction and practice to get to the point where the words take the reader beyond the page into worlds that can be explored and enjoyed. To see the difference, one can well envision a person reading the marks "I love you!" and remaining unmoved. The person doesn't understand how these "letters" open a relation and invite a response. Is it possible that we are each moving through a communicative, meaning-generating world but don't know how to read and respond to it appropriately?[5]

The practical skills that make possible the material intelligence I have in mind have the effect of positioning people in their places and communities in new ways. Skilled engagement makes it possible for people to be more than tourists simply moving *through* places; it situates them *within* places and *alongside* the paths of life that are operating there. Physical work attentively and thoughtfully done puts people in contact with the beauty of this world. That beauty is not to be confused with how people wish things were; rather, it is the beauty of how the world has been created and is continuously loved by God. It is, at times, a hard beauty because it puts people in touch with realities that can wound them, and with a world that is not tailored in all its aspects to making them happy. As Simone Weil understood so well, it takes the discipline of love for beauty of this sort to emerge: "He who is aching in every limb, worn out by the effort of a day of work, that is to say a day when he has been subject to matter, bears the reality of the universe in his flesh like a thorn. The difficulty for him is to look and to love. If he succeeds, he loves the Real."[6] The great danger is to mistake places and creatures for what one wants them to be rather than for what they in fact are. In the process, their God-givenness remains hidden, which is to say the truth of their being. To cultivate material intelligence, what people most need to do is learn to love precisely this world rather than some other, this world with all its frustrations, imperfections, and limits, but also its pleasures, beauties, and never-to-be-repeated incarnations of grace. Manual work is an indispensable apprenticeship in which this sort of love grows.

The work of making, growing, gathering, or repairing is mischaracterized if we think it is a person's imposition of an idea upon the surrounding world. This way of speaking is an (often destructive) mistake because it assumes that people stand apart from or outside of the world that they engage. Human embodiment, especially as revealed in our need to drink, eat, breathe, shelter ourselves, and be creative, teaches that we are always already stitched within places and communities of life and thus grow out of them (more on this in the next chapter). As Tim Ingold correctly notes, making is not reducible to something we do to the world. It is, instead, our growing within a world that is itself constantly growing and developing fresh expressions of life. In an important sense, what we *are* is a world growing in and through us. The question is whether we will in our creative activities learn to appreciate, respect, and honor—and take up a humble role within—the world's transformation of itself.[7]

The activities of making and growing change the world, but they also change us because in the work itself two "openings" occur. First, to participate creatively and sympathetically in the world's transformation of itself opens people to what I call the grace and sanctity of creaturely life. Making a meal or building a garden shed draws people into a deeper appreciation of the vulnerability and the wonder of the creatures and things they use. A bowl of salsa isn't simply a product but a delicious combination of tomatoes, onions, peppers, and spices that (potentially) draws people into the miracles of plant germination, photosynthesis, pollination, and decomposition, just as a 2x4 isn't reducible to a piece of lumber but is a beautiful, useful, material manifestation of a tree that is a member of a forest community that digests carbon, produces oxygen, stabilizes the ground, produces microclimates, and is home to countless creatures large and small. Moreover, salsa and garden sheds are (potentially) repositories and material sites that carry the memories of the skill, devotion, struggle, and care that went into their making or coming-to-be.

When people make things, they invest their attention and care in the thing made. They join their love to the divine love that creates and daily sustains a world that is good, beautiful, fragrant, pleasing, and delicious in so many of its manifestations, and so communicate that this world and its creatures and things are worthy of our cherishing. The importance of this insight should not be underestimated, particularly when we recognize how our world is awash with things we find unsatisfying, ugly, and useless. Would we need to buy so much if the things we had were held as precious because they embodied the skill and love that well-made things communicate? Would we so easily throw things away if we knew them to be the effects of another's, and thus also our own, cherishing and devotion?

Second, practices of making open people to a much more expansive understanding of themselves as they discover more precisely how their living grows out of places and communities and realize that their being is a manifestation of the world growing *through* them. When people engage their neighborhoods and communities in a skillful and knowledgeable manner, they are more likely to discern how their living is made possible by the gifts and the generosity of others. They begin to see in a detailed way the myriad number of blessings that daily come their way in the forms of nurture, inspiration, and love and to recognize that this world is a place where they don't simply reside but *belong*. Put another way, the exercises of nurture and making enable people to know and feel themselves as social, ecological, and sacred beings that both depend on others and can, in turn, be a benefit to others. Agrarian work draws people into their places so they can perceive more clearly how this world is populated by creatures and maintained by processes that, when sympathetically engaged, can build and maintain a pleasing home. It helps people understand that the idea of a life alone is a contradiction in terms and that the diverse forms of loneliness are a derelict condition. All people are sacred beings because they are, quite literally, the outgrowth of divine powers moving through soils, waters, raspberries, bees, chickens, farmers, gardeners, cooks, builders, and friends.

ON DESPISING AGRARIAN WORK

In highlighting the centrality of work to an agrarian position, a problem of great significance emerges almost immediately. Many aspects of agrarian work have been shunned and despised from the beginning. This, in part, is because the care of plants, animals, fields, and homeplaces is exacting, difficult, and unrelenting work. Anyone who has tried to grow a garden knows what I am talking about. Though one might prepare a bed properly, there is no guarantee that the seed will germinate or that, if it does, disease, drought, or some predator will not deprive that gardener of his or her desired flowers or fruit. Moreover, in committing to gardening work, gardeners must learn to face their own ignorance in the face of the soil's and a plant's many needs, their impotence in the face of processes of life and death that cannot be controlled, and their impatience with life cycles and weather patterns that cannot be sped up/slowed down or mastered. The care of plants forces people to realize that plants follow botanical laws and vulnerabilities that cannot be negotiated or wished away. If animals are added to the mix, the daily demands of feeding, watering, and general maintenance are enough to ensure that one is forever "tied down," if not perpetually overwhelmed, by the many requirements of proper care. To be an agrarian is to have one's mind and imagination densely populated by other creatures. It is to unseat oneself as the center or focus of the universe. This can be a lovely thing, since it enables people to feel the kinship of life. But it can also be a burden, especially if the circumstances of one's work are not properly supported and valued.

The histories of food and energy production indicate that agrarian work has rarely been valued or properly compensated. More often than not, agrarian people have done their work in contexts of oppression and exploitation, thereby making inherently difficult work all the more toilsome. The experience of smallholders and migrant agricultural workers today indicates that this situation has not changed. Rather than being geared toward the cultivation of thriving habitats and communities, farm work has been made subservient to the financial gain of an often very small group of powerful (and more recently corporate) elites. The bulk of the wealth agrarian work generates has most often gone to (off-site) land owners, financiers, input providers, marketers, and processors rather than the growers themselves.

If we turn to some of the earliest expressions of permanent human settlement, the time when (some) people committed to the domestication of plants and animals, it is clear that state control of agricultural work developed right alongside it. In *Against the Grain* James C. Scott describes this state of affairs as follows:

Evidence for the extensive use of unfree labor—war captives, indentured servitude, temple slavery, slave markets, forced resettlement in labor colonies, convict labor, and communal slavery (for example, Sparta's helots)—is overwhelming. Unfree labor was particularly important in building city walls and roads, digging canals, mining, quarrying, logging, monumental construction, wool textile weaving, and of course agricultural labor. The attention to "husbanding" the subject population, including women, as a form of wealth, like livestock, in which fertility and high rates of reproduction were encouraged, is apparent. The ancient world clearly shared Aristotle's judgment that the slave was, like a plough animal, a "tool for work."[8]

"Urban" elites—political, religious, economic, and military leaders—had little patience or respect for the forms of work that sustain a community's daily life. Care of land and creatures consistently took a back seat to wealth generation and the accumulation of power (for some). In contexts like these, land ceases to register as a site of grace and a source of creaturely livelihood. It becomes territory instead, an instrument of power, and is useful to the extent that tax revenues and units of production can be extracted from it.

The ancient pattern here briefly described would unfold in numerous variations across the globe. Smallholders and agricultural workers have rarely been able to perform their work in peace and freedom, or in economic and political contexts that protected and rewarded their labors. Coercion and exploitation have, most often, been the governing rule. When we turn to the birth of a modern world, signs of improvement are hard to find. In his erudite history of the development of cotton production and its role in creating modern, mercantile economies, Sven Beckert demonstrates that violence against land and landed peoples was an essential ingredient, which is why he argues that "war capitalism" more honestly describes the economy that birthed modernity.

War capitalism relied on the capacity of rich and powerful Europeans to divide the world into an "inside" and an "outside." The "inside" encompassed the laws, institutions, and customs of the mother country, where state-enforced order ruled. The "outside," by contrast, was characterized by imperial domination, the expropriation of vast territories, decimation of indigenous peoples, theft of their resources, enslavement, and the domination of vast tracts of land by private capitalists with little effective oversight by distant European states. In these imperial dependencies . . . violence defied the law, and bold physical coercion by private actors remade markets.[9]

It would be difficult to overestimate how world-altering this violent approach to land and people was and, in many instances, continues to be. In this approach love is hard to find, which means that the agents of this economic order have lost touch with the Real World as created and loved by God. Rather than being God's creation, the places we now inhabit reflect an Anthropocene world, which is to say a world that is becoming increasingly uninhabitable for people and fellow creatures alike as places and processes are being remade to serve the interests of wealth and convenience (for some).

In addition to drawing a line between an inside/outside world, war capitalism eventually also produced a line between black and white people. As W. E. B. Du Bois famously put it, the economy of the modern world depended on the European invention of a "color line" in which everything "great, good, efficient, fair, and honorable is 'white'; everything mean, bad, blundering, cheating, and dishonorable is 'yellow'; a bad taste is 'brown'; and the devil is 'black.'"[10] From a historical point of view, we know the establishment of this "color line" took some time to develop. In addition to slaves from West Africa, poor, landless, or incarcerated white Europeans—sometimes referred to as the "manure" that would fertilize new lands—were conscripted and coerced to perform the backbreaking work of clearing and "improving" newly "discovered" land for wealthy owners.[11] But it did not take long for a fault line to emerge in which even poor whites could distinguish themselves from, and claim superiority over, black and indigenous people. The net effect of the color line was not only to establish a social and political hierarchy of being but also to enforce an

economic order in which "whiteness is the ownership of the earth forever and ever. Amen."[12]

Du Bois made his observation about unjust white land ownership
and control in the 1920s. The decades before and after reveal a systematic effort by whites to deprive African American farmers of their land,
beginning with the violent effort by southern whites to strip former
slaves of the land promised to them after Emancipation, and the systemic withholding of crop earnings owed to tenants and sharecroppers
for their labor. Consider that by the end of the twentieth century black
farm ownership declined by 98 percent. Various government agencies
like the United States Department of Agriculture (USDA) and the
Farm Service Agency (FSA) were deeply racist and developed numerous strategies to strip black farmers of their land or deprive them of the
financial and technical support regularly offered to white farmers: perpetual delays in the processing of loan applications; trick contracts that
stole farms from illiterate black farmers; local appeals committees
stacked by white men; refusal of loans to do the necessary capital im-
provements (from 1984 to 1985, of the nearly 16,000 USDA loans
given to farmers, only 209 went to black farmers); underfunded black
land-grant schools and experiment stations; and the issuance of loans
that were clearly unpayable and that caused the forfeiture of property.
These discriminatory practices, of course, were built upon a history in
which land was made cheaply available to white settlers, thus creating
the enormous wealth gap that still plagues African American families
and communities today. As Pete Daniel summarizes it, "By the end of
the Eisenhower administration, the rural table had been set to serve the
white male elite and to remove farmers deemed small and inefficient,
including an initiative to remove as many remaining Black farmers as
possible. . . . Discrimination had become regularized to the extent that
it no longer registered as remarkable."[13]

As briefly described here, the abuse and desecration of land and
landed people, and the despising of agrarian work are violations that
directly contravene God's desire that people learn the affections and
skills that nurture the earth and its creatures (Genesis 2:15). By refusing
to care for their places and communities, people also refuse to participate in God's gardening ways with the world and thus deprive them-

selves and fellow creatures of experiencing the Sabbath delight that marks God's own enjoyment of a world beautifully and wonderfully made. The care of earth and each other is humanity's fundamental and abiding vocation. There is no more important work. Its achievement is the basis and foundation upon which all other effort depends and grows. People cannot build a lasting and hospitable home in a toxic landfill or in social contexts saturated with injustice, they cannot do good work if their bodies are sickly from improper nourishment and inadequate exercise, nor can they enjoy good food, clean water and air, and a convivial life if they lack the material intelligence that draws them more intimately and sympathetically into life with others.

To imagine and build a world in which land, fellow creatures, and all people can thrive, the insights of agrarian traditions of work are indispensable. Again, my intent is not to lift up all farming practices, since we know that so many of these have been and continue to be destructive. Moving forward, it will, therefore, be especially important to learn from indigenous and agrarian people who have experienced and resisted the violating practices of the past. It is precisely those "whose dreams of freedom have been denied, delayed, and derailed by structurally racist policies," and who are "spearheading efforts to combat food apartheid, poverty, and poor health," that can teach us the most because they have felt in their bodies and hearts the practices that are life-promoting and those that are not. "Farming is the past, and it is also the future: the key to sustenance and reproduction in the city and the countryside. . . . Our job is to sow the seeds and prepare a place for the ones who will inherit the world. It is time for a collective reimagining that pairs ancestral knowledge with twenty-first century skills and that places Black and other oppressed people at the helm of new ways forward."[14]

In *Freedom Farmers: Agricultural Resistance and the Black Freedom Movement*, historian Monica White chronicles the efforts of Black agrarians—most famously Fannie Lou Hamer, Booker T. Washington, George Washington Carver, and W. E. B. Du Bois—and shows how their initiatives can be an inspiration to agrarian work in the future. What distinguished their effort, among many things, was their commitment to cultivating free people in resilient communities on healthy land in hostile economic contexts. Among their many inventions, like the first models for what today is known as Community Supported Agriculture (CSA), these black agrarian leaders focused on community development as a strategy of resistance. White summarizes their efforts this way:

> In response to extreme conditions of financial, social, and political oppression, black farmers created agricultural cooperatives as a space and place to practice freedom. While their experience with white politicians, landowners, and merchants left them feeling dependent, vulnerable, exploited, and fearful for their very lives, their cooperatives enacted strategies of prefigurative politics, economic autonomy, and commons as praxis. They demonstrated collective agency and community resilience (CACR) in working toward and practicing freedom—freedom to participate in the political process, to engage in an economic model that was cooperative and fair, and to exchange ideas with others who shared their goals. These organizations offered the space to be innovative and practice a liberated community built upon principles of cooperative living and self-sufficiency.[15]

Communities, collectives, collaboration, cooperatives, protecting the commons—these are the key commitments that must guide our experiments into an agrarian future.

The story of black farming in America is surely a story of immense injustice and pain. But it isn't only that. It is also a story about youth empowerment, community development, food security, public health, and personal autonomy and pride. Reflecting on the history of black agricultural work, James Beard Award–winning author Michael Twitty notes, "We knew how to take care of each other. That was the number one dictate of the land: love the others on it just as you love the land and those who gave it to you. Our values were there—to work and celebrate cooperatively, to have humor when it felt there was none, to decorate our lives with the love we never received outside."[16]

As we look to an Anthropocene future, it is hard to know exactly how current realities like food insecurity, the financialization of agriculture, the consolidation and centralization of food processing and distribution, the continued degradation of soils and waters, and the mining for profit of farming communities will develop. What is clear, however, is that people will need to learn and advocate for the skills and policies that increase humanity's collective material intelligence if they are to navigate this earth with appropriate care. They will need to cultivate the sympathies and affections that make the care of lands and communities the top priority, for without these there is no long-term viable or flourishing life. And they will have to do all of this in very tough ecological and social circumstances, which is why the wisdom of the world's authentic agrarian traditions has never been more important.

A HEAVENLY AGRARIAN CITY

It is frequently said that scripture begins in a garden but ends in a city. It isn't always clear what the point is of those who say it. Sometimes it sounds like yet one more swipe against indigenous and agrarian peoples, one more expression of the desire to be done with agrarian work, or one more iteration of the well-established narrative that Progress and the March of Civilizations require people to move from hunting and gathering ways of life, through agriculture, and onward to urban dwelling as the pinnacle of human existence. What troubles me most is the assumption that we already know what a good city is and that by our arriving there the many benefits of urban life will simply disseminate and grow.

As I already noted at the start of this chapter, the future for most of the world's people will be an urban future. Contemporary conditions like food insecurity, unsafe housing, lack of green spaces, and inadequate education and health care—much of it marked along class, ethnic, and racial lines—indicate that for millions of people this development is a grim prospect. This is why it is so important to think carefully about the characteristics of a good city. Does the biblical vision of the heavenly city descending to earth (described in Revelation 21–22) give us some insight into what a God-inspired, creation-affirming city looks like?

It bears highlighting that the holy city glorifies God, which is another way of saying it is a city that communicates through its architecture and infrastructure that this world and its life are sacred gifts to be gratefully received, cherished, shared, and celebrated. If we adopt the (slightly amended) maxim of St. Irenaeus that "the glory of God is a creature fully alive," then a city glorifies God by building, among other things, safe and reliable transportation networks, democratic and healthy food systems, well-funded and readily accessible health care facilities, high-quality housing, clean and transparent energy systems, ample parks and recreation facilities, beautiful neighborhoods, and welcoming plazas and community centers where people can get to know each other and enjoy each other's company. These should be our design priorities because these are the structures that are known to promote flourishing people and vibrant communities.[17]

A look at many of today's skylines does not communicate worship of God. The prominence of banks, corporate headquarters, and investment companies make clear that the pursuit of wealth is the foremost priority. The worship of money, along with the power and privilege it creates, has certainly produced some beautiful buildings. But it has also created inner cities that lack a basic food and health care infrastructure, contain tract housing in which the maximization of profits for developers and investors (rather than well-made homes) is the primary objective, and have segregated communities in which there are few parks, community centers, or public libraries and arts facilities. So many neighborhoods are ugly and alienating. So many schools resemble prisons rather than centers for creative and appreciative inquiry.

Of course, not all cities and neighborhoods reflect the blights I have just described. It would also be a mistake to think that rural communities are somehow immune from the devastation and abandonment that allegiance to profit maximization (for some) creates. My point, rather, is to highlight how far removed much of today's urban development is from the heavenly city that is marked by all-encompassing welcome, generous hospitality, abundant beauty, systemic justice, and the centrality of the community's health and nutrition. As John describes it, the heavenly city does not have a temple. It doesn't need one, because God is intimately present to each of its inhabitants and has become the light by which all members see each other. This is a city where God promises to dwell with mortals in such a way that all their planning, design, building, growing, and engagements reflects the love of God pulsing through them, inspiring and sustaining them so they live in ways that foster abundant life for all. It is a remarkable vision.

> Then the angel showed me the river of the water of life, bright as crystal, flowing from the throne of God and of the Lamb through the middle of the street of the city. On either side of the river is the tree of life with its twelve kinds of fruit, producing its fruit each month; and the leaves of the tree are for the healing of the nations. Nothing accursed will be found there any more. But the throne of God and of the Lamb will be in it, and his servants will worship him; they will see his face, and his name will be on their foreheads. And there will be no more night; they need no light of lamp or sun, for the Lord God will be their light, and they will reign forever and ever. (Revelation 22:1–5)

This is not a city in which gardening ways of being or agrarian sensibilities have been left behind. Instead, they have been intensified and made more deeply and widely incarnate, because God's gardening and farming ways with creatures have taken up permanent residence in the land and with us. This is why it makes sense to specify the heavenly city as an *agrarian* city. The locution is a contradiction only if one believes country and city to be opposed to each other, or if one equates agrarian life with farming. This chapter has argued that is a mistake. No matter where people reside, the flourishing of a human life will always depend on cultivating the practical skills and the affective sympathies that enable people to nurture the places and the fellow creatures that nurture them. The divine command to serve and protect the sources of life, first given to Adam in the Garden of Eden, has not been eclipsed. It cannot ever be eclipsed, because care and celebration of each other and our places is our most blessed way of participating in the nourishing, sustaining, and healing love of an agrarian God.

CHAPTER THREE

Placing the Soul

In abandoning the world we are lost; we are lost again and
again. We may speak poignantly of the experience of being
lost; but we cannot be clear about ourselves and our
situation in so far as our thinking is dominated by that
experience. Disillusionment with the world knows nothing
of the sacrament of co-existence. It can find no place for
the sacramental act.

—Henry Bugbee

In the opening lines to *The Unsettling of America*, Wendell
Berry observed, "One of the peculiarities of the white race's presence
in America is how little intention has been applied to it. As a people,
wherever we have been, we have never really intended to be."[1] Berry
was quick to note that from a historical point of view this observation
is "too simply put," since one can find examples of people who have
been, and continue to be, devoted to the places and communities of
which they are a part. Nonetheless, long-standing philosophical and
religious impulses have encouraged the training of human attention,
care, and desire *against* and *away from* this world. In other words, the
tendencies of some people have often been not only to forsake a given
place—most often for the opportunities and potential wealth afforded
by greener pastures or a "virgin frontier"—but to forsake all physical

places as inherently limiting, defective, and unworthy of their ultimate concern.

Though having roots that extend all the way back to the origins of Greek philosophical thought, and then continuing in varying forms of world-denying, body-despising spiritualities, this otherworldly impulse is alive and well today and is reflected in the work of scientists and wealthy elites who are planning their escape to another planet. Why want to escape? Over its long history, Earth has shown itself to be an inhospitable planet to the 99.9 percent of species that have gone extinct on it. It is only a matter of time before the human species is next. "Nature will eventually turn on us, as it did to all those extinct life-forms."[2] And what nature doesn't do to us, we will eventually do to ourselves by rendering parts of Earth uninhabitable owing to pollution, toxicity, disease, food and resource scarcity, heat death, and the social turmoil and violence that will follow from these degraded conditions.[3] The hope of these futurists is that the fourth wave of science— which centers on artificial intelligence, nanotechnology, and biotechnology—will enable us to genetically redesign humans to travel to and succeed on other planets and, at the same time, engineer (currently inhospitable) planetary landscapes like Mars into new, human-friendly paradises. A tall order.

What these futurists and transhumanists fail to realize is that these newly designed humans will likely degrade or destroy these newly engineered planets, just as they have destroyed this one, if they do not first undergo a moral, affective, and spiritual transformation that inspires them to cherish and care for wherever they are and whomever they are with. It is not a solution simply to transport habits of discontent and degradation to a new location, wherever that may be. That would be to kick the proverbial can down the solar system, and thus merely to delay the most pressing and perennial issue: learning to be at peace with where one is, who one is, and whom one is with.

CHARACTERIZING OTHERWORLDLY IMPULSES

How should we understand and address desires for otherworldly escape?

We can begin by noting that the desire to transcend a finite, mortal condition isn't held only by eccentrics or people on the lunatic fringe but runs deeply throughout Western philosophy, theology, and literature. No physical place can ultimately satisfy or fulfill us because places, like the creaturely bodies of which they are constituted, are *by their very nature* ephemeral and imperfect.

Think here of Socrates's famous and highly influential account of philosophy in the *Phaedo* as a kind of death wish in which philosophers learn to shun attachments to the body and to materiality and instead train their minds on eternal, immaterial, unchanging truths. Bodies get in the way of the pursuit of truth because bodies invariably confuse and tempt people with pleasures and desires that are fickle and dangerous. The body fills people with wants, fears, and all sorts of illusions that invariably put them on paths toward disappointment, frustration, and war, war within themselves over what they crave and war with others as they compete for the wealth and comfort that comes from the acquisition of places and material goods. Socrates put it plainly: "As long as we have a body and our soul is fused with such an evil we shall never adequately attain what we desire, which we affirm to be truth. . . . If we are ever to have pure knowledge, we must escape from the body and observe matters in themselves with the soul by itself" (66b–e). This is why genuine philosophers welcome death as the moment when their souls are finally freed from the frailty of their bodies and the mess of this world. "It seems likely that we shall, only then, when we are dead, attain that which we desire and of which we claim to be lovers, namely, wisdom, as our argument shows, not while we live; for it is impossible to attain any pure knowledge with the body." (66e).[4]

In the *Symposium*, Plato offered another insight into humanity's discontent with this world and this life. In this dialogue, Diotima argued that the pursuit of beauty, though it may begin with attention to beautiful forms instantiated in earthly bodies and things, must ultimately leave worldly things behind because worldly beauty is partial, temporary, and imperfect. True beauty is eternal. It does not wax and wane, come to be and pass away, or share in any way with what is ugly. True beauty cannot reside in any corporeal, earthly thing because all such things are subject to change and are mingled with imperfection.

The beauty of a youthful and energetic human form, for instance, will not last. Bodies that were once virile and capable eventually fail and fall apart, leaving people in pain and bewilderment. Before long, disease and aging will destroy what was, and sadness and frustration will be all that remain.

It isn't difficult to understand the attraction of Plato's position. Spend time with someone living with a chronic health condition, and they will tell you that it can be like torture to live with an uncooperative, unpredictable body that often makes day-to-day life a misery. Listen to a person who has been body shamed—too fat, too thin, the wrong color or gender or sexual orientation—or has been sexually assaulted, and you will soon discover that one's body can be source of agony or revulsion. Take a trip to a nursing home or elderly care facility and it becomes abundantly clear that the vigor and joys of youth eventually end in incontinence, impotence, and pain. Experiences like these, in part, explain why corporeal things should not be worthy objects of our love.

Henry Staten has helpfully described the Platonic desire for an otherworldly absolute as fundamentally a desire to transcend all forms of eros or love that can be disappointed.[5] To lose one's beloved, or to be frustrated by what one loves, destroys human happiness, and that is what people cannot abide. Saint Augustine put this Platonic sentiment powerfully in his *Confessions* (4.6), when he wrote, "I was unhappy, and so is every soul unhappy which is tied to its love for mortal things; when it loses them, it is torn to pieces, and it is then that it realizes the unhappiness which was there even before it lost them." The prospect of mourning in the face of disappointment and loss is why people have been regularly admonished to forsake all love for this world and to practice what the ancient Stoics called "anticipatory detachment." It is why people have sensed, however inchoately, a "hidden and continual grief" (Marsilio Ficino) at the core of their experience of the transitoriness of temporal things.

The mourning that occurs in the face of suffering and loss is so severe because it calls into question the integrity and the value of the self. It isn't simply that people are weak and can't handle some suffering or disappointment. The mourning goes deeper. A self that is subject to the vicissitudes of suffering and pain is also a self that knows itself as vulnerable, shatterable, and incomplete. In the *City of God* (14:25), Augustine wrote, "Even the righteous man himself will not live the life he wishes unless he reaches that state where he is wholly exempt from death, deception, and distress, and has the assurance that he will forever be exempt. This is what our nature craves, and it will never be fully and finally happy unless it attains what it craves."

The experience of the loss of self, what we might also describe as the self's disintegration, is a mirror image of the sadness we feel in the loss of others. If we are disappointed and frustrated by the ephemeral, imperfect existence of others, we must also be frustrated and disappointed in the ephemeral, imperfect existence of ourselves. The best way forward, therefore, is to restrain one's love and not put one's hope in any transitory, suffering thing: "Only a limited or conditional libidinal flow toward such objects is to be allowed, such that the self remains ready and able to retract its substance from the object before the unmasterable violence of mourning might assail it."[6] This hesitant, retractive move, this "anticipatory detachment," is a crucial strategy that gives individuals an escape hatch into the security of themselves, what the Stoic philosopher and Roman emperor Marcus Aurelius called one's "innermost citadel." It is better to seek one's safety in the inviolability of one's own soul and not open oneself too much to the vicissitudes of material life. If one should have any hope at all, it should be, if one follows Socrates, in an immortal soul that is forever in the presence of absolute, ideal forms, or, if one follows techno-humanists, in an immortal, machine-like existence that travels among the stars.

What we can see so far, whether in its Platonic or technophilic guise, is a basic discontent with what can be described as our creaturely condition, a condition that is marked by embodiment, finitude, need, fragility, changeability, imperfection, and ultimately death. It is as though people can be fully happy only if they cease to be creatures and instead become eternal, unchanging, self-subsisting gods living in a heaven marked by permanence and perfection, or infinitely perfectible machines moving within designer universes engineered by steadily improving algorithms. And where is this heaven? Anywhere but Earth, because Earth, perhaps even the whole material universe, is subject to change, suffering, and impermanence.

Do otherworldly desires of this sort reveal a self- and place-despising logic that ultimately assumes it is better not to be than to be? Insofar as our embodied being is continually marked by becoming and change, does an otherworldly desire presuppose that it would be better for us not to have been born at all?[7]

The soul/body dualism that is evident in various Platonic and Christian forms of thought clearly had the effect of disparaging, even sometimes despising, embodiment and materiality in their various forms. But one does not need to be a Platonist to believe that materiality is deficient and doesn't really matter. Modern thinkers like Rene Descartes, Francis Bacon, and Giordano Bruno, though priding themselves on having abandoned the mythological frameworks of the ancients, continued to promote a deprecation of the material world. They did so not by encouraging the soul to flee this life but by denuding materiality of intrinsic or sacred worth and thus opening nature to human mastery, improvement, and possession.

One way they did this was through the elimination of a natural telos in things, the idea that natural things have an end or purpose internal to themselves. If things are without intrinsic meaning or purpose, and do not have in-built ends they are trying to achieve, then it falls to human beings to assign whatever meaning and purpose things can be said to have.[8] Plants and animals are not organisms striving to fulfill their form and function. Nor can they be characterized as having integrity or sanctity that can be violated. They are, instead, more like machines that have no internally derived purpose of their own. They may be complex in their arrangement and in their ability to do things, but there is nothing to prevent people from extracting and redesigning natural elements as they find them.[9] This is why it made sense for Descartes to perform experiments on and dissect living animals, for Bacon to imagine the remaking of an orchard to produce fruit far tastier and sweeter than what nature could produce on her own, and for Julien Offray de La Mettrie to compare the human body to a sophisticated mechanism that could be improved in multiple ways. In this modern sensibility, the classically conceived paradigmatic person as one who contemplates the natural order of things (so as better to fit within it) is replaced with the image of the engineer who redesigns nature (so as to have it serve human interests).[10]

Because the natural or physical world is without intrinsic value (it is brute matter that signifies in quantitative rather than qualitative terms), it cannot possibly serve as a source for moral deliberation.[11] From this presupposition, the "naturalistic fallacy" that sits behind so much modern moral theory—the idea that a moral "ought" cannot be derived from the way the world "is"—easily follows. The natural world cannot be a guide to moral striving, or a check on behavior, because it is without moral charge. Insofar as people subscribe to a moral position, its source must be from within themselves. People are fundamentally disembodied minds imposing meaning and value upon an external, value-neutral world.

It is tempting to view these developments in philosophy and science as being of merely academic interest. That would be a mistake. Once nature is reduced to an amoral realm and a stockpile of "natural resources," then it becomes possible, perhaps even inevitable, that places and the bodies that populate them will be conscripted, often violently, to serve the purposes set by people with power. We see this in the development of modern mercantile capitalism—according to the historian Sven Beckert, more accurately described as "war capitalism"—that violently appropriated land and people to satisfy imperial ambitions. The reduction of places and (human and nonhuman) creatures to units of production to be claimed, controlled, mined to exhaustion, and then abandoned rests upon the small number of philosophical assumptions we have just described, assumptions that are enormous in their practical world applications.

The recent dawning of what is being called the Anthropocene epoch, the time in which the human presence has become so prominent as to become a geological force and a decisive influence shaping Planet Earth from the cellular to the meteorological levels, indicates that the modern dream of human mastery and control has been rigorously applied.[12] There is now no place, no body, and no process that does not, in some way, witness to the human effort to remake this world and this life so that they more readily conform to personal expectations for comfort, control, and convenience. In this remaking effort there have clearly been tremendous benefits in housing, nutrition, mobility, communications, medicine, and life expectancy. But there has also been systemic damage done to most all the world's eco-systems, as reflected in degraded and eroded soils, polluted and de-pleted fresh water systems, plant and animal species extinctions, warming and acidified oceans, and denuded forests (to name a few). How long before multiple regions and coastlines become permanently or seasonally uninhabitable by people? The effort to enhance the quality of life for (some) people has had the paradoxical effect of putting in jeopardy the long-term life prospects for many of the rest.

We can see in this Anthropocene remaking of the world a mani-festation of an otherworldly impulse now expressed in a different key, an impulse born of a similar discontent with the world as given. In this instance, the effort is not necessarily to escape the planet altogether, though, as we have already seen, some are prepared to pursue that path. It is, instead, to transcend this world and this life as they currently are—with all their limits, imperfections, and frustrations—by engi-neering a world and its various plant and animal bodies more to our liking, a world premised on a massive technological infrastructure and then also built environments that have rendered the ideas of "nature" and "the natural" obsolete.[13] This is a "new and improved" world, ma-terially and genetically redesigned from the ground up.

OVERCOMING DUALISM'S DECEPTIONS

Can we be clear and honest about who and where we are so long as various forms of otherworldliness dominate our desiring and thinking? Or, to put the point more practically, can we properly engage the world and each other if we denigrate the bodies through which such engage-ment occurs, or despise the natural bodies upon which our own lives so clearly depend?

One of the lasting contributions of *The Unsettling of America* was to show that on both counts the answer is a resounding "No!" Though we might dream of ourselves as disembodied, immortal souls, or as complex machines or computers that will finally shed all biological and physiological limitations, the fact remains that we live through and *are* our bodies, and these bodies, in turn, necessarily live through the bodies of others—wheat, rice, cows, fish, microorganisms, bees, chickens, and many more.[14] We simply cannot avoid or override the fundamental ecological truth that "our land passes in and out of our bodies just as our bodies pass in and out of our land" and that all the living "are part of one another, and so cannot possibly flourish alone."[15] Insofar as an otherworldly mindset diminishes or denigrates human flesh and the flesh of the world, our ability to live responsibly, perhaps even beautifully, in the here and now is severely compromised because, for a start, we will not give creatures and places the attention and care they deserve.

If we are to resist the world and body discontent that results in otherworldly flight, it is important that we reexamine what we understand a human being to be. As we have seen, various forms of dualism, whether characterized as soul/body, mind/body, ghost/machine, or software/hardware, often underwrite the anthropological accounts I have been describing. What if these dualisms are fundamentally confused? What if these dualisms mischaracterize both human life and the world more generally?

In a series of texts, the British anthropologist Tim Ingold has introduced the concept of a "meshwork" to describe the human place in the world. As we will now see, this concept challenges dualist assumptions about personhood and the nature of the world. Consider first the basic notion, assumed by many, that a place is something like a *container* that holds various objects. Aristotle gave this idea its most succinct and influential articulation when he said, "Place is what *primarily* contains each body."[16] Characterized this way, places do not factor significantly in the constitution or the being of the things they contain: a pebble is basically the same thing no matter what container it is in, and a container remains basically the same no matter what things are in it. Both places and the things they contain are separable, preformed sorts of realities that can be understood in terms of themselves. Things are what they are independent of the places that situate and surround them.

Given these assumptions, it is easy to see how later thinkers would describe the world as a "stage" holding up diverse pieces of furniture and actors that can be moved about to suit the needs of a play, or as a "production platform" that supports the various extractive and constructive activities of human invention, or as a "warehouse/store" that contains multiple natural resources and commodities ready for consumer purchase. Each of these metaphors—stage, production platform, and warehouse/store—simply extends the container imagery. People may be *in* a place, like a pebble in a jar, but they are not *of* it, which is why they can ultimately escape from it. Places are locations, giving people room to stand, move, explore, manipulate, mine, and purchase, but they do not go deeply into the constitution of who and what people are. Even the current use of the word *environment* shares in this logic because environments are understood to *surround* us. If we don't like the environment we are currently in, we can readily move to another.

This picture of the world as a container has as its corollary the idea that persons are fundamentally self-contained, perhaps even self-constituting, entities that can move from place to place.[17] Depending on one's account, one might even believe, as Socrates once suggested, that our souls preexisted this earth and our bodies, reside here only for a short while, and then resume their independent life apart from bodies and places after death. The core of who one is resides not in one's body but in the spiritual or mental core that animates it from the inside out. Moreover, the condition of one's body and the state of one's place should not have an undue effect on who one is trying to be. The real human work is to develop one's interior being, whether characterized as a soul, mind, or personality. This is why various forms of spiritual direction advise ascetic practices that (falsely) treat the body as a problem that, besides needing to be disciplined and kept under control, must finally be discarded and left behind.[18]

The concept of life as a meshwork challenges the twin notions of self-contained places and self-contained organisms. Meshwork thinking requires that we abandon the idea of a world as a collection of bounded, discrete entities because each organism and each thing is what it is only as a result of its entanglement within and codevelopment with a bewildering array of fellow creatures, all moving together within dynamic processes that defy complete description. A life is not a single, separable, self-standing thing. It is, instead, a knotting of lines of codevelopment that are constantly interlacing with multiple other lives and lines of development that together make a tapestry or meshwork. A living body cannot be a single, self-sourcing kind of reality because each body depends on the nurture and support of countless seen and unseen others. Eating, drinking, touching, breathing, and being inspired are the daily proof of that.[19]

As Ingold sees it, dualist anthropologies are held captive to a "logic of inversion." According to this well-established logic, the life of things, rather than being a wide-ranging participation in the life of the world, is turned inward and made to be an internal power contained within individual bodies. Upon observing a living being, what we see on the surface of skin, feather, or fur is an internal power or essence—the power of life—working itself out from the inside (think here of Plato's famous image of an invisible hand moving the visible glove). The shell that we perceive isn't what is most important. It's what is invisibly on the *inside* that matters.

When life is characterized as a power internal to things, then it is apparent that the relationships that join living beings to each other, though important, are not constitutive. What a living thing *is* can be thought apart from the connections it finds itself in. Personal identity is a singular thing. People are thus understood to live within their bodies because life is contained within the boundaries of their skin. If relationships are entered into, it is on a voluntary basis.

Meshwork thinking undoes this inversion by saying that *things are their relations*. Things have no existence and no life apart from their participation in the movements of fellow creatures happening all around and within: "Minds and lives are not closed-in entities that can be enumerated and added up; they are open-ended processes whose most outstanding characteristic is that they *carry on*. And in carrying on, they wrap around one another, like the many strands of a rope. . . . The rope is always weaving, always in process and—like social life itself—never finished."[20] Another way to put this is to say that for an organism "to be" is not only "to become in a place" but also "to become in and through relationships." The relationships to land, water, and fellow creatures are not optional but go to the core of an organism's birth and development. This means that people do not simply enter into (and exit from) relationships in the course of their living. The relating goes deeper than that. For me to exist as the being that I am, I must have always been in relationships with microorganisms, a mother's womb, a life-supporting ecosystem, and myriads of biophysical, meteorological, and social processes that are not optional or always chosen. If this is true, then a living organism is more like a verb than a noun, because life depends on the constant intermingling with and ingestion of others. To understand a life, one must understand, at least to some degree, the *stories* of the multiple lives, large and small, and the multiple places, near and far, that have fed into and supported that life.

Life, in other words, is a constant movement in which openness to (animate and inanimate) others and susceptibility to earth and life processes are the indispensable key.[21] If the movement stops, life stops. Ingold puts it this way: "In a world that is truly open there are no objects as such. For the object, having closed in on itself, has turned its back on the world, cutting itself off from the paths along which it came into being, and presenting only its congealed, outer surfaces for inspection. The open world . . . has no such boundaries, no insides or outsides, only comings and goings. Such productive movements may generate formations, swellings, growths, protuberances and occurrences, but not objects."[22]

Meshwork thinking is so difficult because it compels us to reassess the idea of the world as a collection of bounded, discrete objects. Moreover, it challenges the cherished notion of the invulnerability of the self, the idea that the self is secure in its innermost citadel and immune from the vicissitudes and suffering of life with others.[23] Meshwork thinking teaches us that persons are verbs before they are nouns, and stories before they are discrete entities classified by categories, which means that every attempt to describe a person in isolation and apart from a history of relationships with other creatures is a distortion. Though we may legitimately deploy nouns to distinguish creatures from one another, the fundamental, inescapable truth is that our living depends on our hosting others (like the billions of microorganisms that make up our gut biome) and our being hosted by them (as when soil generates the plant life that feeds us). Persons are not singular, self-standing things that then move within places. Instead, "They *are* their movements. It is in their very patterns of activity that their presence lies."[24] Even in death, a body is not alone or set apart. The eating, breathing, drinking, growing, warming activities that animated a body in life now shift to activities of decomposition and decay that nourish and animate others. What a creature *is* is a feature of the dynamic, complex history of symbiotic interminglings that brought it into being and that maintain it in its becoming. Creatures are not primarily objects to be tabulated and *categorized* like data but stories of codevelopment with others to be *narrated*. To give an accurate account of who and what one is, is thus to narrate the histories of shared life with others, histories that recount the development of a life that has, quite literally, grown out of the ground, been bathed in sunshine, water, and air, and been nourished by honey and bread, tomatoes and cheese, friends and family. . . . The list goes on and on.

Some scholars and scientists have suggested that instead of speaking of single organisms, we should describe people as "holobionts." Derived from the Greek for "whole unit of life," this term helps us resist the notion that organisms are solitary, single things. But even this designation can be misleading if we understand a holobiont as a self-contained unit or assemblage of things that then enters into relationships with others. Creatures are symbiotic realities that depend on the processes of symbiogenesis or co-becoming in which life forms emerge out of the diversity of *life moving together*, even life *inside each other*.[25] The co-*becoming*, rather than simply co-*being*, is key because life is movement. The biologist Lynn Margulis argues that "living beings defy neat definition. They fight, they feed, they dance, they mate, they die. At the base of the creativity of all large familiar forms of life, symbiosis generates novelty. . . . We abide in a symbiotic world."[26] Moreover, according to the geomorphologist David Montgomery and biologist Anne Biklé, the world we live within also lives within us: "The human body is one vast ecosystem. Actually, it is more like an entire planet. . . . From the perspective of a microbe, I am a durable, living trellis—inside and out—on which vast numbers of these microbes cling, climb, and grow. . . . I am their homeland. . . . I am not who I thought I was. And neither are you. We are all a collection of ecosystems for other creatures."[27]

When thinking about human life in meshwork terms, it is important that we not reduce the meshwork to a flat two-dimensional design. If one thinks of a meshwork on the model of woven tapestry that lies on a surface, for instance, it is likely that one will then think of persons as so dispersed, perhaps even dissolved, into the warp and woof of interlacing as to make markers of identity disappear. This would be a mistake. The lines of codevelopment that interlace to make a person's life possible, while clearly reaching out in multiple directions, nonetheless take the form of a recognizable "knot" that emerges from and densifies the weave of the mesh. The knot, of course, is not static or eternally fixed, because one's life is constantly on the move, intersecting with others and being intersected by them. But the knot "stands out" without "standing apart" or "standing outside" the weave within which it emerges. Knots are four-dimensional kinds of realities because they interlace, arise and fall, and bear witness in their form to complex histories of interlacing that are not directly evident in the knot that is currently in view. As Ingold describes it, "Knotting is the fundamental principle of coherence. It is the way forms are held together and kept in place within what would otherwise be a formless and inchoate flux."[28]

It is also important to note that the knotting, interlacing processes that are constitutive of life forms move in multiple registers. To consider the coming to be of individual persons, one must attend to what they have seen, heard, tasted, smelled, and touched—the entire embodied sensorium. The ranges of susceptibility to and resonance with others are enormous and often unthought or unthematized. Why does a particular smell or sight have the power to transport a person to another time or location? Why does a change in the weather affect one's mood and one's ability to interact with others and with particular places? What is clear is that we have never been self-standing beings. We are, instead, sympathetic beings tuned to receive and respond to (seen and unseen) others in a multitude of (known and unknown) ways.[29] Apart from a human being's fundamental openness to others, an openness that is directly and bodily visible in mouths, ears, and belly buttons but is not restricted to these visible marks, life would come to a dead-end stop.

Taken together, these observations on knots and meshworks show that the dualistic anthropologies that underwrite worldly discontent and otherworldly flight are fundamentally *misguided* and *untrue*. There simply is no human life apart from the countless threads of receiving and giving that join human flesh to the flesh of the world and the myriad lines of development that intersect, inspire, and interrupt our own development. Rather than seeking to flee this flesh and this world of codevelopment, the fundamental task is to ascertain how to move patiently and attentively within it, with proper courtesy and care. To be an embodied creature is to be hosted by an unfathomable number of fellow creatures, large and small, and to move within ecosystem processes like birth, growth, digestion, and decomposition that defy comprehension.

Put succinctly, these observations confirm that who you are is not reducible to yourself. You are a zoo of creaturely life, always moving together through ever-changing places and times. Though you might take comfort in a picture of yourself as a discrete *point* in the world, the more accurate description is that each one of us is a well-populated *path* bearing witness to multiple lives in me and I in them. The idea of the self as a point is clearly a more manageable idea because, like Descartes, we can then imagine secluding ourselves in a private room, perhaps beside a warming fire and away from a complex and messy world, to work out the identity and meaning of everything else. But if we understand ourselves as always *in medias res*, in the middle of multiple stories journeying along multiple paths, then the minute you try to fix your identity or future you also discover that there are so many others and places you must also take into account. Ingold refers to this as a riddle of human life: "I carry on, and am in turn carried. I live and am lived."[30] If people are not simply *on a path* but are *a knotting of multiple paths themselves*, then every "I," besides being a verb, is also a social and ecological becoming. To give an account of oneself is also, necessarily, to give an account of so much more.

In addition to falsifying our embodied experience, these dualistic, individualizing anthropologies are also fundamentally *dangerous* and *destructive*, for as Berry notes, "By dividing body and soul, we divide both from all else. We thus condemn ourselves to a loneliness for which the only compensation is violence—against other creatures, against the earth, against ourselves. . . . The willingness to abuse other bodies is the willingness to abuse one's own. To damage the earth is to damage your children. To despise the ground is to despise its fruit; to despise the fruit is to despise its eaters. The wholeness of health is broken by despite."[31]

For too long people have believed they can secure their well-being at the expense of the well-being of others, or that they can build lasting economies at the expense of the land and waters that nurture them. Our Anthropocene condition now teaches that this has been a massively destructive delusion. Oceans, coastlines, glaciers, forests, bees, worms, butterflies, carbon sequestration, hydrological cycles—none of these more-than-human realities can any longer be taken for granted. Human health and planetary health are inextricably linked.

The ecologist E. O. Wilson has argued that we should call our epoch, not the Anthropocene, but the "Eremocene"—The Age of Loneliness.[32] Are we doomed to loneliness? Might there be ways to rekindle humanity's kinship with other creatures?

ON REORIENTING SPIRITUALITY

If we define an agrarian as someone who seeks the flourishing of people and land *together*, and understand by land a field (from the Latin *ager*, which translates as a farm or field) in which diverse species and dynamic ecosystem processes mingle together to create the conditions for life, then it is clear that resisting the desire for a soul's flight will be among an agrarian's highest priorities. Agrarians work to place people in the world by developing in them the sympathies and skills that promote soil fertility, clean water and air, healthy plant, fish, and animal bodies, just economies, and vibrant communities and built environments. They work to help people understand that the full range of human endeavor is necessarily enfolded within complex processes of birth, growth, nurture, death, and decomposition. The best way to come to this understanding is for people to be practically involved, however minimally, in aspects of the production of their own livelihood, since it is through agrarian work that people sense more deeply the character of the entanglements that join people with each other, fellow creatures, and their places.

In retaining the term *soul* in this chapter's title I do not mean to repeat the logic of inversion that reduces a soul to an internal reality—whether a Socratic soul, a Cartesian ghost, or a transhumanist information pattern/software program—confined within a single body. If what I have been saying about life as the power that moves through bodies in places in their various entanglements with each other is true, and if we believe the term *soul* to convey the power of life at work in bodies, then it is clear that a soul cannot be a single, separable thing that is something like a possession held by individuals. A characterization of soul as distinctly mine or yours rests on the mistaken assumption that one's life and identity are one's own and are not profoundly and incomprehensibly rooted in the lives of others.

To be a person is also always to be a social and ecological reality. For you to speak of yourself, even to highlight all the things that make you unique and different from others, you must at the same time also speak of the many influences—family, friends, pets, toys, teachers, schools, doctors, hospitals, houses, kitchens, tools, stores, gardens, watersheds, fields, viruses, diseases, neighborhoods, communities, ethnic traditions, languages, books, songs, and movies (to name a few)—that have nurtured, disturbed, stimulated, hurt, resisted, and directed you. The life-lines that intersect and codevelop with you are far too many to enumerate, let alone fully understand. You may not like these influences and so may actively work to resist them. But even in your resistance, which is an expression of your freedom, you cannot act alone. The movements you make in your life carry within them the movements of countless known and unknown others that have been with you from the beginning. This is why it is so difficult to speak about souls with specificity or certainty. You are not a single self-standing, self-moving creature. Given the many creaturely influences and processes that are constantly weaving in and out of your life, it would be more accurate to say that "you are a zoo!" Your body, quite literally, is a dynamic, hospitable, hosted, fleshy site in which you are constantly receiving from and giving to others.

To appreciate the truth of this insight, try to imagine what it would be like to be you if you were birthed by another mother, formed within a different family or ethnic tradition, or raised in a region of the world quite unlike the one you are familiar with now. Your life and identity, the things that interest, inspire, and move you—in other words, all the elements we might want to associate with your soul— would be profoundly altered because places and cultures, and the many creatures and things that move through it, are all different. The processes of codevelopment would be fundamentally altered and would produce a different life story as the story of you.

Clearly, an articulation of soul in social and ecological terms will be troubling to those seeking to retain a strong sense of individuality. At stake are deep concerns about individual freedom and responsibility. Can I live an authentic life if I am not free to chart my life's journey as I think best? How can I take responsibility for my actions if they are not mine to begin with?

An agrarian position does not require that we give up on notions of freedom and responsibility. What it does require is that we stop thinking of these as if they are not worked out and made possible by the social and ecological contexts in which we live. To be free is to be able to make decisions about how we will engage places and the lives of others, and to accept responsibility is to know we must give an account of how we came to make those decisions. These decisions may be made by me, but they are not reducible to me and my mind or will, because the decision-making process contains within it the multiple influences of the places and communities that have formed me. The great mistake is to believe that a soul or a mind is a single thing housed within a singular body. As Berry notes, there is no mind or soul without a body, and no body without a homeland, and no homeland without multiple creatures. A better formulation is as follows: "Mind = brain + body + world + local dwelling place + community + history. 'History' here would mean not just documented events but the whole heritage of culture, language, memory, tools, and skills. Mind in this definition has become hard to locate in an organ, organism, or place. It has become an immaterial presence or possibility that is capable of being embodied and placed."[33]

Given this agrarian understanding, it is clear that freedom and responsibility are *placed* realities. What you can do, even what you can imagine doing, depends on where you are and the nature of the relationships that are operating there. To see what I mean, consider how freedom and responsibility will take vastly different forms if you are living through a chronically ill body, living in a war zone, working on a farm, shopping in a mall, feeling lonely, or feeling the full support of a loving community. The possibilities that are yours to pursue are always dependent upon and shaped by the contexts you move within.

It is also clear, however, that freedom and responsibility are *shared* realities. For us to promote the freedom of each other, we must also work to help each other in the choice and pursuit of particular objectives because without this help the range of what is possible will be considerably limited. It's hard to be free in oppressive or degrading contexts that have already closed the doors on possibility. Similarly, to promote a culture of personal responsibility, it is important to work to create economies that are local, transparent, and personal. It is very difficult for people to take responsibility for their actions if they cannot see or understand those actions' wide-ranging effects, or if a range of possible actions have been structurally or systematically denied by forces like poverty, racism, sexism, or a degrading built environment. Moral choices are never simply a matter of personal decision-making and thus never simply reducible to individual virtue or vice. Built environments are themselves moral structures because they encourage, sometimes even demand, that people live in particular sorts of ways. As but one example, it is a mistake to blame underpaid and highly stressed workers for buying the cheap unhealthy food our industrial systems make everywhere available.

As we have now to see, *placing the soul* in ecosystems and neighborhoods has profound and practical implications for the way spiritual life is imagined. By "spiritual life" I do not mean an ethereal or disembodied life. I mean a person's overall life orientation and the inspiration and power that moves people to behave in the ways that they do. As such, every spirituality includes an affirmation of what is of ultimate significance and value, some idea of a worthy life goal, and a more or less clear understanding of the best practices that lead to a life's fulfillment. A spirituality need not be ostensibly religious. Capitalism, for instance, can be described as a spirituality because it wields a power and an inspiration in which the remaking of the world for the purposes of commodification and accumulation is a primary goal.[34] Throughout the ages, multiple spiritualities have motivated people. My goal is not to assess them all but to determine what an agrarian approach can mean for one spiritual tradition, namely Christianity.

Throughout their diverse histories, Christians have often been tempted by body-despising and world-denying spiritualities. From the beginning, they have been attracted to various forms of gnostic faith that are ultimately *dis*incarnate in their nature because they deny that God could really and fully become incarnate in the body of Jesus of Nazareth. Sometimes influenced by classical traditions of thought, they have thought it unseemly and beneath any god worthy of the name to mingle with the mess of bodily pains and imperfections, which is why some (Docetic) Christians opted to believe that Jesus only seemed (from the Greek *dokein*, which means "to seem") to have a body like yours and mine. This gnostic impulse, which prioritizes what a person knows and believes over what a person's body experiences in this world, has been a constant temptation and is alive and well today.

To see what I mean, consider two very popular gospel songs that have been favorites of Christians for decades, Albert E. Brumley's "I'll Fly Away" (1932) and J. R. Baxter Jr.'s "This World Is Not My Home" (1946). In the first, Brumley writes, "Some glad morning when this life is o'er, I'll fly away. To a home on God's celestial shore, I'll fly away." The theme of otherworldly escape is clear, as is what drives this desire, namely the experience of this life as punctuated by too much pain and suffering. "Like a bird from prison bars has flown, I'll fly away. . . . Just a few more weary days and then, I'll fly away." In the second, Baxter echoes a similar sensibility: "This world is not my home, I'm just a-passing through / My treasures are laid up somewhere beyond the blue / The angels beckon me from heaven's open door / And I can't feel at home in this world anymore."[35] Why bother too much with this world and this life, or mount an effort to change one's context for the better, if one is only here for a short while?[36]

These songs, as we have already seen, reflect a deep existential sentiment that supposes embodiment and this worldly life to be the source of unending trouble and pain, which is why people must work to escape both. Clearly, there are multiple contexts where embodied life is made more difficult, even sometimes unbearable, by systems of violence and oppression. People should desire to be rid of an unjust social world. But this desire for justice is fundamentally unlike the desire to be rid of the world altogether. The orientation and goal of a spiritual life should be to look, not "up and away," but "down and among," since this is the orientation that the ministries of Jesus reveal to be the life of God with us. Jesus demonstrated that the goal is not to flee this world but to nurture, heal, reconcile, and befriend it.

It is important to attend to these opposing orientations because the more Christians' direction is "up and away," the greater is the likelihood that they will fail to honor and care for the bodies and places that are here and everywhere around them. They may even sanction and contribute to the violation of human and animal flesh, the pollution and poisoning of water, land, and air, and the disintegration of ecosystems and neighborhoods. One does not need to delve far into the past to see that this is in fact what many Christians have done. As Berry puts it, "Christian organizations, to this day, remain largely indifferent to the rape and plunder of the world and its traditional cultures. . . . The certified Christian seems just as likely as anyone else to join the military-industrial conspiracy to murder creation."[37]

If our aim is to address this destructive history and to reorient spiritual life from "up and away" to "down and among," then it is crucial that we attend to the ways Christian scripture presents the identity and vocation of human life. Identity and vocation always go together because our thinking about the goal of a human life depends on what we understand a human being to be. If you think that an interior, invisible soul—some eternal core—is what defines you, then you will likely deemphasize, if not occlude, economic, political, and embodied dimensions in your spirituality.

What does scripture say about human beings, and how does its characterization challenge the dualisms we have seen to be so problematic? Does scripture recommend the despising of creaturely bodies or strategies of otherworldly flight?

One of the best ways to ascertain what scripture says about human identity and vocation is to turn to its creation stories because it is here that we are given an account of why things exist at all and what their existence is for. Rather than being stories of the mechanics of how and when it all began, creation accounts situate and orient creatures in the world so that in their living they can maximally witness to (by sharing in) the Creator's desire that all life flourish and be abundant.[38] In other words, creation accounts tell us why things exist at all and what their significance/meaning is. By having some sense for how God perceives and evaluates creatures, Christians are then in a position to evaluate, however imperfectly, creaturely lives as good, beautiful, and true—or not. To believe that God creates this world and this life as good and beautiful, as Genesis 1–2:4 clearly suggests, is also to believe that God wants all creatures to thrive. It simply makes no sense for God to love creatures into being and then desire that they languish or be destroyed.

In one of scripture's earliest creation stories, set famously in the Garden of Eden, human beings are described as earthen creatures animated by the breath of God: "Then the Lord God formed man [*adam*] from the dust of the ground [*adamah*], and breathed into his nostrils the breath of life; and the man became a living being" (Genesis 2:7). This is a striking characterization that communicates several important points: (1) a human life is not separable (from the ground) and self-contained but is instead an extension of, and in constant need of, the ground out of which it arises and by which it is daily nurtured; (2) a human's life, his or her ability to move and do things, is not internally sourced but is entirely dependent on the breath of God that animates that human being and all the other plant and animal creatures that are also described as emerging "out of the ground" (2:9, 19);[39] (3) life is not a private possession but is a sharing in the divine breath that is the power in which all creatures participate; (4) the fundamental task of humans is not to escape from their garden home but to take care of the ground out of which they come and the creatures they live with (2:15); and (5) human life is defined by need, most basically the needs for nutrition and companionship (2:18).

This scriptural way of speaking about human beings is not confined to the Genesis 2 text. We find it repeated in Psalm 104, where God is described by the Psalmist as constantly facing creatures, sustaining them with divine breath: "When you hide your face, they are dismayed; when you take away their breath, they die and return to their dust. When you send forth your spirit/breath, they are created; and you renew the face of the ground" (Psalm 104:29–30). The book of Job also makes the connection between divine breath and the life of creaturely flesh unmistakable. Speaking of God's presence to creatures: "If he should take back his spirit to himself, and gather to himself his breath, all flesh would perish together, and all mortals return to dust" (Job 34:14–15). Moreover, as the prophet of Ezekiel makes clear, the breath of God is also vitally important to life's re-creative possibility in contexts of violence and desolation. Coming upon a valley of dry bones, the prophet describes a scene in which creatures have been slain. These aren't simply corpses, however. They are dry bones in a parched landscape, signaling abandonment and hopelessness. But God does not abandon his creatures. What they need, in addition to bones and sinews and flesh, is the breath that will animate them into new life. And so God asks the prophet to say to the breath: "Thus says the Lord GOD: Come from the four winds, O breath, and breathe upon these slain, that they may live" (Ezekiel 37:9). The breath that brings soil to life in the myriad forms that creatures can take is also the breath that resurrects and renews bodies that have been abused, violated, and wasted.

These passages make it clear that a person's life is not his or her own private possession. It is a gift and a divine power that moves through them and other living beings at the same time. A specific creature's life is always already creaturely life together because for me to live I must receive my breath from God and my nurture from the divinely animated creatures that move all around and through me. There is no indication here of an individual soul placed within, or elevated above, an individual body.

As Berry and others have noted, one can derive a dualistic conclusion from the Genesis 2 text only by an act of interpretive violence.

> The formula given in Genesis 2:7 is not man = body + soul; the formula there is soul = dust + breath. According to this verse, God did not make a body and put a soul into it, like a letter into an envelope. He formed man of dust; then, by breathing His breath

into it, He made the dust live. The dust, formed as man and made to live, did not *embody* a soul; it *became* a soul. "Soul" here refers to the whole creature. Humanity is thus presented to us, in Adam, not as a creature of two discrete parts temporarily glued together but as a single mystery.[40]

The above passages from scripture give no hint that the point of a human life is to escape its embodied condition. The intimacy of Creator and creatures—experienced daily as the breath within their breathing—communicates that God desires to be with creatures in their embodiment and in their places. The idea that people should want to flee their bodies so as to ascend somewhere else to be with God simply does not make sense, because the place where God is, is the place where creatures are. God is here with creatures, in this world and in their bodies, because God is constantly giving Godself in the breathing that moves the world.[41] To want to flee embodiment and materiality is to want to flee the places where God is at work. It is to suffer from a failure of incarnational nerve. Scripture does not call people to flee their creaturely lives and places. Instead, it calls them to live in places that honor and further operationalize God's life-giving, life-promoting ways with the world. It calls them to participate in God's reconciling and redeeming ways with the whole of creation (Colossians 1:15–20).

This point is made especially clear in the life of Jesus Christ. As Christians tried to understand and give a clear articulation of who this person was, and why he mattered, they said that in his body "the fullness of God was pleased to dwell" (Colossians 1:19). This means that in Jesus's body, God so fully identified with the creaturely condition as to "become flesh" within it (John 1:14), and so work to heal, feed, and reconcile embodied life from the inside. God is not a puppeteer who manipulates creatures from outside. Instead, the power of God is such as to enter into creaturely life in the most intimate way possible—by becoming one flesh with it—and thereby to reorient life so that it might be full and abundant (John 10:10).

The New Testament is clear that people can exist and not really live. They might miss out on "the life that really is life" (1 Timothy 6:19). Owing to physical ailments like hunger and illness, or social ailments like loneliness and alienation, they might be moving through this world in ways that do not realize the potential that is uniquely theirs to achieve. As the life of Jesus makes clear, God does not abandon these people or ask them to wait until they die, and thus indicate that this life is a tiresome existence to be endured until they can escape to somewhere else. Instead, Jesus dwells with them, suffers life with them, and then in the spaces of intimacy works to nurture, heal, and reconcile them. Jesus does not call people out of this life and this world. Instead, he opens fresh possibilities for life within this world and within bodies, possibilities that depend on having Godly power at work within them, or Godly breath circulating through them.

Consider, for instance, the story of the man known as the Gerasene demoniac. Both the gospels of Mark and Luke record Jesus as meeting a man who lives in a graveyard. He is a dangerous man, animated by an evil, death-intoxicated spirit/breath that harms others and himself. This is why neighboring people put him in chains, trying to restrain his violent acts. Their chains, however, are useless. The demon-possessed man easily breaks them. No one in the community has the power to restrain or help him. And so he "lives" night and day among the tombs, howling on the mountains, and hurting himself with stones (Mark 5:5). The fact that he lives alone and in tremendous pain and confusion indicates that his life is a failure, even a perversion of what his life could be if it were animated by a life-giving, life-honoring spirit or breath.

Upon encountering Jesus, the Gerasene demoniac senses a different power and a different way for him to be. The spirit that animates his body is not the same spirit that animates Jesus's body. He runs to Jesus and bows down before him, at once frightened by Jesus and attracted to him. Jesus, meanwhile, perceives that this man is possessed by evil spirits that are destroying him from the inside. The powers that are animating him are powers that lead to desolation, loneliness, and death, which is why he commands the spirits to come out.[42] In performing this exorcism, what Jesus does is liberate the man from the animating powers that have been slowly killing him. He gives him the opportunity to live a different life. Now free, he can reenter a community to start again.[43]

One way to think about Jesus's ministries of healing, feeding, exorcising, and reconciling is to characterize them as giving an embodied expression of creaturely bodies breathing the breath of God. Rather than being animated by powers that lead to "fornication, impurity, licentiousness, idolatry, sorcery, enmities, strife, jealousy, anger, quarrels, dissension, factions, envy, drunkenness, carousing, and things like these"—all described by the apostle Paul as "works of the flesh" (Galatians 5:19–21) that lead to life's ruination and destruction—Jesus shows through his own body, and the way he moves among others, that God wants people to experience "love, joy, peace, patience, kindness, generosity, faithfulness, gentleness, and self-control"—all described by Paul as "fruit of the Spirit" (Galatians 5:22–23) that lead to life's abundance and fulfillment.

The contrast that Paul makes between "flesh" and "spirit" is not a dualism like Socrates's contrast between body and soul. Instead, it refers to two animating powers that move a *whole* person in radically different ways, and with radically different practical outcomes. For Paul and for much of the New Testament, the contrast is not between the material world and an ethereal heaven. The contrast is between creation and new creation. For the dualist, the point is to escape from one's embodiment and from this material world. For the one animated by the breath of God, the point is to participate in God's nurturing, healing, and reconciling of embodied life here and now, and thereby to contribute to the transformation of this material world.[44]

At the close of John's gospel, we are given an especially striking image of how Jesus means to animate the bodies of his followers into new modes of life. It is after Jesus's resurrection, and his followers are huddled in fear behind locked doors. Jesus appears to them, shows them his wounded body, and offers words of peace to calm their fear. He then sends them out into the world to live as he himself has lived. He knows they will need his animating power to do this, which is why we are told, "He breathed on them and said to them, 'Receive the Holy Spirit. If you forgive the sins of any, they are forgiven them; if you retain the sins of any, they are retained'" (John 20:22–23). It is difficult not to see in this scene an echo of the Genesis 2 creation story where God breathes life into the ground to make creatures live. Only now,

Jesus breathes into the flesh of his followers the breath that will animate them into a new life, a life marked by the forgiveness that liberates people from their bondage to sinful ways of being. Jesus instructs them not to flee Planet Earth, but to reenter it empowered to extend his ministries wherever they are.

One might object to this characterization by noting that after his resurrection Jesus ascends into heaven and so seems to model other-worldly flight to be with God somewhere else. What this interpretation fails to recognize, however, is that Jesus ascends *bodily* and promises to return to be with creatures, thereby communicating that heaven, understood as the place of God's own life, is closed to sin but not to bodies. Heaven is not meant to remain a faraway reality reserved for people after they die. It is meant to take root within and transform this creaturely life so that what happens on earth happens "as it is in heaven" (Matthew 6:10). What heaven has no room for is the sort of power that damages and destroys relationships. Moreover, God does not ever leave creatures to themselves, which is why God sends the Holy Spirit as the animating power that will continue and extend God's life-giving breath in the world after Jesus has ascended.[45] Throughout scripture, God's presence on earth with creatures is simply assumed as the breath/wind that moves within, and remains among, things.

This brief account of scripture suggests that a spirituality recommending flight from bodies and places is profoundly mistaken because it moves in a direction that is directly contrary to God's own. At scripture's beginning, we see that God does not stand aloof from the world, holding it in contempt. Instead, God creates the world out of love and desires to be with it, which is why God is presented first as the primordial gardener with knees in the soil, holding the soil so close so to kiss it and breathe into it the life that is our own. At scripture's end, we see again that God does not call people to escape their home and their creaturely condition. Instead, God calls them to be transformed, reconciled, and ready for God's arrival. John's Apocalypse describes the scene in a memorable image in which the heavenly city *descends* and creates a new earth. God is not "up and away" but "down and among" creatures, for "the home of God is among mortals. He will dwell with them; they will be his peoples, and God himself will be with them" (Revelation 21:3).

Much more can and needs to be said about how scripture characterizes human life in creation and with fellow creatures.[46] But enough has been said to demonstrate that an otherworldly spirituality, and the dualistic, individualizing anthropology it presupposes, simply cannot be sustained by scripture. The theological traditions that came after it confirm this conviction, as when in the Apostles' Creed it was affirmed that Christians believe, not in the immortality of the soul, but in the resurrection of the body. The two logics at work in these teachings are directly opposed to each other. Immortality of the soul presupposes that bodies, much as Socrates described them, are fundamentally evil. They are like prisons from which the soul should seek escape. Resurrection of the body, however, presupposes that bodies, as witnessed in Jesus's own healing, feeding, exorcising, and reconciling ministries toward them, are beloved by God, even are the material expression of God's love, and so are not ever be despised or rejected. They are the temple of God (1 Corinthians 6:19), which is to say, they are the places where God dwells and is at work.

———————

Should we say that Jesus was an agrarian?

If we mean by an agrarian someone who is a professional farmer who makes a living through the raising and selling of crops and livestock, then the answer is clearly no. But such a definition is far too limited. The definition of an agrarian should not be reduced to a farmer (of which there have been many types and expressions) but should, instead, include all people who work to promote the health and vitality of creatures in their places. Agrarians understand that a human life cannot flourish apart from good food, clean water, amiable company, good work, excellent tools, fertile soil, pollinating bees, helpful neighbors, protein-producing herbivores, and strong traditions of memory that pass on essential insights and skills to following generations. Insofar as persons work to improve the lives of people and land at the same time, they are agrarians. Characterized this way, it is fairly clear that Jesus was an agrarian because his ministries make sense only in terms that are at once focused on the birds of the air and the lilies of the field (Matthew 6:26–29) and on the most marginalized of humans (the lepers, the prostitutes, the tax collectors), and that extend to "all things in heaven and on earth" (Colossians 1:15–20). Jesus was an agrarian because he focused his love on, and put his body to work for, the well-being of all creatures and the good of all creation.

Agrarian life and work have much to teach us about the meaning of a human being and the purpose of a human life. Moreover, agrarian traditions and practices can help reorient spiritual quests so they become directed "down and among" rather than "up and away." But it should also be clear that agrarians have much to learn from Jesus as the one who demonstrates what a truly life-giving, life-honoring way of being looks like. His movement into life with others, his bodily postures of coming alongside others, the practices of nurture, healing, and liberation that he performs, and his calling of people into communities that will model new social and economic orders based on sharing and service (Acts 2:43–47) signal a profound and practical way of experiencing this life and this world. Attending to Jesus's way of being can help people learn to attend to each other and to their places in fresh ways. It can help them perceive where they are and whom they are with as if all are beloved by God.

To "place the soul" isn't simply to insert people in a location. This is hardly enough because it can, thinking again of the pebble in a jar, leave people mostly unaffected and unchanged. People are not simply *in* places but *of* them, in the sense of a plant growing out of the ground. To "place the soul" is to work to open oneself to the pains and possibilities of this world, like the seed that must open itself to the soil if it hopes to germinate and grow, so that one learns to be a companionable and caring presence wherever one is.[47]

PART II

Agrarian Spiritual Exercises

CHAPTER FOUR

Learning to Pray

Absolutely unmixed attention is prayer.
—Simone Weil

The apostle Paul believed that followers of God should rejoice always, pray without ceasing, and give thanks in all circumstances (1 Thessalonians 5:16–18). It is a lot to ask, especially given the many circumstances where rejoicing, praying, and thanksgiving may not be foremost in people's minds. How do people become capable of this sort of life? In this chapter I will focus on what unceasing prayer is as a daily *way of being* and what it involves. My assumption is that praying without ceasing describes a God-inspired set of habits—a nimble, improvisational *posture* and a disciplined *focus* for action—that reorients people in their places and communities so that life is cherished and God is honored. It is a cultivated mode of life that transforms how people perceive, feel, receive, and engage their world. In other words, while prayers can take multiple well-known (spoken) forms like petition, adoration, and confession, unceasing praying is foundational because it works at a person's (often unspoken) demeanor or comportment, what we might describe as his or her basic manner of relating to anything at all. What I want to suggest is that prayer is fundamentally an embodied and affective posture that by opening people to the presence of God also positions people to be available to each other in God-honoring ways.

According to Aristotle, prayers are forms of speech that are not susceptible to truth or falsity.[1] Unlike declarative statements like "It's raining outside," or "That is a big dog," prayers do not increase our knowledge of the world in the way that descriptive or factual statements do. Prayers cannot be tested according to the rigors of scientific procedure or verified by the methods of empirical observation. How, for instance, would one empirically verify statements like "Lord, you have known me, even while I was in my mother's womb" or "Our Father, who art in heaven, hallowed be thy name"? Is verification even the right sort of thing to try to do? These examples suggest that prayers follow a different grammar and obey rules of use in which considerations other than factual truth or falsity come into play.

Aristotle makes a good point. Rather than being statements of fact, prayers are often more like promises that express a commitment to behave in the world in ways that nurture and honor its God-givenness. But he also happens to miss something vitally important about a praying way of being, which is that praying seeks to reorient people so they can live in their world in a more compassionate manner. A compassionate stance, however, changes how one perceives and what one understands to be the truth of reality. Insofar as people learn to encounter their places and fellow creatures as beloved by God, they also come to a fresh understanding of *where* they are, *whom* they are with, and *how* they should behave. In other words, persons who pray ought to *perceive* their world differently than those who do not pray. They should also *engage* it differently by responding to others as sacred gifts to be cherished and celebrated. By changing how people encounter and engage others, praying also changes what they think, feel, and understand about them.

Another way to frame this is to say that in a praying mode of being people learn to tell the stories of their lives with God as a central character within them. God's ways of being with others and God's ways of naming and narrating the significance of what is happening—especially as these have been revealed in scripture and in the life of Jesus—reframe how people understand the characters and events of their own lives. The meanings of day-to-day dramas and the values by which people evaluate the action of life are transformed because now the whole of existence is illuminated by the divine presence that creates, nurtures, heals, reconciles, and perfects it. People who pray may not provide a swath of new scientifically verifiable facts about the world, but they do invite others to experience places and fellow creatures as imbued with divine significance. For instance, whereas a strictly scientific account of a newborn child can say a lot that is of great value about the physiological aspects of the birth process and the child, a prayerful way of being characterizes newborns (and all people) as "children of God." So named and narrated, people must now relate to the child in distinct ways that honor its life *as a gracious gift.* The significance of the child's presence, its reason for being, and thus also how one should engage it throughout its life, changes when the stories of its existence are enfolded within the stories of God.

To pray is to desire to relate to God in some way. It is to invite God to be an inspiring and instructing presence in the details and demands of one's life. This desire, however, is anything but simple, since people can be confused or mistaken about who God is, where God is, or what God wants. They may also fail to appreciate what it takes to be in relationship with God (or with anything else, for that matter). The issue isn't simply that there can be an incongruity between what one says, what one is deeply committed to, and how one lives.[2] We must also consider the personal and practical conditions that make something like a genuine encounter possible at all. Preparing to come into the presence of others, and then learning to respond to them, requires that one first be attentive and open to them, and that, as we will now see, is not easy.

THE PRACTICE OF ATTENTION

The prospect of cultivating habits of unceasing prayer depends on developing a capacity for attention. Being open to and in communication with God presupposes that one is attentive to what God has to say and show. Otherwise one's communication, however pious sounding, will not be a genuine dialogue with God but a monologue or echo chamber instead. This is why Simone Weil believed that "attention, taken to its highest degree, is the same thing as prayer. It presupposes faith and love. . . . Absolutely unmixed attention is prayer."[3] Weil is not alone in speaking this way. Writing in the fourth century, Evagrius of Pontus, one of the great monastic masters of contemplative practice, said that "nothing is more essential to prayer than attentiveness."[4] But what is attention, and how does one cultivate it?

In her analyses of modern moral thought, Iris Murdoch argued that an egocentric conception of persons renders genuine attention all but impossible: "Our picture of ourselves has become too grand, we have isolated, and identified ourselves with, an unrealistic conception of the will, we have lost the vision of a reality separate from ourselves, and we have no adequate conception of original sin."[5] The issue isn't simply or solely self-aggrandizement. It is also the constant temptation to deform the world by fantasy, which is the desire to engage a world as we wish it to be rather than as it really is. One needn't think this to be a malicious gesture. One can just as well characterize it as reflecting discontent, exhaustion, fear, or boredom in the face of realities that either resist, frustrate, or disappoint us. It takes considerable patience and resolve—one has to slow down, make time, concentrate, and commit—and a good amount of confession and mercy, not to walk away when confronted with others that are fundamentally a mystery and that resist comprehension by us. To engage others in a serious and sustained manner is to discover how often we are mistaken about them. It is a lot easier to live with the ideas and the simplifying stereotypes and caricatures we have of others than to engage them on their own (almost always) complicated terms.

Murdoch turned to art to help us understand the difficulty because it is in artistry that we often see "the almost irresistible human tendency to seek consolation in fantasy. . . . Almost all art is a form of fantasy-consolation and few artists achieve the vision of the real." To see the real, artists must learn the moral discipline to "silence and expel self." Great artists practice detachment and self-renunciation, not because they despise themselves, but because they see how their needs and desires can get in the way of a faithful perception of what they are looking at. This gives to the greatest art an "impersonal" quality. It is art that "shows us the world, our world and not another one, with a clarity which startles and delights us simply because we are not used to looking at the real world at all."[6] Great art does not reflect the artist's imposition of him or herself upon the world but grows as a response to a reality that has been patiently and precisely perceived and deeply felt.

The sculptor Auguste Rodin understood this process better than most. As described by the poet Rainer Maria Rilke, Rodin managed the kind of attention that excised whatever was extraneous and unimportant. "But to what is important he throws himself open, and he is wholly open when he is among things or where animals and people touch him quietly and like things." Compared to people who live among things as though sleeping, absent-minded, or unsympathetic, or to people who walk through life constantly scanning it for the next possibility, Rodin is "the lover who continually receives, the patient one who does not count his time and does not think of wanting the next thing. For him what he gazes at and surrounds with gazing is always the only thing, the world in which everything happens."[7] When he sculpted a hand it was as though the hand was the sole thing God had created, so fully did Rodin create the glory and grace of what a hand is. When he sculpted *The Kiss* it was as though he saw that we need to receive and give love to others and that this is the only action that can fulfill a person's life.

Rodin's powers of perception developed when he was a lowly handworker, exercising his craft in obscurity. His abilities were refined in drawing exercises that trained him to see deeply into the life of things and to recognize the energies of nature that issued in the surfaces and contours of things. In a sense, he did not sculpt things as he wanted them to be. Rather, he sought to sculpt things as nature gave them to him. His sculptures of things are so moving because one sees in them what we might call their essential being or inner power, the freshness of their emergence into the world. Rodin understood that what he wanted was irrelevant to the truth of things. Instead he gave himself, and turned his talent and skill, fully to the task of creating sculptures that have and express their own voice. The cultivation of this habit of attention enabled Rodin to find joy and beauty in the smallest of things because he sensed the miracle of their being in ways that few people do. Rilke writes, "This wise and great man knows how to find joy; a joy as nameless as that one remembers from childhood, and yet full to the brim with the deepest inducement; the smallest things come to him and open up to him. . . . Everything speaks as though it had been in the wilderness and had meditated and fasted. And we have almost nothing to do but listen; for work itself comes out of this listening."[8]

In Murdoch's terms, Rodin excelled in the capacity to love, since love is the capacity to direct one's attention to others in ways that are genuinely open and responsive to their alterity, or what I call their sanctity and grace. "It is in the capacity to love, that is to *see*, that the liberation of the soul from fantasy consists. The freedom which is a proper human goal is the freedom from fantasy, that is the realism of compassion."[9] Love is the crucial capacity to cultivate because love exercises the patience and kindness that enable people to meet others as they are. As Paul puts it, love "is not envious or boastful or arrogant or rude. It does not insist on its own way; it is not irritable or resentful; it does not rejoice in wrongdoing, but rejoices in the truth. It bears all things, believes all things, hopes all things, endures all things" (1 Corinthians 13:4–7). One's going out to the world, in other words, requires that people also turn inward to cultivate the conditions for genuine receptivity. Without this interior work, what the Australian indigenous author Alexis Wright calls an "inward migration," people will perceive what they encounter in terms of their fears, anxieties, and ambitions, or in the thoughtless ways of cultures bent on suicide and ecocide. "This inward migration—removing oneself to a place of concentration, imagination, and wondering—is the mind working and sifting through the essence of things; it's where you begin to try to comprehend the complexity of the endless interconnectedness of place, and what it means to be in place with your homeland, and to visualize faraway places and all of the ideas that arise from curiosity."[10]

Murdoch was in agreement with Weil, who argued that without the discipline of attention people close themselves off from the grace of the world and consequently run the risk of embracing a counterfeit world, a world primarily of their own desiring or imagining. Fear, anxiety, arrogance, and apathy act like screens or filters that prevent the alterity of others from reaching us, which is why people must do the interior work that removes their influence. "Attention alone—that attention which is so full that the 'I' disappears—is required of me. I have to deprive all that I call 'I' of the light of my attention and turn it on to that which cannot be conceived."[11] Weil feared that prayers run the risk of projecting upon God what people want for themselves. The problem with prayers of wish fulfillment is not that people (often legitimately) want things but that their wanting can become dominant and the primary prism through which others are perceived and related to. This is why she insisted that "attention consists of suspending our thought, leaving it detached, empty, and ready to be penetrated by the object."[12] In making personal wanting the animating impulse of prayer, people may (unconsciously) communicate that they do not trust God to provide for them and so must secure their needs for themselves. In this grasping and securing posture, however, the sanctity of others cannot shine because who they are is now a feature of how they service a person's need. This is why the discipline of attention is so important for prayer: it makes it possible for monological speech to be transformed into a true dialogue with God in which our pleas, laments, questions, hopes, and desires can be informed and corrected as one learns to listen to God. The connection between prayer and attention is crucial because attention is the discipline that trains the ego and opens the heart so that a humble, compassionate, and just regard for others can occur. By cultivating a capacity to welcome and receive another *as other*, attention shows itself to be a generous and kind posture.

Since the time of Murdoch's and Weil's writing, the day-to-day contexts in which people live—what Yves Citton calls the "ecologies of attention"—have shifted dramatically. The transformation has happened at multiple levels. Consider, for instance, how the advent of a screen culture now gives people the prospect of creating and inhabiting virtual or fantasy worlds that can be tailor-made to suit their preferences. As people spend more and more of their time on laptops, tablets,

VR headsets, and smart phones, worlds are presented to them that are highly stylized, choreographed, and cropped to serve someone's financial or ego interests. If viewers become bored, they can simply opt out and scan for new possibilities. The point is that you as the viewer should not have to face a reality if you don't want to. You set the terms and frame the image for what you want to see. Though people give their gaze to what they are looking at, what they see will likely not have the feel or significance of Rodin's encounter with the alterity and mystery of being. Rather than (possibly) meeting the grace of God in fellow creatures, it is all the more likely that people will encounter a projection of their desires or a marketing pitch. Perception becomes pornographic in the sense that others are encountered and engaged not in terms of their integrity or sanctity—as sacred gifts—but in the instrumental terms of what they can do for us.

It would be a mistake to blame individual people for this. This is because we live in economies long in the making that are prone to objectifying and commodifying everything and every place within reach. It is important to underscore that these economies developed alongside a new self-understanding of persons as historical agents who control and possess the world. As described by Pierre Manent, to be modern is to be self-conscious and autonomous agents who design and engineer the world according to their own liking. The laws of nature or God no longer play a defining or determining role.[13] As a result, other people do not signify as children of God, nor do plants and fellow animals appear as creatures beloved by God. Practically speaking, this means we have increasingly come to inhabit built environments that reflect entirely human goals and concerns. In a world populated by simulacra and spectators, genuine attention becomes difficult.

It is also important to appreciate how in recent decades the functioning of economies has shifted in important ways. In thinking of production economies, the crucial limiting or enabling factor has traditionally been the scarcity of material inputs. Today, however, it is the scarcity of a people's capacity to notice, let alone purchase, what companies produce. This is why technologies and communications media have proliferated to the extent that they have. Anyone with something to sell or announce wants your attention. Unsurprisingly, people in-

creasingly feel under assault from the barrage of robo-calls, screen no-
tifications, event announcements, and automated sales pitches.
Suffering from solicitation overload, people succumb to attention exhaustion. In what business people call the "attention economy," the
most marketable entity is not a consumer product but a consumer's
attention. Internet platforms like Google need to keep track of your
every gaze and movement because it is your attention that they can sell
to advertisers and marketers.[14] This is why a casual search for some
consumer product results in advertisements for that product that are
specifically targeted at you for several days thereafter. Citton observes,
"*Our attention has a price*, and it is pretty high. For the moment, however, it is not paid *to us*: others skim off most of the profit."[15]

Today's attention exhaustion didn't just happen. It is the inevitable
result of major trends in modern cultures that premise (personal, political, economic) "success" upon the intensification and widest possible extension of stimulation. Jonathan Crary puts it this way: "It is
possible to see one crucial aspect of modernity as an ongoing crisis
of attentiveness, in which the changing configurations of capitalism
continually push attention to new limits and thresholds, with an endless sequence of new products, sources of stimulation, and streams of
information, and then respond with new methods of managing and
regulating perception."[16] For most people it is becoming harder and
harder to escape from relentless solicitation. The result, however, is
that people have less and less ability to choose and take their time to
linger with things, or to reflect patiently on the paths of life they wish
to travel. If it is true that people signal what matters by what they
give their attention to, and if moral and spiritual character mature
in the sustained engagements people have with others, then attention overload and exhaustion—along with the withdrawal from reality
they occasion—are phenomena of the profoundest significance. Can
people be thoughtful about what they want, or be clear about who
they want to be, if their attention is perpetually distracted, dispersed,
or assaulted by countless solicitations? Can people nurture the world
that nurtures them if they do not have the attentive capacities to sense
places and communities as media of blessing? If it is the case that we
are transformed by what we give our attention to, then the giving

and withholding of attention are matters of the highest practical and personal concern.

How does Jesus help us direct and give our attention?

ATTENDING WITH JESUS

When Jesus was asked by his disciples how to pray, he told them to say, "Our Father in heaven, hallowed be your name. Your kingdom come. Your will be done, on earth as it is in heaven. Give us this day our daily bread. And forgive us our debts, as we also have forgiven our debtors. And do not bring us to the time of trial, but rescue us from the evil one" (Matthew 6:9–13). In Luke's gospel, the prayer is similar, but shorter: "Father, hallowed be your name. Your kingdom come. Give us each day our daily bread. And forgive us our sins, for we ourselves forgive everyone indebted to us. And do not bring us to the time of trial" (Luke 11:2–4).

This Lord's Prayer is well known and practiced by countless Christians. It is, in multiple respects, a foundational prayer because it reflects Jesus's own practice of communicating with his Father. Attending to it, we not only gain some insight into what Jesus was saying and doing in his own prayer life. We also begin to appreciate what he thought praying is meant to do. Stated succinctly, to pray is to want to participate in the coming to earth of God's kingdom, the assumption being that the best life is one where the power of God's love is the only power at work inspiring our attention and animating our action. To participate in this life, however, is not automatic. People must prepare themselves daily with prayer, much like musicians who regularly practice the scales that will open a world of music to them. Prayer reorients people so that they perceive, feel, and engage life in a new way. When looking to Jesus's prayer, we can see that three elements emerge as essential. Prayer (a) transforms a person's desires; (b) teaches people to receive life as a sacred gift; and (c) calls them to practice forgiveness. These elements enable people to relate to others in a God-honoring manner. They are not accomplished once and for all but are daily and ongoing, which is why praying, at its core, is an unceasing activity.

Transforming Desire

To say, "Your kingdom come. Your will be done, on earth as it is in heaven," is to want existing ways of being in the world that lead to division, degradation, and death to be reformed so that they witness to the Godly ways of being that nurture, heal, and liberate life. Earth and heaven are not opposed to each other. Nor do people need to wait until they die to experience life with God because in the embodied life of Jesus the "fullness of God was pleased to dwell" (Colossians 1:19). To see how Jesus lives is to see how God has always lived. To participate in Jesus's ways of being is thus to participate, however imperfectly and incompletely, in God's ways of being. In other words, the extent to which people live like Jesus—and in ways that are unique to each person's specific potential—inspired and animated by the love of God as he demonstrated it, is the extent to which they live the life of heaven.

To call upon heaven is not to long to get to another location. It is, instead, to long for sinful ways of thinking and relating to be defeated so that God's ways of mercy and justice become a reality here and now. *Transformation* of this world, rather than *transportation* to another, is the key. But for transformation to occur, people must, as some ancient variants of Luke 11:2 put it, ask that the Holy Spirit descend upon them and cleanse them of former ways. This means that prayer is fundamentally a cleansing activity in which sinful ways of perceiving, feeling, thinking, and engaging are washed away. The Psalmist modeled this way of praying when he said, "Create in me a clean heart, O God, and put a new and right spirit within me" (Psalm 51:10).

Put formulaically, to pray is to open yourself to the Holy Spirit so that it can activate the love of God that is (always already) the essence of your being and that is uniquely yours to express in the world. In opening yourself to the power of God, two possibilities of the highest importance come into view: (a) the activation of God's love within you enables you to live into the fullness of your distinct life and thus experience what Jesus calls life's abundance; and (b) this same activation enables you to love others truly and thus to contribute to the healing and flourishing of the communities and places through which you live. The Spirit of God has never been foreign to anyone because it is only the power of God's love that (from the inside) sustains people in their being.

Somewhat paradoxically, praying is the activity that, by calling upon God, recalls people to themselves so they can appreciate and activate the divine love that has been implanted within and among them from the beginning: "The kingdom of God is among/within you" (Luke 17:21).[17] When people pray, they invite Jesus into their hearts so he can clear away the dispositions that make people either negligent or destructive and then install the habits that serve and celebrate others. A "pure heart," in other words, is a heart in which the strategies that block God's love from being active are removed. It is a heart in which the love of God is operative and freely flows. This means that praying is an exercise in which, like Paul, a person learns to say, "It is no longer I who live, but Christ who lives in me" (Galatians 2:20). To pray is to ask that the love of God should grow and become ever more deeply rooted in one's life, and thereby transform the ways one relates to everything else.

Scripture presupposes throughout that people can be animated by a false spirit. This is why it is so important that people learn to test and discern the spirit. One of the best ways to do this is to evaluate the forms of life that grow as a result of a spirit's influence. If one's life results in "fornication, impurity, licentiousness, idolatry, sorcery, enmities, strife, jealousy, anger, quarrels, dissensions, factions, envy, drunkenness, carousing, and things like these" (Galatians 5:19–21), then one can be sure that one's life is not animated by the Spirit of God. But if one's life produces "love, joy, peace, patience, kindness, generosity, faithfulness, gentleness, and self-control" (Galatians 5:22–23), then one can know that the power of God that sustains and perfects all of life is also at work within oneself.

A clean heart is animated by a desire for others, or by what Willie Jennings calls an eros for others. This desire is fundamentally a desire to live into deep communion with others.[18] As God said when first creating the world, it is not good for a person to be alone (Genesis 2:18). Lonely or alienated life is a contradiction in terms and must, therefore, be distinguished from times of solitude or "inward migration" that can play an important role in a person's spiritual development. The best life is a companionable one in which people know they are nurtured and supported by fields and watersheds, neighborhoods and communities, and families and friends. In creating a garden world, God made it clear that human kinship is to be so broad and deep as to include the animals and all the life of the garden. In making care of the garden humanity's fundamental and abiding vocation, God also made it clear that it is through the exercises of care that people learn the depth, the requirements, and the blessings of that kinship. For people to thrive, they need to know that they *belong* in their places and communities, grow out of and are benefited by them, and can only fully flower if they make *mutual* flourishing their central concern. People must constantly be on the lookout for misdirected and disordered desires because these lead to the unraveling of life.

The prophets spoke regularly of the need to care for and protect those who cannot protect themselves because they understood how easily desire turns inward and becomes self-serving. Disordered desire does not remain at the personal and interpersonal levels. It ramifies in the creation of economies and institutions that fragment and exploit life and that consign creatures to abuse and abandonment. This is why they argued that justice demands new economies and political forms that provide for the needs of every person. In the words of Isaiah, "Wash yourselves; make yourselves clean; remove the evil of your doings from before my eyes; cease to do evil, learn to do good; seek justice, rescue the oppressed, defend the orphan, plead for the widow" (Isaiah 1:16–17). What is so striking about the prophets is that they did not confine their vision to the care of fellow human beings. It extended to every creature under heaven, and to the land itself, because God's covenant is with the whole creation. "I will make for you a covenant on that day with the wild animals, the birds of the air, and the creeping things of the ground; and I will abolish the bow, the sword, and war from the land; and I will make you lie down in safety" (Hosea 2:18).[19] To do evil is to violate another's life in some way. It is to be prone to the blindness that does not see others as the cherished gifts and beloved children of God that they are.

In his life and ministries Jesus demonstrated that a desire for others and a desire for God are inseparable. When describing those who will inherit God's kingdom, Jesus says they are the ones who feed the hungry, give water to the thirsty, welcome strangers, clothe the naked, take care of the sick, and visit those in prison (Matthew 25:32–46). He does not distinguish what is done to people and what is done to him: "Truly I tell you, just as you did it to the least of these who are members of my family, you did it to me" (25:40). Jesus's point is not that people may elect to serve others as a way of serving him. It is, instead, to insist that the two desires are inseparable. John's first letter states the matter unequivocally: "Those who say, 'I love God,' and hate their brothers or sisters, are liars; for those who do not love a brother or sister whom they have seen, cannot love God whom they have not seen. . . . Those who love God must love their brothers and sisters also" (1 John 4:20–21).

Given what we have already said about the difficulties of coming to attention, we should expect that having a desire for others is not easy. Those who want to follow in the ways of Jesus must give themselves away and be baptized into the way of his self-offering death (Romans 6:3). Speaking this way does not amount to a despising of oneself because a faithful life presupposes and is rooted in the conviction that each creature is loved by God *as it is*. Rather, it expresses how important it is to ground each person's self-understanding in the knowledge that God's love for them is unconditional. Apart from this understanding, it is all too likely that people will love themselves improperly or not love themselves at all, as when they become mired in guilt, insecurity, or self-loathing. When a desire for oneself is put to death, people give up the need to grasp, secure, and control life for themselves. They are freed to receive their life as a gift and as the expression of God's love for all creatures, and thus are also opened to give that love to others in return. Jesus is the model here because he exhibited in his embodied movements what it looks like to be completely open to receiving God's love and completely free to give that same love to everyone. Being maximally "for us," he also shows us what it takes for us to be maximally "for others."[20]

Attention is crucial for the cultivation of a desire for others. It is also crucial for the work of justice. In a conversation with Mary Zournazi, Rowan Williams noted that "both justice and love depend on a sustained paying attention to what is there before you, putting aside your own agenda, your own preoccupations or fears or preferences and seeking to see clearly. Generosity begins not in the overflow of warm feeling, but in a patient looking and listening. It's why love needs contemplation."[21] From a scriptural point of view, justice has less to do with a settling of legal claims between disputants than with, instead, a proper alignment that develops between people when they appreciate how much they need and depend on each other. It isn't enough to follow some rules. Instead, people must learn to apprentice themselves to God's ways of being because these are the ways of presence, patience, and compassion that equip us to take care of each other. Proper care presupposes that people are attentive and attuned to each other and thus know when their actions are genuinely helpful or not.

People yearn to be seen and engaged without the agendas, caricatures, and misconceptions that invariably harm them (Murdoch observed that people often make up pictures of what they think other people are and then persecute them with those same pictures). People want to be known in a merciful and compassionate way. For that to happen, however, prayer is essential because it activates the attention in which the anxieties and ambitions of the "I" have been put away. This is another way of saying that prayer teaches people how to love unconditionally. The model for this unconditional love is God, who creates every creature not as the expression of some lack or need but as the embodiment of an overflowing generosity that delights in creatures being themselves. "God . . . is the power that simply makes things to *be what they are.* God has no interest to serve. God has no needs to satisfy. Therefore, when God makes what is other, God affirms the other unconditionally. That's it." God doesn't make creatures to fill some lack in God's life. Nor do God and creatures exist in a competitive relationship where the greatness of the one depends on the diminution of the other. Instead, God is glorified all the more as creatures maximally realize their free life. "And this means that God's perception of the real is utterly without distortion: God saw what he had made and, behold, it was very good."[22]

The goodness of creatures and the sanctity of their lives are presupposed by all of Jesus's ministries. Again and again we see that he did not engage others in an instrumental or idolatrous manner. He did not heal or feed or forgive others because they satisfied some ambition of his or fulfilled some personal need. Instead, he provided the nurture and friendship others needed so they could truly *become themselves.* Jesus reminded people again and again that they are children of God meant to live a life of love. If one is to live this way, however, the conditions within (like fear, anxiety, and hubris) and without (like ostracization, abuse, and injustice) need to be cleansed and corrected. In all his ways of relating to others, he showed us what this cleansing way looks like. For people to pray that God's kingdom come, and that God's will be done on earth as it is in heaven, is to want to journey along the ways of love that Jesus embodied.

Receiving Life as a Gift

To say, "Give us this day our daily bread," is not a simple matter, especially for people who have been trained to purchase bread as a commodity. As such, it appears as a more or less self-contained package in which the vestiges of its complex (and vulnerable) coming-to-be have been shorn away. But for those who know better, bread is something of a miracle because they understand that there is no bread without grain, no grain without seeds, no seed germination without fertile soil, no fertile soil without billions of microorganisms, no plant growth without sunshine and rain, no vitality without plant health, no grain fields without farmers and farm communities, no dough without the creativity of bakers, and no life without God's animating breath circulating through all of it. Bread does not have to be. Its existence should not be taken for granted. Bread is but one nurturing and delectable instance of a world that reflects the God who perpetually *gives life.*[23] As the Psalmist says, God covers the heavens with clouds and prepares the rain the earth needs; God makes the grass grow and gives to the animals their food; God fills us with the finest wheat, and gives snow like wool (Psalm 147:8–16). "Taste and see that the Lord is good" (Psalm 34:8) indeed!

One of the tragedies of living within a commodified world and its objectifying logic is that people feel cut off from what we might call life's liveliness and ever-fresh generativity. Things just are what they are. The sense that things are the material manifestation of a divine intention that *desires for them to be* and that values their being as *good and beautiful*—this is what is lost when bread ceases to be a sacred gift. The bread may still taste good. But in a thoroughly commodified world, what you eat more likely reflects someone's business plan rather than the blessing of God. Marketers want you to eat their food (which is why they spend millions on advertising) so they can boost their bottom line. Compare this with a baker who presents you with a loaf as the expression of their love for you and then sits down with you to share in your life. When bread is received as a loving gift, it isn't only a source of immediate nourishment. It is also an invitation into fellowship, friendship, and communion with others. Would we not be more satisfied and contented in our lives if the things we used and consumed were known to be the expressions of another's love and care for us?

The conviction that bread is a gift communicates an essential insight: *life happens within a receiving and giving dynamic.* As historians and anthropologists have long observed, societies that foreground the importance of gift exchange also understand that life is a relational reality. To receive but not give in return (noting that there is an etiquette to what proper return entails) is to be confused about what life is. More seriously, it is also to short-circuit the flow of life, because now one takes out of circulation—by keeping for oneself—what is to be shared with others. When a gift is taken to be a private possession, and when owners believe they can do with their possession whatever they choose, the conditions are set for the exploitation, even abuse, of what one owns. The evidence of this danger abounds in factory-farm animals that are abused as "units of production" rather than cherished as creatures beloved by God; in agricultural fields where soils are eroded and mined of their nutrient value, and waters are polluted by the steady application of ever more toxic herbicides and pesticides; and in communities turned into "sacrifice zones" where labor and infrastructure are exploited and then abandoned. In a world governed by a commodification logic, creatures and places are reduced to "natural resources" to be mined as efficiently and profitably as possible. Consumers, meanwhile, are treated as more or less gullible "units of consumption" meant to bolster shareholder profits. In a world like this, nothing and no one can signify as a precious gift. This is a horrifying world because in it no creature, not even you, is the embodied expression of the love of God.

This brief description helps us see that the postures and the overall comportment of the person who *receives* are fundamentally different than the postures and comportment of the person who *grasps*. Grasping reflects a desire to control things, since ownership often confers the right to do what one wants with what one owns. The control of places and creatures, however, means that one does not engage them *as they are* but as owners *want them to be*. The ability of places and creatures to express and develop themselves is thus either frustrated or denied. There is in this grasping posture an abiding presumption that reality should conform to one's expectations and do one's bidding. A receiving posture, by contrast, is constantly learning to relinquish the desires for possession and control. It has to, because individuals do not control the giving or the timing of a gift, nor do they determine what the gift is. To receive is to trust that what the giver gives is good. To receive is to hold onto what is given with a gentler and more appreciative touch.[24] To grasp is to close one's hand around something, whereas to receive is to come with open hands that remain open for the purpose of further sharing.

On those special occasions when gifts are given, it is customary for people to say thank you. Expressions of gratitude matter because they communicate that the gift did not have to be given. It is gratuitous, and a manifestation of another's care. Saying "Thank you," however, easily becomes hollow if it does not follow from a grateful heart. What is a grateful heart? It is one in which people learn to make themselves a giving and generous presence in the world. If an expression of gratitude signals that a gift has been received, a generous disposition signals that the recipient has been transformed by the gift. As Lewis Hyde puts it, "Passing the gift along is the gift of gratitude that finishes the labor. The transformation is not accomplished until we have the power to give the gift on our own terms."[25] Stated theologically, a grateful heart is a conduit organ that continuously *receives* the love of God and *gives* it to others. A grateful heart is a clean heart that has learned to clear away the impediments that sequester, divert, or frustrate the flow of God's gracious gifts.

If these reflections on the gift are true to the Spirit of God, then Jesus's admonition to receive bread as a gift is not only for the purpose of evoking words of gratitude—as important as they are—but also to transform people so they become generous in the care and nurture they give to others. When people receive a gift properly, they understand that the world exists, not to be hoarded, but to be shared. They appreciate that life is a relational reality and so must be governed by a covenantal rather than a contractual sensibility, a sensibility in which people are committed to being with each other in the modes of listening, nurture, and celebration. Put in economic terms, this means that wheat will be grown in ways that build soil fertility, conserve fresh water, respect animals, compensate farmers and bakers, and honor eaters by providing them bread that is nutritious and delicious.

Jesus gave a memorable image to describe the receiving/giving dynamic of life when he spoke of a seed that germinates and produces much fruit only if it gives itself to the nurturing soil that is the matrix for all growth. There can be no flowering life if a seed holds to itself or tries to secure itself by itself (John 12:24–26). A self-enclosed seed remains dormant because it deprives itself of the nurture that only others can provide. As dead to the world, it cannot contribute to the world's ongoing life. For a seed to grow and flourish, it must, therefore, cease to be an individual, self-standing thing and instead become a conduit that is open to receiving God's love but also oriented (in its fruitfulness) to giving that love to others in return. People, like a seed, must give themselves unreservedly to the nurture of the contexts that nurture them if they want to experience "the life that really is life" (1 Timothy 6:19).

It is understandable that people will resist this self-giving mode of being because such a life is supremely vulnerable to another's abuse or neglect of it. This is why people often choose to build walls of protection and then work to fortify their lives by *grasping* and *controlling* the world rather than *receiving* and *sharing* it. But as multiple histories of violence and abuse demonstrate, paths that choose self-fortification eventually (and literally) lead to a dead end. They also precipitate the loneliness that comes from removing oneself from the flows of a giving/ receiving life. To receive life's nurture as a gift is to know that the best life is lived, not alone, but in a community that welcomes what people have to give and that provides for each other's needs. It takes courage to give oneself to others. It takes trust to believe that what one has to give matters. And it takes tremendous patience and humility to receive gifts that do not always match up with what one desires. Given these multiple layers of vulnerability, we can now see why ecclesial life, or the life of a community inspired and animated by the love of Jesus, is central to Christian formation. Nurturing contexts, though not without their problems, give the support people need to give themselves to others. Caring communities that work for the good of each other help people handle the vulnerabilities that accompany a self-offering life.

Life is a relational reality in which people are constantly receiving from others and giving in return. When people pray to God, "Give us this day our daily bread," they are not only asking to be nurtured every day. They are also asking that their lives be transformed in ways so that they can, in turn, and in ways specific to their abilities, become gifts that nurture others.

Forgiving Indebtedness

To say, "Forgive [*aphes*] us our debts [*opheilemata*], as we also have forgiven our debtors," is to recognize that personal and communal life are undermined by forms of indebtedness that either frustrate the flows of a receiving and giving life or deny that life is a gift meant to be shared with others. There is, of course, more than one kind of indebtedness, but what Jesus's prayer is alerting us to is the fact that indebtedness often creates forms of bondage that prevent people from being maximally present and attentive to each other. This is why people need to be released (*aphes* can be translated as release, pardon, remission, and forgiveness) from the division and oppression that indebtedness often creates. They must be on the lookout for the forms of debt that prevent people from freely relating to each other, the assumption being that people cannot really experience the blessings of life together in contexts that establish (and legally enforce) hierarchies that divide people into creditors and debtors, masters and slaves, or haves and have-nots. Forgiveness is such a radical gesture because it addresses what we can call the "debt imaginary" that determines how people think life should be organized. Jesus's prayer says it is time for people to stop the forms of indebtedness that lock them in forms of bondage that stifle their ability to grow and experience life's abundance.

Jesus's prayer highlights that forgiveness, while clearly speaking to interpersonal relations, is fundamentally an economic reality. To appreciate what Jesus is yearning for, it helps to situate his prayer in terms of how he understood his own mission. When Jesus first began his ministry in Galilee, he took up the prophetic mantle, declaring, "The Spirit of the Lord is upon me, because he has anointed me to bring good news to the poor. He has sent me to proclaim release [*aphes*] to the captives and recovery of sight to the blind, to let the oppressed go free, to proclaim the year of the Lord's favor" (Luke 4:18–19). Quoting Isaiah, Jesus is drawing our attention to how poverty and oppression are forms of bondage that prevent people from living well with each other and on the land. The "year of the Lord's favor" refers to the year of Sabbath Jubilee when land was restored to families who had lost it owing to financial hardship.[26] Jubilee marked the cancellation of financial debts and indicates that the Lord's justice demands that no individual be allowed to amass a private fortune at the expense of others who are rendered permanently destitute. The good news that Jesus proclaims releases people from economic bondage and liberates them from oppression. Forgiveness and freedom go together. Being forgiven, people can explore and develop the God-given potential that is uniquely theirs to achieve. Being liberated, they can creatively extend to others the love they daily receive.

Debt is a complex, pervasive, and often debilitating phenomenon. On the one hand, it seems morally obvious that people should repay their debts. But on the other hand, it is also clear that the moneylenders who lock people in debt are commonly reviled for the usurious practices that capitalize on another's need or misfortune. Though people are often advised to "save their money" and resist taking on debt, they also know they will likely not get an education, drive a car, or purchase a home without loans or a mortgage. Banks and credit card companies encourage and depend on rising consumer indebtedness because debts (and the interest payments they require) are highly profitable to those in the lending business. As the global financial collapse of 2008 demonstrated, governments will go to great lengths to protect systems of indebtedness, even if it requires the ruination of millions of lives. When we turn to the level of international relations, debt is again a pervasive and pernicious presence that takes the form of economic policies that require farmers to grow and workers to produce commodities for export (to pay off national debt) rather than provide for their community's needs. Colonized nations are thus crippled by the debt payments they owe to the very countries that looted and pillaged them in the first place. To appreciate the oppressive power of indebtedness in the lives of people, we should recall that revolutionary movements in the ancient world centered on a unified platform to cancel the debt and redistribute the land.[27] It is a hope that still animates millions of peasants, renters, migrant workers, refugees, and homeless people around the globe today. Jesus's proclamation of the year of Jubilee and his prayer that we "forgive everyone indebted to us" (Luke 11:4) need to be understood in this light.

As these examples show, financial debt saturates and defines day-to-day living for billions of people. It weighs on individuals and countries like a heavy chain that stifles possibilities and makes people anxious. It has become so pervasive and (seemingly) normal that many people find it hard to imagine what they would do with a debt-free life. What would life look like if economic indebtedness and land/wealth consolidation did not play this determinative role? How would a debt-free and more evenly wealth-distributed world alter the ways people related to their places and communities? What new dreams and possibilities for personal and communal life would emerge in a world defined by debt forgiveness and committed to economic reparations?

A debt-forgiving world would not be a world without obligations. In part, this is because not all forms of obligation are oppressive. Some are life-nurturing and life-giving, which makes them essential. Consider the fact that every individual depends on others for his or her birth, nurture, instruction, and support. I could not be the person that I have become apart from parents, siblings, friends, teachers, coaches, farmers, pets, grocery stores, utility companies, construction workers, doctors, bankers, chickens, cattle, wheat fields, pastures, earthworms, bees, and so on. The list goes on and on and reaches to the unfathomable. Quite literally, I owe my life to everyone, everything, and every place because my life is inescapably entangled and stitched within social and ecological meshworks that defy precise or complete enumeration. This is why it is impossible to construct a detailed, credit/debit ledger in which costs are comprehensively listed and payments are fully made.[28] One way to distinguish an obligation from a debt is that the latter can be precisely quantified and monetized, whereas the former cannot. To appreciate the difference, imagine what it would be like if a parent came to his or her now-adult child with an invoice detailing the multiple expenses accrued along the way. The child would be appropriately horrified by the parental injunction "It's time to pay your debt," because the care of another, if it is genuinely motivated by love, cannot be monetized. At the same time, parents would be appropriately dismayed if their children abandoned them in their need. Love seeks to bind people to each other, but not in ways that are oppressive. The love that is inspired by Jesus nurtures, liberates, and empowers others to become themselves.

Debt thrives in a monetized world governed by contracts. It assumes that the relationships between parties of the contract are impersonal and temporary: when the debt is paid, the deal is done, and the relationship comes to an end. Obligation, however, moves in a personal world governed by a covenantal sensibility that seeks to deepen a person's relationships with and responsibilities for others. As people know from personal experience, the appearance of money within a covenantal relationship invariably complicates and troubles it. Money can certainly change hands, but when it does it usually takes the form of a gift, or sometimes as a loan that, importantly, is without interest.[29] As David Graeber rightly understood, the reason money is so troublesome in a personal, covenantal setting is that money turns what is a moral relation into a matter of impersonal arithmetic. Should financial cost-benefit analysis be the overriding mechanism through which I determine whether to have children, pursue a friendship, or commit to a neighborhood? History teaches that when financial ledgers determine relationships and responsibilities, all manner of actions that would otherwise seem improper, if not immoral, now become justified.[30]

From the beginning, God calls people into covenant relationships with each other, with the land, and ultimately with God. This is because God has created a world in which creatures are defined by their need for nurture and support. To be a creature is to be self-*insufficient*. This means that life alone is a contradiction in terms. The best life is a communal one in which the power of God's love is animating how people are relating to each other. When love is the determining power guiding what people do, then the whole of creation has the greatest chance of experiencing the abundance God desires for it. When people appreciate the life that flourishes as *life together* in fertile and fecund places, then they also recognize how important it is to nurture the communal contexts that nurture them. This is why covenantal obligations are not to be avoided. Instead, they are to be honored and cultivated because each individual life excels to the extent that all the places and lives that touch and influence it are respected and nurtured at the same time.

I have emphasized the placed, embodied, and economic conditions of personal life because too many accounts of forgiveness frame it in the narrow terms of the wronged person, the wrongdoer, and the wrong act. In framings like this, the focus is on a particular event that is more or less abstracted from the ecological and social contexts that brought it into being. It is important to have environmental and economic factors constantly in view when considering the work of forgiveness because factors like financial debt, income inequality, racist policing and zoning, wealth consolidation, land dispossession, housing inequities, gender discrimination, and ethnic and class prejudice often inspire and fuel the resentments, insecurities, jealousies, and anxieties that precipitate wrongdoing. As people feel abandoned or devalued, perhaps even despised, it is all but inevitable that they will also act out in injurious or destructive ways. When this happens, people now find themselves doubly bound: bound by the weight of an unjust economic order and bound by the moral guilt of wrongdoing.

When Jesus instructed people to pray, "Forgive us our debts, as we also have forgiven our debtors," he was reminding them that the best life flourishes in communal, covenantal contexts where every effort is made to absolve people of the forms of bondage that oppress and degrade them. He was asking that people put aside credit/debit ledgers and cost-benefit analyses when assessing their responsibilities in a world that is saturated with divine gift giving. Ledgers and analyses of this sort are not wholly illegitimate, but they must not be allowed to dominate or finally determine how our dealings with others are decided. Followers of God forgive because they know that debt and guilt prevent people from living out the fullness of their lives. Indebtedness short-circuits the flow in which people humbly receive and generously share the gifts of God. Like God, people forgive because they know that forgiveness frees people to receive gratefully what God and others provide, and it inspires them to live in ways that are a gift to others. Forgiveness does not condone wrongdoing, nor does it magically make everything smooth and all right. Instead, it highlights how wrongdoing injures life together and violates communal responsibilities. Forgiveness, in other words, removes the shame that prevents people from being present and attentive to each other in ways that foster mutual flourishing. To be forgiven is to know that one can start afresh in one's relationships with others. The goal of forgiveness is a reconciled and mutually enhancing life, which is to say that it is the kind of life that characterizes the kingdom of God. "Forgiveness is a characteristic of the kingdom of God. Those who practice the ethics of the kingdom of God (and these include love and mercy) will demonstrate the kingdom of God—its irruption into human society and the evidence of its reality—in the here and now."[31]

––––––––––

I began this chapter with Paul's admonition to rejoice always, pray without ceasing, and give thanks in all circumstances. Given my accounts of the importance of attention, the transformation of desires, our attunement to a receiving and giving life, and the role of debt forgiveness in fostering a communal and covenantal sensibility, we can now better see why prayer is fundamentally an unceasing and daily way of being and a set of practical habits that reorient people in their places and communities so that the love of God might move more freely through them. At its core, prayer is the daily action whereby people open themselves to receiving the love of God and letting it become operational within, all with the aim that whole persons—body, heart, and mind—are now directed to being a nurturing presence wherever they are and whomever they are with.

This prayerful way of being is closely tied to the prospects of rejoicing and thanksgiving because prayer most basically is one's ever-deepening immersion and participation in the ways of God's love as these are embodied in habitats, neighborhoods, plant and animal creatures, and the wide diversity of fellow human beings. To engage God's love is the climax of life, since it is here that people encounter the divine power that creates and sustains a beautiful world. A prayerful life is not without pain because in too many places and times what people encounter is life's neglect, abuse, and violation. But it is the way of being that draws people into the world so that they might share in the joy and delight that marks God's own *Shabbat*.

CHAPTER FIVE

Learning to See

Love is the soul's looking.
—Simone Weil

To look and to see are not the same thing. Though individuals may "look" at the same scene, what they "see" can vary considerably. This is because viewers come equipped with different habits of attention and are motivated by varying desires and interests. To look inevitably presupposes a perspective or point of view that is itself a reflection of one's physical *location* (am I close enough to see details?), one's *time* (medieval peasants looked at things differently than today's typical suburbanites), and one's *standing* within a culture (marginalized people see things that those at the center of power often do not). Moreover, one's own seeing can change dramatically over time, as when adults say they see the world differently after becoming parents. Then again, who hasn't had the experience of remarking, "How did I not see that before?"

Though *looking* may presuppose little more than the physiological capacity for sight, *seeing* presupposes what Hans-Georg Gadamer called a "hermeneutical consciousness" that appreciates the *significance* of what one is looking at. To see is to interpret, and to interpret is to put to practical use ideas and concepts of varying kinds that enable people to articulate the meaning of what they look at. Depending on who we are and what our training has been, each of us will understand or deem important what another may find irrelevant or uninteresting. This is why a home builder sees things about a house that a typical home buyer doesn't appreciate, or why an experienced painter can admire the virtuosity of a painting in ways that a casual onlooker cannot. To see, in other words, is to look with particular kinds of sensitivities or interests, and thereby also to ascertain the significance of what one is looking at in specific ways.[1]

The discipline of hermeneutics teaches that there is no unmediated encounter with the world because to be in a world is "always already" to be engaged in acts of interpretation that, like a camera lens, "open" the world and bring it into focus. Drawing on the work of his teacher Martin Heidegger, Gadamer argued that the work of understanding is not something people elect to do from time to time. It is what they do all the time, no matter what stage of development they may be in, because people are the kinds of beings that are driven to experience their world as meaningful.[2] To be without understanding, unable to assess the significance of what one is looking at, would be like living in a world that was always blurry. Of course, what people believe the meaning of the world to be has varied dramatically from culture to culture. But the essential point is that people do not exist in a meaning-neutral space. None of us simply "look" at things, having no interest in or grasp of what is observed. From the moment we are born we are being educated, whether formally or not, to see, to focus, to evaluate, and thus also to engage our surroundings in the unique ways that we do. "Don't go there. It's dangerous!" "Isn't that a lovely spot?" "That was great. Let's do it again!"

How people have understood the world *as a whole* has varied greatly through time. Sticking to the ancient Greek philosophical context, when Democritus (5th c. BCE) looked at the world, he "saw" invisible, indivisible *atomoi* in perpetual motion. The various things that make up the world, things like trees, rivers, animals, and rocks, were to him but the random effect of various *atomoi* coming together. There is no force or intelligence directing their coming-to-be or their falling apart. Stuff simply happens! This picture of an atomist, pluralist world was in striking contrast to that of his contemporary Anaxagoras, who believed that the various elements of the world share in each other and in the whole. No particular thing is finally cut off from any other thing because each has within itself a portion of everything else. Moreover, there is nothing that is accidental or random about this world because *Nous* or Mind permeates the whole, giving it the shape and form that it does. For Anaxagoras the world he "saw" was an ordered and intelligible whole, a *kosmos*.

Why these dramatically different ways of seeing the world? Is it that Anaxagoras's picture (potentially) yields a more rational, regular, and reliable world in which people can say that whatever happens, happens for a reason? Was Democritus deeply frustrated by the desire to make sense of things? What this contrast reveals is that a picture of the world is also, in some sense, a picture of the people that develop it and so communicates what they want or hope or fear their world to be. How people position themselves in a place depends on what they understand their place to be. A mechanical picture of Earth and earth-system processes, for instance, is ideal for people who want to control the world and engineer it to fulfill their aims.

Following Pierre Hadot, it is important to underscore that ancient philosophy, and the "science" it made possible, were first and foremost about the advocacy for a way of life and the disciplines that enabled its practitioners to live well (however that was conceived). *Theoria,* the way of seeing being recommended by a philosophical school, was inextricably connected to an *ethos* or practical way of being in the world. To the extent that one's picture of the world did not help people live better lives, one ceased being genuinely philosophical. The whole point in serious contemplation of the world was to effect self-transformation, which meant that an *ethos* was accompanied by an *askesis,* a form of asceticism or personal discipline that aligned the life of the wisdom seeker with the truth of the world.[3] *Theoria, ethos,* and *askesis* were inextricably intertwined and influenced each other in important ways.

Though more contemporary philosophical schools may not appear to be in service of what is believed to be a better *ethos* or *askesis,* it is nonetheless apparent that people are encouraged to see and understand the world in ways that serve some interest or goal. *What* people are asked to see, the *modes* and the *tools* they are given to look at it, the *categories* and frames they are provided to organize what they see, and the *significance* they are supposed to discern as a result of their looking—all these are more or less established as cultural or professional norms while people set about doing their work. Hadot observes: "University philosophy therefore remains in the same position it occupied in the Middle Ages: it is still a servant, sometimes of theology, sometimes of science. In any case, it always serves the imperatives of the overall organization of education, or, in the contemporary period, of scientific research. The choice of professors, course topics, and exams is always subject to 'objective' criteria which are political or financial, and unfortunately all too often foreign to philosophy."[4] How and what we see, in other words, are always influenced by the cultural priorities, business institutions, professional norms, and streams of financial funding that establish the protocols for research.[5]

My point is not to say that we see whatever we want. It is, rather, to note that the *theoria* that enables us to make sense of what we are looking at always develops within an *ethos* or practical way of being that enables people to live in their world in particular sorts of ways. It would be myopic to think that we could evaluate what others are telling us about the world without also attending to the practical forms of life their seeing grows out of and encourages. To appreciate what I mean, it is helpful to look at the process of seeing as it happened in the work of Charles Darwin.

CONSIDERING DARWIN

In his autobiography Darwin tells us that the "gloomy parson" Thomas Robert Malthus's essay on population played a decisive role in his own work because it gave him the categories that brought what he looked at into a more compelling focus: "Fifteen months after I had begun my systematic inquiry, I happened to read for amusement Malthus on Population, and being well prepared to appreciate the struggle for existence which everywhere goes on, from long continued observation of the habits of animals and plants, it at once struck me that under these circumstances favorable variations would tend to be preserved and unfavorable ones to be destroyed. The result of this would be the formation of new species. Here I had at last got a theory by which to work."[6]

Here we can observe how Malthus gave Darwin the optics or interpretive lens by which to see the world as signifying in particular sorts of ways. Darwin had been looking at plant and animal species for a long while, but he had not yet found the interpretive framework that enabled him to make satisfactory sense of what he was looking at. Malthus gave him the hermeneutical framework he longed for. His *theoria* enabled Darwin to see creatures of all sorts as waged in competitive struggle so that they might increase themselves in the face of scarce and diminishing resources. As Darwin would write in *The Descent of Man*, all organic beings expend effort to increase their numbers. These populations, much like the human populations Malthus described, increase geometrically, and in places that cannot keep up with such rapid levels of increase. "Hence, as more individuals are produced than can possibly survive, there must in every case be a struggle for existence, either one individual with another of the same species, or with individuals of distinct species, or with the physical conditions of life. It is the doctrine of Malthus applied with manifold force to the whole animal and vegetable kingdom."[7]

Darwin's seeing of the world is saturated with an *ethos* of scarcity that also reflects an *askesis* of unremitting struggle and competition. It yields a vision of the world famously described by the poet Alfred Lord Tennyson as nature "red in tooth and claw." To look at any organic being is to see a drive to grow and reproduce itself. If such a being is to survive it must adapt to changing circumstances or die because it is only the "fit" beings, those who can best utilize the place they are in to improve reproductive potential, that can carry on.[8]

As a way of seeing the world, a Malthusian/Darwinian *theoria* clearly has considerable explanatory power. A lens focused on the struggle for survival brings multiple elements of the world into clearer view. Moreover, his insight that creatures are embedded within and in continuity with other creatures in their places is, in my view, essential. It would be naive, however, to think that Darwin's account of the world is "objective" or "comprehensive" in any straightforward meaning of the terms, or that it brings everything into focus. What does his *theoria* leave out of view and out of consideration, and what might it prevent lookers from seeing? Why put the focus on competition among individuals rather than cooperation among groups? Why assume scarcity in a world that might also be characterized by great abundance? Why believe that the drive to live is a drive primarily to "survive" rather than to "thrive" or "delight"? These are just some of the questions we can ask about the kind of seeing that follows from a Darwinian framework. This way of seeing, as valuable as it is, does not exhaust what is to be seen. As just one powerful counterexample, it is worth noting that it is common to find indigenous peoples picturing a world governed by kinship and generosity rather than competition and scarcity. What do they see that Darwin did not, and why?

It is important to consider carefully Darwin's vision of the world because several of his key concepts—fitness, scarcity, survival of the fittest—have made their way into the diverse disciplines of today's education. Darwin is invoked not only to describe what we might call the natural world. He has also given the basic tools by which social worlds are described and explained and (sometimes) justified, which is to say that in Darwinism we now find a *theoria* of the world that is in service to an *ethos* or particular way of being in the world. Numerous scholars, for instance, have noted that Darwin's picture of ecology is strikingly similar to Adam Smith's picture of economy: both presuppose a vision of things in which individuals operate in ways to maximize self-interest. Both assume processes in which the weak are eliminated to make room for the strong. Both assume a picture of individuals fearful of not getting enough.[9]

My aim is not to dismiss Darwin's scientific observations. As a *theoria* for understanding how species adapt and evolve through time, it has tremendous explanatory power. But it would also be a mistake not to note the narrowness of what might be called its moral vision. Marilynne Robinson, for instance, observes: "That human beings should be thought of as better or worse animals, and human well-being as a product of culling, is a willful exclusion of context, which seems to me to have remained as a stable feature of Darwinist thought. There is a worldview implicit in the theory which is too small and rigid to accommodate anything remotely like the world."[10] What is missing is a world that makes room for the soul.[11] What is missing is a world in which charity—the very virtue that would enable us to see and address the misery of the weak—has much force.

This brief look at Darwin helps us see that a *theoria* is never neutral or innocent. Each *theoria* moves within and often justifies an *ethos*, and that means our looking is invariably in service of or in response to particular ways of inhabiting the world. Though people might think that their *theoria* is obvious, logical, objective, perhaps even comprehensive, the history of humanity's reasoning shows that efforts to clarify or make sense of the world often have the effect of distorting, dissimulating, even brutalizing it. Idolatrous seeing, which is an instrumental form of looking that frames places and fellow creatures in terms of what they can do for us, is an ever-present temptation.[12] It is important to remember that the long march of Western philosophical and scientific development has facilitated the imperial conquest of the world's continents, the genocide of many of its indigenous populations, the enslavement of millions, and the systematic plundering, pollution, and degradation of most all the world's habitats. Never before in the history of humanity have we been able to look upon the earth with such precision and breadth. Concurrently, never before have we witnessed so much degradation that is the practical/economic result of how we see.

Our present predicament suggests that we are in the midst of a crisis of seeing. The faith once given to philosophers has been transferred to technicians and economists who, it is commonly believed, will present the world "truly" and give the means by which to live conveniently and comfortably within it. But even this faith is wavering as people see various forms of environmental catastrophe threatening the viability of the world that scientists and technicians are helping create. To be sure, scientists have given us a great number of gifts in the forms of engineering, medicine, and education, but it would be naive to ignore that today's research institutions and machinery are leading us to the extinction of human life.[13] Our doom may not come about in one great cataclysmic event, taking instead the form of an inexorable and mostly unnoticed "slow violence" that systematically undermines the health of all life.[14] Or it may be the remote-controlled, tele-murder violence "without hatred" that governs today's military operations.[15] However the crisis is characterized, it seems that we are in need of an alternative *theoria*, a different way of seeing, that will animate an *ethos* enabling people to cherish the world and live more peaceably within it.

A CHRISTIAN WAY OF SEEING?

Is there something like a distinctly Christian way of seeing the world? When followers of Jesus Christ look at the world, what do they see or understand to be there? Put slightly differently, how does the *askesis* or discipline of Christian living—living that is patterned after Christ's own way of being in the world—give rise to a *theoria* that opens and newly focuses the world, enabling people to determine the significance and meaning of things in fresh ways?

To begin, we can say that Christians see the world as God's *creation*. It is the work of God's hands and the expression of God's love and delight (one can wonder if the parson Malthus had much inkling of this). But this can be only a beginning, for it is not entirely clear what it means to say that we live in a created world, or what practical difference it makes. It is important to ask this question because many Christians assume that there is little difference between a world seen/interpreted as creation and a world seen/interpreted as nature. The world "is what it is," with the key difference being that for Christians nature has its origin in God. In other words, the natural world becomes a created world the moment God is positioned at its beginning as the One who got it all going. As this telling continues, God put in place the natural laws that keep the world functioning in the regular patterns that it does. Every once in a while, however, God is thought to intervene in a special way by interrupting, suspending, or perhaps even abrogating, natural laws so as to produce a miracle.

This more or less deistic characterization of creation is a profound mistake. Why? Because it does not at all reflect a biblical understanding of the world as the material place in which God's love is continually at work birthing, nurturing, healing, reconciling, and liberating creatures into the fullness of their being. As the Psalmist puts it, God continuously and intimately faces the world and breathes upon it, because without God's animating breath or Spirit (*ruah*) the whole of life collapses into dust (104:27–30). Focusing exclusively on origins ignores the fact that in scripture creation is as much about the salvation and the final consummation of things as it is about their beginning. More fundamentally, however, is the fact that a deist characterization of the world has no room for creation understood as the action of the Triune God: *from* the Father, *through* the Son, *by* the Holy Spirit. Creation, rather than being a single event that happened a long time ago, signifies God's ongoing involvement in an economy and ecology that join creaturely life with the life of God.[16] As such, the doctrine of creation is about the *character* of the world, communicating important insights about its significance and purpose. Though it clearly matters that God is understood to be the One who creates "in the beginning," what is of utmost importance is the realization that the world is the place where God is daily at work inspiring and nurturing all life into the fullness (salvation) of its being. Creation thus names a moral and spiritual topography of creatures called to be responsive to each other and to their Creator, and in their shared life to witness to the love of God.[17]

Equally important, this deist rendering ignores the fact that Christian theologians from early on advocated a Christian *theoria physike* or manner of seeing that enabled people to perceive the world as the place where God was intimately at work.[18] But to engage in this form of *theoria* it was essential that people also practice the *askesis* or discipline that purified seeing of the passions (like fear, insecurity, sloth, or the drive for power) that distort the world and reduce it to the satisfaction of human impulses. Stated succinctly, to see the world in a Christian manner required of people that they learn *to see everything as God sees it*. It was considered important for Christians to develop this way of seeing so that places and fellow creatures could be engaged in a manner that brought honor to God and healing to the world.

But how is it possible for people to see the world this way, especially given the assumption that people are creatures and not the Creator? The answer given was that people can learn to see as God sees insofar as they become disciples of Jesus Christ and participate in his *ethos* or way of being in the world. It is a core Christian position that God bridged the chasm between Creator and creation in the incarnation of Jesus Christ. The eternal divine way of being that creates, sustains, heals, and beautifies life became embodied and operationalized in the person and ministries of Jesus of Nazareth.[19] The prologue to John's gospel gives this memorable expression by describing Jesus as the divine, creating Word or *Logos* become flesh: "All things came into being through him, and without him not one thing came into being. What has come into being in him was life, and the life was the light of all people" (John 1:3–4). John's gospel, however, is hardly unique in this regard. The early Christian hymn in Colossians speaks similarly of Christ: "He is the image of the invisible God, the firstborn of all creation; for in him all things in heaven and on earth were created, things visible and invisible, whether thrones or dominions or rulers or powers—all things have been created through him and for him. He himself is before all things, and in him all things hold together" (Colossians 1:15–17). The letter to the Hebrews describes Jesus as God's Son, the one who is "heir of all things," and the one "through whom he also created the worlds" (Hebrews 1:2). And in the first letter to the Corinthians Paul describes Jesus Christ as the one Lord "through whom are all things and through whom we exist" (1 Corinthians 8:6).

Passages like this make it abundantly clear that the earliest Christian communities understood creation in a decidedly Christological way. Jesus's life was understood to be the incarnation of the very life that God eternally is, a life that creates and loves and nurtures and heals and reconciles all things that it touches. Jesus shows definitively that for God to create is also for God to redeem. New Testament scholar Sean McDonough summarizes it this way: "The mighty works of Jesus, his proclamation of the kingdom of God, and the climactic events of the crucifixion and resurrection, clearly marked him as the definitive agent of God's redemptive purposes. But these mighty works could scarcely be divorced from God's creative acts. The memories of Jesus preserved in the gospels depict a man who brings order to the threatening chaotic waters, creates life out of death, and restores people to their proper place in God's world."[20]

Jesus is not simply a moral teacher. In his embodied life and way of being, Jesus shows what it practically takes for creatures to live the abundant life God has wanted them to live all along. His miracles, rather than being an interruption of the laws of nature, are acts of liberation that free people from the destructive bondages of demon possession, hunger, illness, alienation, and death. Jesus is the complete, embodied realization of life's possibility as a way of love. To see him is to see the divine love that created the heavens and the earth. To participate in his life is to take on his point of view and thus to *see everything in a completely new way*. As Paul would put it, to be "in Christ" means that we no longer see others from a human point of view: "if anyone is in Christ, there is a new creation: everything old has passed away; see, everything has become new!" (2 Corinthians 5:17).

To proclaim Jesus as creator is, therefore, to open up a new understanding of the world as the place of God's ongoing, redemptive work. It is to see each creature as blessed by God and each person as a child of God. Jesus, in other words, is for Christians the interpretive lens that enables them to see everything in terms of a new framework of significance and meaning. To participate in his *ethos* is to see every creature and every place as a sacred gift.

THEORIA IN MAXIMUS THE CONFESSOR

It took many years to develop the insight that in Jesus Christ a new way of seeing the world came into being. One particularly important place, however, was in monastic and mystical traditions that stressed ascetical disciplines as a way for people to share in the divine life and the divine way of seeing reality. As one example, I will focus on the seventh-century Byzantine monk Maximus the Confessor because it is in him that we find a Christian *theoria* developed in a rigorous and fruitful manner.

Maximus says that with Jesus "a wholly new way of being [*kainoterou tropou*] human appeared. God has made us like himself, and allowed us to participate in the very things that are most characteristic of his goodness."[21] Christ is the center of the universe and the gate through which true and complete life moves because in him we find the definitive, embodied expression of the divine love that is life's beginning, sustenance, and end. As John's prologue put it, all creatures came into being through Jesus, who is the divine *Logos*. "All of Maximus' thinking about the created world comes under the economy of the incarnation of the Word, which is the entrance of the God beyond being into being."[22] The remarkable thing is that Jesus invites people to participate in God's way of being and to be, as John's gospel put it, the friends of God (John 15:15).

For Maximus it was of utmost importance that both divine and creaturely natures were fully affirmed and respected in their union in Christ. Jesus shows that becoming human does not denigrate divinity, nor does being divine obliterate creatureliness. He also shows that in their coming together a new mode of life or *tropos* (in Greek) becomes possible in this world. Lars Thunberg provides a helpful analogy for thinking about this dynamic coming together: "It is a union which can be characterized as similar to that between fire and iron. Iron glows in fire but remains what it is in itself. In one and the same hypostasis iron and fire are found together, but the piece of iron effects exactly that which is in accordance with its own nature—as well as that which belongs to both—i.e., it glows, but in a way that is proper to iron alone."[23] Union without confusion, interpenetration yet distinctness— these are each important to remember because the path of salvation (what Greek theologians often described as *theosis*, a creature's participation in the life of God) means that creatureliness is never denied, destroyed, or left behind. Rather, what happens is that distinctly human life is lifted up into the divine life, where it realizes its full potential. Because Jesus is at once fully human and fully divine, he can lead people into the perfect realization of their humanity.

The task of Christians as followers of Christ is to help fellow creatures move into the fullness of their life in God. They are, as Paul put it, to be "ministers of reconciliation" in the world (2 Corinthians 5:18). But to do this Christians must learn to see the world as God sees it. They need the proper *theoria*. For Maximus, having the proper *theoria* means learning to see creatures in their relation to Christ. Using his technical language, people must learn to see how the *logos* that defines each creature is related to the divine *Logos* made incarnate in Christ. Why? Because if creatures are created through and have their being in Christ, then their lives are at their best when they exist in ways that resonate with his way of being.

Logos is a Greek term that is notoriously difficult to pin down because of its wide usage in ancient philosophical and spiritual contexts. As employed by Maximus, however, it is fairly clear that it refers to something like the dynamic principle of order and coherence that enables each creature to be the unique being that it is. To know a creature's *logos*, in other words, is to know its capacities and potential. To say that Christ is the eternal *Logos* continuously and intimately present to each particular created *logos* is to say several things. First, no creature is the source of its own life. It depends on the power of God to sustain it in its being. Second, no creature is complete in itself. All creatures are created to be in relationship with others, drawing their daily nurture and help from them. When creatures properly receive and give help, the webs of creation are strengthened. The trouble, however, is that sometimes creatures are prevented from realizing their potential. Their *logos*, which enables them to express their unique capacities, is frustrated by (alienating, fragmenting, or violating) ways of being that bring harm rather than healing, deprivation rather than nurture. To say that a creature is prevented from achieving its potential is also to say that its *logos* is being derailed, distorted, or denied. Third, if creatures are to maximally realize the potential that is unique to their *logos*, they need to live in ways that lead into ever-greater communion with God and fellow creatures. This is what Jesus does with his *tropos* or mode of life. He models the ways of being that produce abundant life. The task of creatures is to participate (in ways appropriate to their natures) in his way of life by bringing their *tropos* as closely into alignment as possible with his *tropos*. The moment when full alignment is achieved is also the moment when God is all in all (1 Corinthians 15:28).

Admittedly, this is a very abstract way of speaking, but its implications could not be more mundane and practical. Consider how Jesus moved among the society of his world. Upon meeting people who were hungry, he fed them. Upon meeting people who were sick and outcasts, he healed them and welcomed them back into community. If people were under the influence of an evil spirit, he exorcised it, and if they found themselves to be lonely or at the margins, he befriended them. Again and again, we discover that Jesus's mode of engagement with others is determined by mercy and compassion. When he looked at suffering or abused humanity, *he saw what their lives could be* if they were liberated from their oppressive contexts. He understood that each person has potential that is unique to that person, which is why he offered his love as the way to activate and realize it. His divine, creative, and nurturing *Logos* was in touch with the *logos* of those he met in ways that enabled him to diagnose a better way of life for them. His looking, in other words, did not remain at a surface or superficial level. He saw into the divine depths of each person and found there the divine love that wants to find expression.

Put another way, Jesus introduced into the world a divine way of being that enabled people to *see* how life is being degraded, frustrated, or impoverished *and* how it might be nurtured, healed, and made abundant. He revealed the social and economic mechanisms that prevent people from living into the fullness of their lives, things like wrongdoing, shame, guilt, fear, and debt, and invited people to live in ways inspired by his self-offering love because love is the way that enables people to maximally realize their *logos*. His love is the best way of life—the ideal *tropos*—because his love is the divine power that creates, sustains, redeems, and perfects life.

Maximus believed that the healing and redemption of the world depends on each creature living the self-offering way of being that Jesus modeled in his ministries. Of course, not all creatures will participate in or exercise this love in the same way: the ways of being a cloud or butterfly, for instance, present possibilities that are unique to them. Even so, what is striking about Maximus's vision is that his Christological development of the divine *Logos* as present to every created *logos* allows him to say that God's love is the principle of intelligibility at work within all things.[24] If we look deeply enough we will see God's creative, dynamic love at work in each creature, sustaining it in its being. Divine love, in other words, is the source of the liveliness of a world brimming over with fertility, fecundity, diversity, and flowering.

This is a breathtaking vision in which not only humanity but the whole of the created world is invited to participate in the divine life of love. According to Maximus, a creature is properly known when it is seen to be a material expression of God's love.[25] The incarnation of God's love, in other words, does not end in Jesus Christ: "For the Word of God and God wills always and in all things to accomplish the mystery of his embodiment."[26] To be formed by Christ is to participate in his loving ways and thus also to see and engage creatures in ways that help them realize their God-given potential.

Again, the implications of this teaching are both practical and economic because what it entails is that people engage their places and fellow creatures in noninstrumentalizing and nonviolating ways. Whereas multiple forms of economic development often depend on extracting and appropriating the wealth of communities and habitats (as when farmers mine the soil of its fertility, fishers deplete oceans of fish stock, foresters clear-cut a valley, and financiers champion policies that either exploit or abandon neighborhoods), the goal of Christ-inspired and Christ-animated development is to *work with* habitats and communities so that mutual flourishing is optimized. This is not a simple or easy process because people do not always know or can be mistaken about what a place or community most needs. This is why attention and listening—the work of prayer—are crucial. The essential task is to come into the presence of others with a student mindset that seeks to learn from them what is advisable to do, and a servant disposition that commits to come alongside them and help them realize their potential.

Wendell Berry argues that this is what traditions of husbandry do at their best. He notes that upon commencing to farm, a farmer will often have multiple visions of how this land and its livestock will realize possibilities he or she most desires. As is also often the case, these visions tend to reflect what the farmer wants rather than what the farm itself recommends. But if the farmer stays attentive while working, and acknowledges how personal wants can sometimes damage or frustrate the farm's life, then something very important can occur. One's vision alters so that it is no longer an imposition upon a place: "if one's sight is clear and if one stays on and works well, one's love gradually responds to the place as it really is, and one's visions gradually image possibilities that are really in it. Vision, possibility, work, and life—*all* have changed by mutual correction. Correct discipline, given enough time, gradually removes one's self from one's line of sight. One works to better purpose then and makes fewer mistakes, because at last one sees where one is."[27] Husbandry is the *askesis* that opens a *theoria* in which creatures can be engaged in ways that honor their life as blessed by God.

Maximus's account of a Christian *theoria* is grounded in the conviction that each creature in its very physicality is the intimate expression of God's love. In *Ambigua* 46, for instance, Maximus refers to God as the Sun that shines divine rays of light and life on each creature so that in its growth and coming to ripeness God's wisdom and providence are revealed. This means that all claims that denigrate materiality as the realm to be abandoned or left behind would amount to a rejection of the incarnation of God in Jesus. Thunberg says, "The presence of the Logos in the *logoi* is always seen as a kind of incarnation—a parallel to the incarnation in the historical Jesus—and thus an act of divine condescension."[28] God's presence to creatures, however, does not prevent creatures from being themselves. As the power that creates, nurtures, and heals, God's presence is hospitable, welcoming, and respecting of the alterity of others so that they can maximally be themselves. "A God who himself exists in a self-communicating manner, in Trinity, engages in conversation with his creatures, one by one and all together, and they in turn exist in order to converse with him their own existence, to be themselves and with each other, in his own life. He moves right inside their being to give it its very own mind, voice and life, to bring the finite beyond its finitude and into his life of eternity."[29] There is in this account an understanding of God's creative love (which is meant to find expression throughout the entire universe) as fundamentally empowering and liberating. Jesus invites people to participate in ways of love that disarm the powers that harm creatures.

Maximus believed that no particular creature could exist if it did not participate in God's life. But not all things participate in the same way. Each thing expresses its own distinct *logos*, which means that it has unique capacities and a distinct way of being that are specific to it. The *logos* of a tree, for instance, is to give physical and dynamic expression to all the characteristics that enable a tree to be the thing that it is: sink down roots and absorb nutrient energy, transform sunlight into carbon, grow and produce seed, et cetera. The *logos* of a worm clearly differs because it does not have the powers of photosynthesis or carbon production. Even so, it gives expression in its own life to a *logos* that enables it to be the unique, soil-enriching thing that it is. Neither tree nor worm can be said to be insignificant in the eyes of God because each of these creatures expresses a *logos* that is always already in communication with the divine *Logos* who is Jesus Christ. Being in such communication they are also being directed toward each other to create the possibility of symphonic life together. Jesus is the power of sympathy and compassion that, by nurturing each individual life, also tunes creatures to be responsive to each other and thus to contribute to the conditions for mutual flourishing. Maximus concludes:

> We are speechless before the sublime teaching about the Logos, for he cannot be expressed in words or conceived in thought. . . . Nevertheless we affirm that the one Logos is many *logoi* and the many *logoi* are One. Because the One goes forth out of goodness into individual being, creating and preserving them, the One is many. Moreover the many are directed toward the One and are providentially guided in that direction. It is as though they were drawn to an all-powerful center that had built into it the beginnings of the lines that go out from it and that gather them all together. In this way the many are one.[30]

Maximus gives us a breathtaking vision of the expansiveness of God's love in which every creature participates and to which every creature gives witness when it realizes the life God has given it. In our looking at things we cannot ever simply look at the surface because deep within them there is the power of divine love at work. Tsakiridou gives this summary:

> Reaching out to each and every creature, this love whose source is the Trinitarian life, defines Maximus' vision of a resurrected universe in which "the unique divine power will manifest itself in all things in a vivid and active presence proportioned to each one." Here, *energeia* describes the diverse (open) and binding communion

between creation and God in which beings shine with "dignity and splendor." . . . Creatures emerge as the vibrant and self-contained recipients of a hypostatic redemption by means of which they can (now) truly belong to themselves—because they finally belong (actively, communicatively) to God and to each other.[31]

HOW LOVE LOOKS / WHAT LOVE SEES

When Simone Weil said, "Love is the soul's looking," she was communicating an essential insight: people are drawn to see and be in touch with the sources of their own livelihood. People want to be in places and communities that nurture them and inspire them to live well. They want to be in resonant relationships that make them feel more alive and that challenge them to discover and realize their potential. And they want their efforts to contribute to the flourishing of the world, since contributing to the good of others is one of the best ways to acknowledge and testify to the goodness people believe to circulate through themselves. Life is driven by hunger—for food, companionship, beauty, goodness, and fulfillment. "The soul knows for certain only that it is hungry. The important thing is that it announces its hunger by crying. A child does not stop crying if we suggest to it that perhaps there is no bread. It goes on crying just the same. . . . The danger is not lest the soul should doubt whether there is any bread, but lest, by a lie, it should persuade itself that it is not hungry."[32]

The trouble, however, is that people can be confused about what they think will satisfy their hunger. They might embark upon satiation strategies that not only leave them dissatisfied but do damage to the sources of nurture and support they most need. In other words, their living might be animated by a disordered and misdirected love. They are looking in the wrong places and in an inappropriate way. This is why spiritual writers have often spent so much time attending to the disciplines or *askesis* that reorient love so that it comes into better alignment with the love of God.

Maximus believed that we can understand things and ourselves in a Godly way only when the movements of our entire life—the movement of our minds, the ordering of our affections, the practices of our bodies—are brought into conformity with Christ: a Christian *theoria* needs a Christian *askesis*.[33] Christian discipleship is the key to the right ordering of ourselves and the right ordering of our vision so that we can see each other and everything as God sees it. In the incarnation of Jesus Christ, God entered and "maintained the *logos* of creaturely origin while also wisely restoring humanity's means of existing to its true *logos*."[34] God does not alter human nature by making it something else. Rather, God in Christ changes "the mode and domain of action proper to their nature."[35] In other words, God does not desire creatures to be something else. God only ever asks creatures to be themselves truly and fully, a capacity that has become clouded and distorted because of sin.

A reality as complex as sin can be described in multiple ways, but for the purposes of this chapter the most salient point is to note how sin obscures a person's ability to see reality as loved by God. Sin clouds and blocks our doors of perception so that, as William Blake maintained, one cannot see things as infinite, but only through the "narrow chinks of his own cavern."[36] One way to describe what Blake meant is to note how people can come to view others through the narrow frame of their own concerns, worries, or ambitions. When that happens, people are not perceived on their own terms or in ways that respect their sanctity. Instead, they are seen and engaged in terms of what they can do for us. Writing in the throes of the industrial revolution, Blake realized that people now found themselves in an economic order and a built environment that abused and degraded them at every turn. Politicians and factory bosses did not see workers as children of God to be cherished and celebrated. They saw them as so many expendable units of production that could be used up and discarded as necessary. Their distorted vision was destroying the world.

When Maximus spoke of sin he often referred to it as people coming under the influence of various passions. Passions cloud vision. They prevent people from seeing others as creatures beloved and blessed by God. A life lived according to the passions—traditionally seven in number: gluttony, unchastity, avarice, anger, dejection, listlessness, and pride—is so dangerous because it results in the tyranny of creatures and the degradation of the created world.[37] The passions mobilize an improper self-love in which others must serve my hunger, my sexual ambitions, my desire for wealth or power, my frustration with circumstances and events, my insecurities and boredom, or my need to be important. The issue is not self-love itself, since the ministries of Jesus affirm again and again that each creature is loved by God. The key is to understand how the love of God is always a self-offering love in which the building up of one's community contributes to the well-being of all its members, including oneself. Outward-directed love positions people vis-à-vis others so they can be open to them and see and welcome them on their terms. Christ-like love is the kind of love that is patient before and solicitous of another. It is courteous and considers what creatures can become if people make their lives conduits for the extension of God's compassion and mercy. It is at its core a hospitable gesture that, by creating a nurturing home, also takes care of all the creatures that enter into it.[38]

Maximus's account of asceticism—the *askesis* that informs the *ethos* that makes possible a Christian *theoria*—does not condone the denial or denigration of the material world. This it simply cannot do, since such denial would void the fundamental truth of creation as loved by God. It would reject the incarnation as God's full embrace of embodiment. Instead, the goal of ascetic practices is to foster a new vision in which people are able "to perceive every creature in its first-created, victorious beauty."[39] Genuine asceticism opens people up so that they can become vessels that receive and give again the Christ-like love that leads to the world's healing and reconciliation. It re-forms people so that St. Isaac the Syrian, another seventh-century monk, can say, in response to the question, "What is a compassionate heart?,"

It is a heart on fire for the whole of creation, for humanity, for the birds, for the animals, for demons and for all that exists. At the recollection and at the sight of them such a person's eyes overflow with tears owing to the vehemence of the compassion which grips his heart; as a result of his deep mercy his heart shrinks and he cannot bear to hear or look on any injury or the slightest suffering of anything in creation. . . . This is why he constantly offers up prayers full of tears, even for the irrational animals and for the enemies of truth, even for those who harm him, so that they might be protected and find mercy. . . . He even prays for the reptiles as a result of the great compassion which is poured out beyond measure—after the likeness of God—in his heart.[40]

Maximus did not sentimentalize Christ-like love. He understood that Jesus's self-offering love, though welcomed by people in pain and by those who had been marginalized, was a threat to people in power. His way of being, though being the way of being that creates, nurtures, and beautifies the whole world, was despised by Roman authorities who subscribed to forms of power that dominate, violate, and ultimately destroy life. Jesus's crucifixion is the site where contrasting forms of power and contrasting visions of life clashed. This is why Maximus argued that the hearts and minds of people must go through a cruciform experience that purifies the ego of all coercive and violating tendencies. "All visible things [*phainomena*] need a cross, that is, a capacity that restrains the affection for them on the part of those who are sensibly attracted to them. And all intelligible things demand a tomb, that is, the complete immobility of those who are intellectually inclined toward them. For when natural activity and movement are removed along with the inclination for all these things, the Logos who is alone self-existent, reappears as though he were rising from the dead, circumscribing everything that originates from him."[41]

In a manner reminiscent of Paul's description of baptism as the believer's old self being crucified with Christ so that he or she might also be resurrected into newness of life (Romans 6:3–14), Maximus is describing a process in which our vision and our understanding are cleansed and our priorities reoriented so that the life we live is now in conformity with the life God has intended all along. Living this cruciform life, a life in which love directs people to seek the good of others rather than pleasures for themselves, people come to see everything in God. They come to see that each thing is the unique expression of God's love and exists for no other reason than in its flourishing to give glory to God as the giver and nurturer of its life. The essential task is to learn to love properly, for it is in the mode of love that the human presence on earth becomes one that heals and reconciles all things in their individual being and in their life together.

We can now appreciate that a Christian *theoria* gives rise to a striking vision of the world as the material expression of God's love. It is an iconic seeing of the world that presupposes an *ethos* and an *askesis* in which human passions are purified and practical ways of being are disciplined so that each creature can be met and engaged as the unique, sacred gift that it is. This world and its creatures are never to be despised. They are only to be loved.[42]

CHAPTER SIX

Learning Descent

[God] is at a total remove from every condition, movement, life, imagination, conjecture, name, discourse, thought, conception, being, rest, dwelling, unity, limit, infinity, the totality of existence. And yet, since it is the underpinning of goodness, and by merely being there is the cause of everything, to praise this divinely beneficent Providence you must turn to all of creation. It is there at the center of everything and everything has it for a destiny.

—Pseudo-Dionysius

The way I go is
marriage to this place,
grace beyond chance,
love's braided dance
covering the world.
    —Wendell Berry

In "The Long-Legged House," Wendell Berry wrote that as a writer his struggle had not been to find a subject but rather to know what to do with the subject he had been entrusted with from the beginning. The subject he was referring to was his farm in Henry County,

Kentucky, the region of his birth. "I was so intricately dependent on this place that I did not begin in any meaningful sense to be a writer until I began to see the place clearly and for what it was."[1] But seeing a place clearly is "an enormous labor" that begins with the realization that we belong to a place rather than the other way around. To know that we are not the owners or possessors of the world amounts to a "startling reversal of our ordinary sense of things," and it culminated, at least for Berry, in what became his governing ambition: "to be altogether at home here." The ambition to allow oneself to be entirely governed by a place and by one's belonging to, for instance, thrushes and herons is "a spiritual ambition, like goodness." While other creatures may live instinctually where they are, human beings must make the choice—informed by intelligence, propriety, and virtue—to *be and become* in a place. "It is an ambition I cannot hope to succeed in wholly, but I have come to believe that it is the most worthy of all."[2]

In "A Native Hill" Berry spoke similarly of the transformations of perception and mentality that overcame him when he left New York City and chose to make his Kentucky farm his permanent home. No longer thinking that he would be here only for a while or until some other, potentially better opportunity came along, Berry says that the choice to stay for the rest of his life was determinative: "Once that was settled I began to *see* the place with a new clarity and a new understanding and a new seriousness." This was a difficult perception because it required Berry to give up the idea that he, having been raised there, already knew this place. He didn't, or at least not in a satisfactory or faithful way. He needed to reenter and learn again by walking, looking, listening, smelling, touching, tasting, and becoming altogether more attuned to his place if he was to discover its real abundance and depth. He needed to learn the names and histories of places, creatures, and things. He needed to work with the place by applying his attention and skill to it. He needed to reconsider and reorient his mind as a root system going ever deeper into the ground, rather than as an organ that stands apart from the world to make judgments about it or impose a plan upon it. The revelations that followed were many, but what was fundamental was that "I came to see myself as growing out of the earth like the other native animals and plants. I saw my body and my daily motions as brief coherences and articulations of the energy of the place, which would fall back into it like leaves in the autumn."³

My aim in this chapter is to explore the difference it makes to say that one *grows out of* a place rather than merely *lives on* it, and to explore the forms of understanding that accompany this realization. It is to assess how a decision to make one's place a *permanent home*—a place of belonging—rather than a *temporary residence* changes the way we think about this world and our place within it. How is the characterization of a spiritual journey transformed when, as Berry put it, one sends one's mind "into the place like a live root system"? Put another way, my aim is to explore some of the commitments and forms of knowing that accompany humanity's *creaturely* condition.

To admit to being a creature is to appreciate one's finitude and need, and to know that we do not live from out of ourselves but must constantly receive from others the power and nurture that animate our being. It is to acknowledge that we are not self-possessed or in control of our lives but, *as rooted beings*, live by the mercies and blessings of what our neighborhoods make possible. It is to realize that our bodies are not self-contained and self-propelling entities but sites of ongoing exposure to and vulnerability before others. This is a heartening discovery that introduces us to the kinship of life and to a realization of what we might call the fundamentally hospitable character of this world that is populated by so many beautiful sights, pleasing sounds, reassuring touches, fragrant aromas, and delectable flavors. But it can also be discomforting because one realizes that a habitat's creatures and processes are not always or exclusively tailored to satisfy our specific pleasures and preferences.

The effort to plumb the depths of human existence is sometimes characterized as a mystical pursuit in which people seek to understand the mysterious *source* and *ground* of reality. It is, in certain respects, an uncommon pursuit because it requires of people a concerted effort to move beyond surface appearances of reality and their packaged and (increasingly) marketed forms. It requires that people not take themselves or their world for granted but work to interrogate the difference between life as they want it to be and life as it is. This is a difficult pursuit insofar as people must learn to shed the ideas and attachments that prevent apprehension of the real, which is why mystics sometimes speak of entering a cloud of *un*knowing on the way to a more genuine "knowing" of the conditions for the possibility of any life at all.

Berry does not write as a self-professing mystic. Even so, I think we can develop Berry's spiritual ambition to belong and be entirely at home in his place by putting it in conversation with mystical ways of understanding. How does his ambition and his affirmation that he grows out of his place challenge and potentially correct how we characterize a mystical path? Insofar as Berry's aim is not *up and away* (into a cloud) but *down and around* (into the soil), his is not a mystical *ascent* but rather a *descent* into the literal ground that is the material and dynamic site of his livelihood. What we might call an agrarian mysticism introduces us to the *dark night of the soil* because it reframes and reorients the mind (and heart) as a root system that grows ever more deeply into the soil that is the source of life's nurture. This is a journey that seeks an intimate knowledge of forests, fields, watersheds, and skies, but also regions, neighborhoods, and communities, and then sympathetic attunement to the human and nonhuman communities that live within them. If our aim is to plumb the enabling conditions of our embodied life, we must focus our attention down and around because it is among rhizomes and rivers, bees and butterflies, bakers and builders, and then also within the complex processes of germination, decomposition, making, and neighborliness (to name a few), that life's nurturing contexts are prepared. If our aim is to encounter the grace and gratuity of life's happening, and thereby come to the realization that this life is a sacred gift, then it is to this world and not some other that we must turn.

For some, casting a spiritual life as a *descent* into earthly neighborhoods will appear counterintuitive, since so much spiritual writing charts the path to transcendence as an upward journey. This is a mistake. Scripture does not reveal a god who is distant and aloof. It presents God as the One who is constantly coming near and becoming involved in the lives of creatures as a nurturing, healing, and justice-working presence. Recall that Christian scripture begins with God kissing and breathing a divine breath into creatures, animating them from within, and then ends with God descending to earth to make a divine home among mortals. Insofar as our spiritual lives are to be patterned on God's own life, our aim ought to be to live with others in ways that make God's creative and loving ways incarnate here and now. From a scriptural point of view, the thought that the destination of our spiritual ambition ought to be somewhere beyond earth is misguided because God's orientation, especially as revealed in the becoming flesh and becoming practical in the life of Jesus, is *down*, *around*, and *with* creatures in their places. The "beyond" implied by transcendence, in other words, is not opposed to immanence but refers us to the unfathomable and mysterious divine power moving *within* creation. If we seek to be with God, then creation ought to be our focus and destination.

RECONSIDERING MYSTICISM

It is unlikely that many people would call Berry's ambition mystical, particularly if we go by popular characterizations of the term referring it to esoteric teachings or exceptional, ecstatic experiences providing direct access to the divine. According to this common view, a mystic is someone who has extraordinary states of consciousness in which unity with God is achieved. As William James famously put it, a mystic has a special faculty, much as the musician has a special ear, that is open to particularly intense states of feeling into depths of truth "unplumbed by the discursive intellect" and beyond the reach of institutional religious authority.[4] Mystics, in other words, are people possessed by special powers that take them out of the realm of the ordinary, out of the places of daily life and struggle, and into the holy realm of an ineffable God.

For a number of reasons this characterization of mystics, though having historical precedent, needs to be challenged and corrected.[5] We do better to understand mysticism, not as a peculiar type of experience or paranormal state of consciousness, but as a practical process and a way of life that are, in principle, available to all if they make the effort. Though the goal is often an encounter with God, a mystic is someone who is particularly open and earnest in his or her search for God as the unfathomable Source of this life and world. What the "presence of God" means, or who the God is that we surrender ourselves to, is, of course, not something that can be determined beforehand. Indeed, and as the witness of many mystics confirms, the God we meet on a mystical path is most often quite unlike the God our traditions and communities teach us to expect, imagine, hope, or fear. This is why they speak so often of a "God beyond God."[6] Given our propensity to worship the gods of our own making, that is, the gods who will best sanction and further the agendas we prefer, Meister Eckhart advises the following prayer: "I pray God to rid me of God."[7] Sometimes the path to God requires that we first shed the ideas of God we have been given.

The narrowing of mystical sensitivities, and their presumed extraordinary character, are also attributable to the influence of modern deistic notions that assume God to be far removed from this world. To gain access to this God, one supposes, would require some supernatural, perhaps paranormal effort that would make us unscientific or plainly kooky. If God appears at all it will be in the form of a "miracle" that is an interruption or suspension of the laws of nature. But why think of God as separate and so far away? The Psalmist, for instance, declares God to be intimately present to this world in the water that enriches it and the fertility that produces a luxurious harvest (Psalm 65), or as the foundational power that secures earth system processes and as the animating breath within each living being (Psalm 104). To the Psalmist it simply does not make sense to go in search of a god "outside" this world if God is the Creator underpinning the goodness and sourcing the liveliness in all that is. What we need to learn is that God is not "somewhere else," sequestered in some special place or realm beyond our experience. As we develop a contemplative and mystical way of living it will be important to keep Pseudo-Dionysius's point that God, though of an entirely different order of being when compared to creatureliness, is nonetheless at the core of our being and at the heart of the whole of creation as its animating, pulsating life. There is, in other words, a chasm of "natures" or "being" separating God and creatures, but not ever a spatial or temporal chasm, since God is "at the center of everything."[8] Were God ever to "remove" Godself spatially from creation—an unimaginable prospect when considered from the perspective of the logic of creation—all creatures would die "and return to their dust" (Psalm 104:29).[9]

It is important to be clear that not all mystics or spiritual guides would be in agreement with this point. Insofar as these writers are influenced by gnostic or Platonic commitments, one can find in their writings strands of antimaterialism and otherworldliness that see little or no value in being altogether at home in our created world. In the name of detachment, for instance, we are told to be "receptive of nothing but God" (Eckhart), or to become forgetful of everything beneath us, and to concern ourselves with "no creature whether material or spiritual nor with their situation and doings whether good or ill."[10] The assumption here is that people can have a direct or unmediated relationship with God that bypasses creatures and created places. The central problem with this position is that it denies that God has made Godself known and present precisely in the materiality of this world. What is crucial to remember is that creation is God's love variously made tactile, visual, auditory, fragrant, and nutritious. This is not to say that creatures are divine. It is, instead, to note that God is always with and within creatures as their creating, animating, nurturing, and sustaining Source. There simply is no such thing as a world without God. To think that people can approach God without the world is to assume that one can abandon the very places and creatures God loves and is daily at work within.

This is why it is important to think carefully about what "detachment" means and what it practically entails. It should not ever mean the denial, abandonment, or denigration of material creatures. Instead, we do better to think of it as the denial of certain kinds of attachments that elevate the self at the expense of creatures and thereby distort what creatures in reality are: sacred gifts loved into being by God and bearing their own worth and sanctity. Put succinctly, when we make ourselves the measure of what creatures are, then we also (eventually) think of creatures as means in the service of our own ends. They cease to be what they are *in themselves* because their significance and value are features of what they are *for us*. Our goal ought instead to be to perceive and engage creatures as God does, recognizing that God relates to creatures not through instrumental means but in the mode of unconditional love. As the healing, feeding, exorcising, and reconciling ministries of Jesus make clear, God's love for creatures is not tied to God lacking something. God does not have any need or desire to make creatures fulfill what we might call a divine deficiency, which is why God can love creatures completely *for themselves* and in a detached manner. Think here of Thomas Merton's precise formulation regarding our detachment: "We do not detach ourselves from things in order to attach ourselves to God, but rather we become detached *from ourselves* in order to see and use all things in and for God. . . . There is no evil in anything created by God, nor can anything of His become an obstacle to our union with Him. The obstacle is in our 'self,' that is to say in the tenacious need to maintain our separate, external, egotistic will."[11] On this view, the goal is not to become free of creation but to be freed of certain ways of being within creation, ways of perceiving, thinking, and acting that inhibit or prevent a deep encounter with creatures and with God.

Learning the art of detachment is not easy, especially in cultural contexts that prize commodity accumulation and personal self-possession and invulnerability. It is difficult to appreciate how we live through our dependence upon others—most directly and evidently through bodily acts of touching, eating, drinking, and breathing—if the stated goal of a successful life is to be without need. When self and world mastery are the goal, the sanctity of creatures erodes. This is why we need to recover an understanding of Christian practice and discipleship as a "schooling in the ways of creatureliness" where we learn "that courtesy to creatures in which reverence for the Creator finds expression."[12] To believe that God is the Creator is to perceive all creatures as having their source and sustenance *in* God. It is to sense, however imperfectly, the divine presence moving through things. No thing simply exists as a brute, valueless fact. Rather, each thing is the material expression of a divine desire that it should be, and that its being is good and beautiful. This is why courtesy before fellow creatures ought to be the daily, abiding human posture that governs our approach to those we meet.

To be courteous is to acknowledge that who we are, even *that we are*, is a feature of our having received the divine love that delights in the beauties of this world. Pseudo-Dionysius, speaking of the beauty and goodness of God, put it this way:

> Beauty is the cause of harmony, of sympathy, of community. Beauty unites all things and is the source of all things. . . . From it derives the existence of everything as beings, what they have in common and what differentiates them, their identicalness and differences, their similarities and dissimilarities, their sharing of opposites. . . . Hence, the harmony and the love which are formed between them but which do not obliterate identity. Hence, the innate togetherness of everything. Hence, too, the intermingling of everything, the persistence of things, the unceasing emergence of things.[13]

There is, in other words, a correspondence among creatures, a mutual and created harmony and sympathy that finds its unity and potential in God as the One who desires for life to grow together. If we are to come into the presence of God, we must learn to find our place *in* this created correspondence and live responsibly and charitably within it, rather than seek an *escape* from it to be with God somewhere else.

Learning the courtesy that *corresponds* with creation is of tremendous significance because it means that a search for the ground of existence is false when commitment to and fidelity with fellow creatures come apart. The art of correspondence requires people to become fully present in and attentive to the places in which they move and live, for without this basic courtesy people will likely behave in violating or negligent ways. Signaling humanity's long-standing destructive behavior, the geologist Marcia Bjornerud says, "Like inexperienced but overconfident drivers, we accelerate into landscapes and ecosystems with no sense of their long-established traffic patterns, and then react with surprise and indignation when we face the penalties for ignoring natural laws." This is why she argues that if people want to fit harmoniously in this world they must first expand their conceptions of the time of Earth, appreciate how multi-billion-year-old earth systems have established patterns and processes that enable life's diverse flourishing, and then give up the notion that they are timeless beings that can somehow flourish in violation of these patterns and processes. We must stop "treating the planet as if it were a simple, predictable, passive object in a controlled laboratory experiment" and must instead take our respectful place within Earth's gradual, interwoven, and very long development.[14]

To correspond with another being is not a simple thing because correspondence requires people to stop thinking of others as simple, static, and clearly defined objects. Creatures are alive with possibility and thus are characterized by their movement and development. This is why Tim Ingold says, "Only when we appreciate things as their stories can we begin to correspond with them."[15] When we appreciate that creatures are stories that are themselves bound up in ever-expanding stories that *involve* creatures with each other in their places, then it becomes clear that people must always make a choice about whether to honor another's story by taking the time to discover the various events and processes that enabled the other to be who that person has so far become. "How have you been doing?" and "What was your upbringing like?" and "How are you handling the struggles and opportunities that have come your way?" are the kinds of questions people committed to correspondence ask. They must also decide how they will weave their story within the stories of others, and whether their involvement is respectful or not, mutually enhancing or not, by asking "How can I help and support you?" Creaturely life is an entangled life in which people constantly move with and through others, prompting Ingold to note that "all living, and all knowing, is intrinsically social, whether it be of trees in a wood, beasts in a herd or human beings in a community. Social life is one long correspondence."[16]

Correspondence is a fully embodied and ecological reality. It is important to stress this point because mystical paths often seem to be a disembodied affair that takes little notice of quotidian matters like the cleaning of kitchens, the changing of diapers, or the sorting of garbage.[17] A disembodied and dualist approach must be resisted because the only life we know, the life God deeply loves, is an embodied one. This realization changes how we might think about a spiritual journey. Consider Rowan Williams's description of contemplation as one central spiritual exercise: "Contemplation, then, cannot properly be a prostration before a power outside us; it is a being present to ourselves *in* our world with acceptance and trust. Hence . . . the importance of attention to the praying *body*; the contemplative significance of taking time to *sense* ourselves in prayer, to perceive patiently what and where we materially are."[18] Indeed, because God, however mysteriously, is made manifest through the work of creation, we can make no claim to being present to God except insofar as we tune our living so as to be in harmony with God's life-giving presence among us. If to be alive is to be created, then to live well is to live in such a way that our own creative gestures—as witnessed in our eating, teaching, building, parenting, playing, and loving—increasingly bear witness to and honor the continuing creativity of God. "If the 'mystical' ultimately means the reception of a particular *pattern* of divine action (creative love, self-emptying incarnation), its test will be the presence or absence of something like that pattern in a human life seen as a whole, not the presence or absence of this or that phenomenon in the consciousness."[19]

This characterization of mysticism as a journey into the presence of God via correspondence to creation as the place of God's abiding work is central to a recovery of the sense of human beings *as creatures*. A great deal hinges on whether people can affirm their creaturely status, for as Berry once observed while commenting on the violence committed against Kentucky's lands, "There appears to be a law that when creatures have reached the level of consciousness, as men have, they must become conscious of the creation; they must learn how they fit into it and what its needs are and what it requires of them, or else pay a terrible penalty: the spirit of the creation will go out of them, and they will become destructive; the very earth will depart from them and go where they cannot follow."[20]

It is when we make ourselves the goal of the world, as when we redesign the earth and its creatures to satisfy self-chosen and self-enhancing aims, that the correspondences of creation begin to unravel. We stifle creation by making personal pride and greed "the standard of our behavior toward the world." By failing to live patiently and with a measure of propriety, attentive and attuned to our fittedness within multiple webs of interdependence and responsibility, we destroy the beauty and goodness of creation. "The world is lost in loss / Of patience; the old curse / Returns, and is made worse / As newly justified. / In hopeless fret and fuss, / In rage at worldly plight / Creation is defied, / All order is unpropped, / All light and singing stopped."[21]

PATHS OF TRANSFORMATION

The first thing to say about a path of genuine transformation is that it is a *path* and not a *road*. Roads are constructions that aim to get people across a place as quickly and efficiently as possible. They tend, as much as possible, to be straight and smooth, which means that the land has to be bulldozed and graded for the road to fit within a predetermined line. Whatever obstacles are in the way must be removed because one's focus is primarily the destination rather than the places along the way. A path, by contrast, is born of a much slower movement and proceeds by direct contact and familiarity with the contours of the land. It meanders, often forks, and prefers to go around obstacles. A path, in other words, communicates respect, even affection, for a place by showing the willingness of people to adapt their movements to what the place recommends. If, as Berry suggests, a road acts like a bridge that avoids contact with places conceived as abstract spaces, then a path takes people into places that personal experience has taught them to be of value.[22]

It is worth asking how many prescriptions for a spiritual journey assume a road rather than a path. Do the varying soul/body or heaven/earth dualisms communicate a desire to avoid the messy, often recalcitrant and matter-of-fact character of fleshly and social life by taking a direct road to an ethereal and decidedly disembodied destination? A desire for flight from flesh is understandable given the frustration that is built into living with (often) uncooperative or heartbreaking others. But if we dig deeper it is also clear that a basic impatience with life's slow and complex unfolding often fuels the desire for flight that subverts the spiritual descent that makes possible our being "altogether at home" in our places. Put another way, one reason for choosing a road over a path is that the latter requires forms of patience and reckoning that the former does not.

To appreciate the character of our impatience we can consider briefly the nature of root systems that should serve as a pattern for the proper working of our minds. Scientists have learned that a single rye plant will in the course of just four months grow fifteen million roots that have a combined length of roughly 380 miles. If one adds the many more millions of hairs that are attached to these roots, then the overall length of the plant's engagement with its soil home extends to 7,000 miles.[23] It is astonishing to think that the vitality of one rye plant requires such a bewildering array of paths of nurture. If we broaden our scope to include tree communities, then the complexity of just plant nurture becomes unfathomable.[24] How much patience and what forms of study does it take to follow and appreciate these many webs of need and support? What these scientific studies make clear is that soil is not a simple *container* of organisms but a complex and hospitable *home* in which roots, fungi, worms, water, and untold numbers of microorganisms grow together to create the conditions for fertility and fecundity. This is the ground out of which people grow. "The more we learn about the life of soil, the more apt our language's symbols become: 'roots,' 'groundedness.' These words reflect not only a physical connection to place but reciprocity with the environment, mutual dependence with other members of the community, and the positive effects of roots on the rest of their home. All these relationships are embedded in a history so deep that individuality has started to dissolve and *uprootedness is impossible*."[25]

Individuality begins to dissolve as people realize the many ways soil nourishes the life that roots in it. Each root punctures the idea that an organism is a self-enclosed or self-standing thing. Humans are not exempt from this picture.

My point is not to suggest that humans are reducible to plants. It is, instead, to point to the fact that our embodiment *roots* us in the earth.[26] To eat, drink, breathe, and provide for their livelihoods, people must turn continually to what soils, plants, waterways, insects, bacteria, fellow animals, families, fellow workers, neighborhoods, and communities provide. In other words, the paths of nurture that sustain each human life are bewildering in their complexity and unfathomable in their extent and depth because they take us into ecological and social worlds that cannot be fully enumerated or neatly circumscribed.

A lifetime would not be enough for a person to attempt to trace all the paths of nurture and support that make their living possible. This is why it is so important for people to exercise the propriety that honors their need of others. It is also why a human life must be governed by the patience that enables people to slow down, attend to where they are and whom they are with, and then appreciate how their development must always acknowledge the gift of (the sometimes difficult and unasked-for) nurture that others are to us. Patience takes time, but one of its greatest benefits is that in tracing paths of nurture people discover how rocks, worms, and bees, but also teachers, cooks, and builders, are a blessing to us. But paths of patience can also be painful as people, in tracing the roots of their lives, discover histories of wrongdoing and violation.

To practice patience people must resist the temptation to deny their need of others and ignore the many paths that are in fact the source of their nurture. This is why it is important to speak of a need for a perpetual *metanoia* or continuous turning round of direction of the mind and heart in order for us to enter into communion with each other and with God. The change of direction that marks conversion is not simply from earth to heaven but from a straight road onto the many forking and intersecting paths of nurture that ultimately connect us to God as the divine Source that is the condition for the possibility of any path of nurture at all. *Metanoia* communicates a change of heart in which we welcome and respect our interdependent need rather than resist or take flight from it. It is the sort of change that will enable people to correct what Berry calls our "habit of contention—against the world, against each other, against ourselves." The breaking of this habit, this "intransigent destructiveness in us," will require us to change the assumptions by which we often live our lives. "It is not from ourselves that we will learn to be better than we are."[27]

One important way to effect this change is for people to become *apprentices* to creation, and thereby to embark on paths of knowing that make cooperation with fellow creatures and attunement to life-creating processes a determining aim.[28] But cooperation and attunement are difficult to achieve apart from a concerted effort to come into the presence of fellow creatures by subjecting oneself to their influence and making oneself a student of their lives. Berry describes the character of our submission in the following:

> Until we understand what the land is, we are at odds with everything we touch. And to come to that understanding it is necessary, even now, to leave the regions of our conquest—the cleared fields, the towns and cities, the highways—and re-enter the woods. For only there can man encounter the silence and the darkness of his own absence. Only in this silence and darkness can he recover the sense of the world's longevity, of its ability to thrive without him, of his inferiority to it and his dependence on it. Perhaps then, having heard that silence and seen that darkness, he will grow humble before the place and begin to take it in—to learn *from it* what it is. As its sounds come into his hearing, and its lights and colors come into his vision, and its odors come into his nostrils, then he may come into *its* presence as he never has before, and he will arrive in his place and will want to remain. His life will grow out of the ground like the other lives of the place, and take its place among them. He will be *with* them—neither ignorant of them, nor indifferent to them, nor against them—and so at last he will grow to be native-born. That is, he must re-enter the silence and the darkness, and be born again.[29]

In this passage Berry is clear that the exercises of knowing and conquest are often indistinguishable. Fellow creatures and their places have often not been encountered or cherished as the sacred gifts that they are because the intent to know them is driven by the more expansive intention to conscript, commodify, and possess them. Even a brief look at the history of human settlement reveals that when people have come to a place they have often come as investors, prospectors, surveyors, miners, farmers, and engineers looking to make a profit and then move on. Their settlement has not been faithful or authentic because they have not truly come into the presence of where they are or acknowledged the many paths of nurture reflected in the many creatures they share their life with.

If people desire to come into the presence of a place and its life, it is essential that they learn to correspond with where they are by ceasing to make themselves the center of what they do. This is an embodied effort in which we physically leave "the regions of our conquest" but also leave the built environments that suggest that the world exists primarily, if not exclusively, for us.

> Sometimes I can no longer think in the house or in the garden or in the cleared fields. They bear too much resemblance to our failed human history—failed because it has led to this human present that is such a bitterness and a trial. And so I go to the woods. As I go under the trees, dependably, almost at once, and by nothing I do, things fall into place. I feel my life take its place among the lives—the trees, the annual plants, the animals and birds, the living of all these and the dead—that go and have gone to make the life of the earth. I am less important than I thought, the human race is less important than I thought. I rejoice in that. My mind loses its urgings, senses its nature, and is free. The forest grew here in its own time, and so I will live, suffer and rejoice, and die in my own time. There is nothing that I may decently hope for that I cannot reach by patience as well as by anxiety.[30]

In this passage Berry is not only describing a need for encounters with wildness. He is also alerting us to a posture or bodily comportment in which people open themselves to the many diverse life forms and ecological processes that intersect with and move through their living.

Given the storied and social character of life, we should also expect that paths of transformation will require people to know the histories of their community's coming-to-be. To go deeply into a place is not only to encounter wildness. It is also to learn the stories of how your place came to be the specific place that it is. How have the events of the past shaped what is happening here now and what is possible in the future?

To see why attention to history matters, consider the "Pilgrimages of Pain and Hope" that are organized by DurhamCares in Durham, North Carolina.[31] The aim of these pilgrimages is for people living in Durham to understand how their neighborhoods came to be and how their coming-to-be is affecting the life that is happening there now. Histories of the displacement of indigenous peoples, slavery and a plantation economy, but also Jim Crow and redlining policies, are still working themselves out today as African Americans and other people of color struggle to achieve equity and justice in housing and business development. Durhamites need to understand, for instance, that the construction of the Durham Expressway did not simply make it easier for some residents to travel from one location to another. It also cut through the heart of established African American communities and thereby effectively undermined their future development. They need to know how the financial backing of preferred industries and businesses created forms of employment and salary structures that, in turn, fostered social hierarchies and neighborhood inequities that have yet to be addressed.

These pilgrimages are so important because they get residents to walk through their neighborhoods so they can physically see how events of the past have shaped their place's architecture and design. Speaking with local residents, they can hear the stories of what happened and can better understand the continuing effects of past decisions. Knowing past injustices, they are now better positioned to work for a more just future. Knowing a place in greater detail, they can also work more carefully to develop its unique potential. If our aim is to correspond with a place and community, and if our desire is to work toward a future of mutual flourishing, then pilgrimages like the ones organized by DurhamCares need to be held in the many places of our shared life. To go on a pilgrimage is like sinking a root into the nooks and crannies of a place. The health and resilience of communities depend on residents growing the multiple roots that draw them more deeply into the places that are the sources of their nurture and strength.

An apprenticeship is the labor by which a worker slowly and carefully learns the skills that promote correspondence. The worker does not simply impose his or her ambitions on the work but rather lets the materials (their availability and quantity), the needs of the community in which the work is performed, and the possibilities of good, safe, beautiful, and useful design determine the character and extent of the work. The quality of the work is indicated in the durability, usefulness, and beauty of the thing made, the health and happiness of the community in which the work is performed and the product is used, and in the long-term viability of the work itself (i.e., the work does not presuppose the degradation of the sources or workers that feed into the work). Good work that reflects a successful apprenticeship aims to make healthy, flourishing habitats and dynamic, convivial communities—exactly the sorts of places from which one is less likely to seek an escape.

DARK DESCENT

It is not uncommon for writers to describe a spiritual journey as entailing a form of personal death. The apostle Paul, for instance, describes the baptism that is one's entry into a Christian way of life as a baptism into Christ's death and as a crucifixion with him (Romans 6:1–11). Though it sometimes happens that followers of Jesus become martyrs, the larger point Paul is making is that sinful ways of being must die so that a new way of life can emerge. Those who live "in Christ" no longer perceive others from a strictly human, more or less self-serving, point of view but engage them as Christ did because Christ has taken up a transforming and inspiring residence within them (Galatians 2:20). What Paul means by the crucifixion of self is open to multiple interpretations. I would argue that this injunction is fundamentally about persons learning to offer themselves in service to the benefit of their community. If so, the death referred to is not about one's *cessation* but about one's *opening* to others so that the flows of a giving and receiving life can be maximized. In other words, the self that must die is a self-enclosed, self-securing self.

This interpretation follows from Jesus's own injunction to his followers in John 12 that they, like a grain of wheat entering the soil, must die to self by breaking out of the shells of self-containment and venture to send roots deeply into the nurturing environments around them. Growing roots is the key thing.[32] To hold onto oneself and to resist being rooted is to close life's possibilities. The image of a germinating seed demonstrates that the effort to protect and keep oneself apart from others is fundamentally self-destroying. To bear fruit and live abundantly one must learn to give oneself away because self-offering is the movement that strengthens the community that nurtures each of its members in return. Jesus's healing, feeding, befriending, exorcising, and reconciling ministries are the practical expressions of what a root-extending, self-offering life looks like.

The transition from an old to a new life is not easy. Much of it happens in a kind of epistemological darkness as people discover that they cannot comprehend all the roots that nurture their lives. It is also inherently risky and disorienting because in giving oneself away one also gives up control and makes oneself vulnerable before others. This means that the markers and guideposts by which persons determined where they are and where they should go have changed. One no longer walks on a straight, friction-free road. Instead, one now moves slowly and patiently as one responds to the places and the fellow creatures among which one moves. This is why the death of old ways is often described by mystics as a person's entrance into darkness. Darkness descends as people work to shed the various forms of rationalization—the "light" of their own minds—that authorize and legitimate the construction, direction, and ordering of a world as they want it to be.[33]

There is a great deal that one can say about spiritual darkness. One could, for instance, describe it in terms of extinguishing the light that frames and focuses others in terms of how we want to see them. When we perceive and engage fellow creatures in terms of what they can do for us, we do not perceive or engage them in terms of the divine love that desires for them to realize the life that is uniquely theirs to achieve. The divine light that enables us to see creatures as sacred gifts, and thus worthy of our respect and cherishing, is blocked when we place ourselves between God and creatures (or presume to be a god over creatures). The result is that people darken the world and cannot see creatures properly because they have put it all in shadow.[34] This is why it is so important for people to acknowledge God as the Creator. The value of creatures, along with their purposes and ends, is grounded in their God-given sanctity rather than in what we decide to make of them. The goal of our knowing, therefore, ought to be to see creatures in the light of God. For this to happen, however, the exercises of human reason need to be chastened and disciplined by love.[35]

The love that chastens reason is not a sentimental love. In the 1980 "Sabbath Poem VI," Berry offered a meditation on precisely this theme:

The intellect so ravenous to know
And in its knowing hold the very light,
Disclosing what is so and what not so,

Must finally know the dark, which is its right
And liberty; it's blind in what it sees.
Bend down, go in by this low door, despite

The thorn and briar that bar the way
                              (*TC*, 30)

Here Berry puts his finger on the grasping and acquisitive nature of an intellect that serves to reduce creation to a utilitarian or market-driven role. He signals his opposition to the sorts of scientism epitomized in modernity's ambition to take control of the world by force and with the aid of technologies that mask our fragility and dependence upon others.[36] Through scientific and economic reductionism the intellect has become blind. Though it looks, it no longer sees truly, since it has lost the imagination to see the sanctity of created beings.

This is why Berry instructs us to "bend down." Our bending, as the thorns and briars make plain, is hardly a straightforward or smooth effort, since it must fully come to terms with the harvest of human sinfulness. As Berry continues,

. . . greed and sloth
Did bad work that this thicket now conceals
                              (*TC*, 30)

Human sinfulness is not an abstraction or reducible to a personal mistake. It is made manifest in soil washed into the sea, in watersheds poisoned by the use of synthetic fertilizers and pesticides, in mountaintops blown up and then removed for their coal, in rural communities destroyed and emptied out by the "career of money," and in minority and poor neighborhoods abandoned by politicians and business leaders who see them of little value. When we bend down, we are signifying a humble disposition that is prepared to learn from creatures and be taught in the ways of interdependent living. To bend, like a servant, is to give up the hubristic assumption that we can live well alone and through the forceful imposition of our will upon the world.[37]

O bent by fear and sorrow, now bend down,

Leave word and argument, be dark and still,
And come into the joy of healing shade.
Rest from your work. Be still and dark until

You grow as unopposing, unafraid
As the young trees, without thought or belief;
Until the shadow Sabbath light has made

Shudders, breaks open, shines in every leaf.
(*TC*, 31)

The divine love that creates and sustains all life defies human comprehension. It is not tailored to secure each individual's happiness, nor is it to be corralled and controlled by us, because when people do that they invariably restrict, distort, and subvert it. The challenge is to live well in the midst of so much incomprehension.

The mind that comes to rest is tended
In ways that it cannot intend:
Is borne, preserved, and comprehended
By what it cannot comprehend.

Your Sabbath, Lord, thus keeps us by
Your will, not ours. And it is fit
Our only choice should be to die
Into that rest, or out of it.
(*TC*, 7)

When we trace the many roots that nurture us, and then recognize in these paths the presence of the life-creating and life-sustaining God, the possibility emerges that people will want to give their love to the divine love that is already there. When that happens, the divine command to till and keep the garden of life appears no longer as a curse but as an invitation to join with God in the maintenance and celebration of life. Speaking of sowing clover and grass, Berry says in his poem "Enriching the Earth,"

> All this serves the dark. I am slowly falling
> into the fund of things. And yet to serve the earth,
> not knowing what I serve, gives a wideness
> and a delight to the air, and my days
> do not wholly pass. It is the mind's service,
> for when the will fails so do the hands
> and one lives at the expense of life.
> After death, willing or not, the body serves,
> entering the earth. And so what was heaviest
> and most mute is at last raised up into song.[38]

Self-submission is at the heart of a spiritual life. It is not a solo or Promethean enterprise, however, but happens best within a community where each member, as Paul noted (in 1 Corinthians 12), is devoted to the care of each other. Neither is it a disembodied affair, since our submission is enacted daily in our need to eat and drink, but then also ultimately in our dying into the earth at burial. What self-submission communicates is that we recognize our lives to depend on our being rooted in networks of nurture and support that can sometimes harm and terrify us (when the ground is barren or toxic) but that also bless us with their goodness and grace (when the soil is healthy and fertile). To submit to the land and to others is finally a hopeful exercise in which people demonstrate their trust in the resurrecting God who assures us that a self-offering life will be like a seed that germinates, grows, and provides much fruit for all to share.[39]

Can we be at peace with each other and with God, and so be "altogether at home" in creation? Berry offers no simple or painless solutions. What he recommends is love's labor, a labor informed by virtues of modesty, attention, fidelity, humility, thrift, propriety, generosity, mercy, and gratitude, and punctuated by the practices of confession and repentance. What we need to learn to do as much as possible—and for this we will need the help and guidance of spiritual traditions, the insights of ecology, the support of a community, and the memory of good work—is place our minds in this world like roots in the ground, since it is here and now that the incomprehensible, gracious givingness of God, what Berry sometimes calls "Sabbath light," already shines.

If a mystical path is one in which the traveler learns to submit to God, then it is the virtue of agrarian life to show us that our submission is authentic only as we commit ourselves to the health and vitality of forests, fields, watersheds, cities, and neighborhoods, for it is here that God's ways, however mysteriously, are being worked out. It is here, in the soil beneath our feet and among countless communities, that God meets us in a grace that exceeds our comprehension and our wrongdoing.

> For we are fallen like the trees, our peace
> Broken, and so we must
> Love where we cannot trust,
> Trust where we cannot know,
> And must await the way-ward coming grace
> That joins living and dead,
> Taking us where we would not go—
> Into the boundless dark.
> When what was made has been unmade
> The Maker comes to his work.
>
> (*TC*, 74)[40]

CHAPTER SEVEN

Learning Humility

Humility consists in knowing that in what we call "I"
there is no source of energy by which we can rise.

—Simone Weil

It is difficult for people to be true to their creaturely condition, especially if we define creatureliness as a person's *vulnerability* and *self-insufficiency*. Whether out of fear, blindness, or hubris, an abiding temptation is for people to evade their *dependent* standing in the world. Rather than patiently and honestly living up to their *neediness* before others—by acknowledging and honoring the breadth and depth of the meshworks people inescapably live through—they are tempted to deform need into fantasy, establish themselves as invulnerable, and then remake the world to suit personal concerns. Rather than being grateful for the contributions others make to their well-being and joy—most basically through acts of companionship and nurture—people either neglect or destroy (often in the name of self-preservation) the very sources of life upon which they depend.

There are good reasons for this. That people work to become *in*vulnerable is a sign of how often situations of vulnerability are turned into sites of denigration, abuse, and violence. Children, women, indigenous peoples, ethnic minorities, poor peasant families, communities of color, migrant workers, refugees, and LGBTQ persons are just some of the people who have lacked the backing and protection of powerful elites and thus have been exploited, displaced, or killed. Given this sordid history and its continuing momentum, it is not surprising that people should do what they can to become inviolable. To be vulnerable is to be weak and inferior. To be dependent on others is to be at their (often unreliable) mercy.

What is lost and what is falsified in the pursuit of invulnerability? In her book *The Ethics of Vulnerability: A Feminist Analysis of Social Life and Practice*, Erinn Gilson argues that the elevation of autonomy and control as moral ideals deprives us of essential insights about what it means to be human. As embodied and social beings, people are necessarily dependent on a host of fellow creatures ranging from bacteria and bees to families and strangers. When we deny this fact we also forfeit the occasions in which empathy, compassion, and solidarity can be cultivated as personal ideals. Moreover, "The valorization of independence and self-sufficiency . . . reduces care to a means to an end (that of independence) rather than a value in itself. . . . If the reality of human life is that we are always dependent to varying degrees, then our conception of autonomy ought to reflect such facts of dependence, interdependence, and the significance of care-giving and receiving rather than relegating them to the status of the exceptional and abnormal."[1]

But there is more. The denial of our need for relationship deprives us of what Anne Dufourmantelle calls the wisdom and power of gentleness. "Gentleness is primarily an intelligence, one that carries life, that saves and enhances it. . . . It is an understanding of the relationship with the other, and tenderness is the epitome of this relationship."[2] What Dufourmantelle's analyses help us appreciate is that creaturely life is always life together with others who are similarly insufficient, helpless, suffering, weak, fallible, irritating, disappointing, and sometimes stupid. The infrastructures of steel, concrete, and glass notwithstanding, we live in a wounded world populated by permeable, sensitive, and soft flesh, flesh that carries the histories of the traumas inflicted upon it. This is why tenderness is so important, since it communicates an appreciation for our *shared* vulnerability and a commitment to be a solicitous and protecting presence to those we are with. It takes attention, intention, and practice to cultivate a considerate and gentle intelligence.

My aim in this chapter is to develop an account of humility that is attuned to creaturely need and vulnerability but is also directed to cultivating the sympathy and gentleness that are crucial for the healing of our wounded communities and places. My inspiration for this way of thinking begins with scripture's earliest account of humanity's creation in the Garden of Eden. As is well known, God creates the first *adam* (human) out of the *adamah* (humus) by breathing into the latter God's form-giving, life-giving breath. Along with other plant and animal creatures, human beings are soil divinely animated, and humanity's fundamental and abiding task is to serve and protect the garden that is its nurturing home. The point of this work isn't simply to grow some food or flowers. It is to cultivate a detailed understanding of this world as *a vulnerable membership of life* in which creatures provide for the needs of each other and then learn the skills necessary to fit harmoniously within this membership. Humility is at the core of this task, not only because it is reflected in the etymological connections between *human, humus,* and *humility* but more fundamentally because humility communicates an overall orientation for daily life in which people keep the needs of others foremost in mind and heart. Put another way, when people embody humility they witness to the truth of their humanity *as creatures* called to praise God precisely *in the honoring of this world and its life*. The world God creates is a vulnerable world susceptible to pain and suffering. To live well and beautifully within it, people must not only affirm the good of their need. They must also learn the skills of gentleness and compassion that are essential to life that is always life together. Humility takes us to the heart of a spiritual life that is faithful to the world as a place of belonging and responsibility. This is a thesis that needs clarification and defense.

As I develop my account I will draw on Jean-Louis Chrétien's phenomenological description of the call-response structure to human life, since it alerts us to the *sympathetic* and *resonant* nature of embodied life. As he rightly sees it, no human being lives alone or in isolation.

Though people may think of themselves as individuals, and may even work to separate and protect themselves from others, the experience of touch reveals our being and our every movement to be another's being and movement reverberating *through* us. "Each and every sensation starts by consenting to the world, and from this ground only can it ever return back to itself. The joy of being is of another order than self-sensation and self-enjoyment."[3] Put in auditory terms, "We speak for having heard. Every voice, hearing without cease, bears many voices within itself because there is no first voice. . . . Between my voice as it speaks and my voice as I hear it vibrates the whole thickness of the world whose meaning my voice attempts to say, meaning that has gripped it and swallowed it up, as it were, from time immemorial."[4] On this account, to fail to attend and listen to others—recognizing that "listening exceeds by far the sense of hearing. Everything in us listens, because everything in the world and of the world speaks"[5]—is to be guilty of the spiritual malfunction that precipitates the undoing of communities and the created order.

CLEARING AN OPENING FOR HUMILITY

The call to be humble is often framed by spiritual writers as a call to be *nothing*. Simone Weil, for instance, says, "We should renounce being something. That is our only good." This is because, in and of themselves, individuals can be and do nothing: "Everything without exception which is of value in me comes from somewhere other than myself. . . . Everything without exception which is in me is absolutely valueless; and, among the gifts which have come to me from elsewhere, everything which I appropriate becomes valueless immediately I do so."[6] Speaking this way, Weil reflects a tradition in which people seeking humility are regularly admonished to acknowledge their worthlessness and to esteem their powers as little more than rubbish.[7] Humility develops best, they are advised, in contexts where individuals are held to be of no repute.[8]

Unsurprisingly, it is precisely the call to see ourselves "as nothing" that has caused calls to humility to be met with resistance, even scorn.

It is just too depressing, and it stifles human potential and achieve-ment. Critics ranging from David Hume to Friedrich Nietzsche rou-tinely deride spiritual writers who, in their calls to humility, refer to the sinfulness and contemptibility of the human race. Norvin Richards is representative when he asks, "If humility is low self-esteem, where does this leave the rather *splendid* among us . . . ?"[9] On this view, hu-mility is a vice and a blemish on the strength, daring, ingenuity, and dignity that elevate us as a species. It is the surest and most miserable sign of self-imposed decadence and therefore ought to be rejected as a valued character trait. Failure to banish humility from a list of virtues will inevitably lead to forms of self-hatred and self-loathing that have done so much personal and social harm.

What should we make of this criticism? Are calls to humility just another way of keeping oppressed and beleaguered people down? Is humility finally a form of self- and world-hatred that has roots extend-ing all the way back to Jesus's injunction that "those who love their life lose it, and those who hate their life in this world will keep it for eternal life" (John 12:25)?

It would be puzzling, if not contradictory, to think that Jesus wants people to hate life or themselves when he also says, "I came that they may have life, and have it abundantly" (John 10:10). It would also be incongruous given Jesus's daily commitment to heal, feed, exorcise, befriend, and reconcile personal bodies. Jesus's overall life is a rebuke precisely to those people who think this world and its life do not matter and therefore can be ignored, demeaned, or abused.[10] His ministries of touch and his compassionate presence to others witness to God's inti-mate and abiding love for each and every created being. If this is the case, then the call to be nothing cannot mean we should despise our-selves or others. Why? Because God never despises creaturely life. It is important to recall that creatures are not simply the *objects* of God's concern. They are the *embodied expressions* of God's creating and sus-taining love, which is why God enters into covenant relationship with them, promising to be with them always as the Source, Nurturer, and Healer of their lives. As we must now see, the call to humility is ulti-mately a call to reframe how we understand what a human being is and what a human life is ultimately for. Humility should not be about loathing oneself but about coming to understand oneself *as a gifted and cherished creaturely being* that needs and lives through the nurture and love that others must provide. It is about living in ways that honor the divine power that animates our life together. Humble people have learned to position themselves gratefully, graciously, and generously within a world that moves through the receiving and sharing of the gifts of God.

We can return to Weil's text *Gravity and Grace* to see what is involved. She writes, "Humility is the refusal to exist outside of God." The great mistake is for me to think that I can live on my own or that I can secure life for myself, even draw life from out of myself. This I simply cannot do. I did not create myself. To live, I must constantly *receive* the power of life from God as a gift. I must *participate* in a meshwork world where this divine power is constantly circulating through all the bodies and processes that intersect and pulse through me. The danger in pronouncing myself to be a self-standing, self-sourcing "I" is that I might separate myself from others and believe I can make it on my own. This is an illusion that is also destructive because the drive to secure and protect the "I" has the effect of blocking (by hoarding for oneself) the flows of life that I must receive and extend to others. The key is to understand myself, not as a sovereign, self-enclosed, self-standing, and object-like *subject*, but as an enmeshed, needy, dynamic *conduit* or *vessel* through which God's life-creating love can freely move. "In so far as I become nothing, God loves himself through me." "God can love in us only this consent to withdraw in order to make way for him, just as he himself, our creator, withdrew in order that we might come into being. This double operation has no other meaning than love."[11] Each life is at its best when divine love flows in an unimpeded manner through the breadth and depth of relationships that constitute it. When people appreciate that they live only through receiving the diverse gifts of birth, nurture, and companionship, then the call to be nothing can be understood as a call to remove from myself any and all obstacles that would subvert or stall the action of God that moves *through* me (and others).

Weil's description of humility alerts us to the porous, vulnerable, and rooted character of a human life. To be human is essentially to be

open to others like a seed that opens to its soil environment by extend-
ing roots that receive and give nurture in return (John 12:24).[12] Apart
from this openness people cannot be the sympathetic, ecstatic, and
erotic beings they are created to be. The eroticism I have in mind is not
anything like the pornographic impulse that reduces others to
self-pleasing objects. It is, instead, the eroticism of God's compassion
that goes ever more widely and deeply into the world, nourishing bodies and inspiring them to extend this love to others in return. When
people stall, stifle, or block God's love they not only hinder creation's
ongoing development but also mistake themselves. The key to a right
and honest understanding of a human creature is to know that the
desire to assert oneself gets in the way of a true life, which is life for
others. Weil puts this point succinctly when she says, "I must withdraw
so that God may make contact with the beings whom chance places in
my path and whom he loves."[13] It is important to see in this statement
an echo of Paul's description of Jesus as the one who emptied and
humbled himself so as to serve others. This emptying or withdrawal
was not in the service of self-loathing or self-annihilation. It was in the
service of embodying a self-offering life that gives to others without
remainder (Philippians 2:6–8).

The *kenosis* or self-emptying character of God as revealed in the
self-offering life of Jesus alerts us to a crucial point about creation and
all the life that moves within it: this created world is the material expression of a *hospitable* God. God creates (and saves and fulfills) by
making room for others to be, *welcoming* them into the divine nurturing presence, and then *liberating* and *empowering* them to live into the
fullness of their lives. This means that as creatures, human beings are
fundamentally *hosted* and *hosting* beings called to participate and extend God's hospitable ways in the world. This is a radical hospitality
that is already deep inside of creaturely bodies in the form of a gut
microbiome that we feed in our eating and that feeds us in the form of
facilitating digestive processes. More than we know, but in ways that
our bodies nonetheless exhibit, every human being is a multitude of
beings engaged in complex processes of mutual nurture. People do not
choose, nor can they opt out of, the receiving-giving dynamic of created life. What they can (in varying degrees) do is decide how they will

participate. The essential fact is that people cannot live into their humble, hospitable role if they deny or close themselves off from the receiving-giving dynamic that is at the heart of life's hospitable movement.

The close connection between humility and creatureliness enables us to rethink the "nothingness" that people are called to keep constantly in mind. Recall that in Christian theological traditions, the whole of material reality is believed to have been created *ex nihilo* or "from nothing."[14] This nothing is not a mysterious or highly esoteric "something" but aims to communicate the utterly gratuitous nature of this world. Nothing has to be. That anything is at all must, therefore, be the result of a divine love that delights in something other than God being what it is. In other words, creation *ex nihilo* is also creation *ex amore* or "from love," since it is only love (rather than some divine lack or external pressure placed upon God) that prompts God to create at all. Saint Bonaventure understood this, which is why he insisted that humility is core to humanity's self-understanding as gracious and gifted beings.[15] We have not made ourselves and cannot make ourselves but are creatures who are dependent upon God as our Creator. Bonaventure describes our complete dependence in terms of the nothingness of creation: "Therefore, since all things, which have been made, abide by the one principle and were produced from nothing, that man is truly wise who really recognizes the nothingness [*nihilitatem*] of himself and of others, and the sublimity of the first principle."[16] Here again we can see that the invocation of our own nothingness is, at a deeper level, an affirmation of each human life as the embodied expression of a divine love that desires for it to be and to flourish.

The anthropological insight that human life is utterly gratuitous and moves via the reception and sharing of gift upon gift is of the greatest practical and material significance. Consider how across times and cultures people have constructed built environments that have as their aim to reflect human prowess and power. Various ever more sophisticated technologies have been developed so that people can engineer their worlds more and more to their liking.[17] There has been considerable good in this effort but also a lot of violence because creatures, whether human or nonhuman, have often not been received as sacred gifts but grasped as objects to be possessed and controlled. So many places have been wasted or polluted, while countless lives have been sacrificed on the altars of personal ambition, private accumulation, and financial profit. Far too often the construction of our farms and cities communicates a spirit of acquisition and control rather than humility and gentleness. How would daily life differ if people worked and played in places—the schools, houses, workplaces, playgrounds, and hospitals—that *in their design and construction* communicated that all creatures are to be welcomed and cherished?

The design and development of places are radically transformed when people see others as gifts to be received and cherished rather than as objects to be owned and manipulated.[18] One's feel for life, but also what one expects out of it and what one believes its point is, shift dramatically, and this shift is reflected in what we do and make. For instance, in a world where life is believed to be sacred, neighborhoods are constructed that communicate welcome and sociability and so emphasize the construction of sidewalks, front porches, parks, public benches, and plazas where people can freely and spontaneously gather. Farms are kept that facilitate good work and honor multispecies life, and so are kept small enough that farmers can exercise the detailed attention that is a prerequisite for good care of the soil, watersheds, and animal livestock. Processes of manufacture are guided by the commitments to preserve the health and vitality of the habitats from which raw materials are harvested, that honor and properly compensate the skills of workers, and that respect consumers by making products that are useful, durable, and beautiful. The idea that any place can be rendered toxic, putrid, or ugly by the human activity that occurs within it is rejected, not only because it is (literally) self-destroying, but because it is a fundamental dishonoring of God and the works of God's hands.

Our built environments reflect, sometimes more honestly than our spoken words, what we think life is about and what it is for. In the things we make we communicate whether we believe this world is worth cherishing. That our farms and cities are populated with so many monuments praising the accumulation of wealth and power reflects not only a rejection of, but a rebellion against, humility. To refuse humility is to build the material infrastructures—the financial institutions, insurance plans, military complexes, incarceration facilities, and gated communities—that hide our need and deny our vulnerability. It is to think we can be fully human without exercising the hospitality that welcomes and respects others and the gentleness that witnesses to an understanding of our shared vulnerability. When a spirit of humility goes to work, the goal is to make and maintain places so as to highlight their goodness, beauty, and sanctity.

These observations enable us to appreciate that humility is much more than a personal virtue. It is a way of coming to truthful terms with the kind of world we are in, the kind of creatures we are, and what is proper for us to do in our world and with others. It is not reducible to a self-despising or a self-effacing gesture because at its core what the practice of humility does is enable people to face each other and fellow creatures in the ecstatic, erotic movement that extends to them the divine, creating love that is always already being received. To walk in a humble way is to acknowledge our need of others and to be grateful to God for the gift of this world and its life. It is to make oneself a courteous, gentle, and nurturing *conduit* that witnesses to and honors the creating hospitality of God.

TURNING TO THE BODY

Quite rightly, people are suspicious of those who speak loudly and confidently about their own humility. It isn't only that such talk displays a performative contradiction. It is also presumptuous. If it is true that we live through the reception of innumerable gifts that exceed our calculating and comprehending, then we should follow Chrétien, who describes human life as a perpetual experience of excess: "the excess of a human being over himself, an excess of what one is and can be over what one can think and comprehend."[19] It is simply impossible for us to enumerate and completely know the myriad bodies (ranging from microorganisms in the soil to stardust in far-away galaxies), or fully appreciate the complexity of processes (ranging from the actions of germination and growth to the origination of anything at all), that feed into and make our being possible. Bathed as we are in an overwhelming number of influences and interchanges, sometimes the most honest thing to do is to speak with restraint and as a witness to the unfathomable depths and intricacies of this life.

To appreciate life's excessive character we should turn to the experience of a living body, for it is here that the roots of authentic humility grow. This is easier said than done, because spiritual traditions—whether in philosophical or religious guise—have elevated the soul or mind over living flesh. They have assumed that a material body is something that one (sometimes only temporarily) *has* rather than *is*. This preference and way of thinking has been a disaster insofar as it has underwritten the abandonment and abuse of the earth and its many creatures. But it is also fundamentally dishonest because it obscures the fact that what we know, believe, and experience depends upon points of access that each have their root and inspiration in a living body. Jean-Yves Lacoste is right to say, "No experience of the self can bracket the body, and thus bracket the relations of proximity to which the body binds us; the experience of the self is the experience of place as much as of time."[20] Every human life is necessarily a rooted life that *through our flesh* binds us to the earth and entangles us with other creatures.

When thinking about embodied life, it is important to resist the elevation of *sight* as the preferred sense for self-understanding and to consider the centrality of *touch* instead.[21] In part, this is because sight can suggest a separation between observer and observed and can thus occlude the intimacy of involvement within a world that an observer's position presupposes: in order for a living body to look at a world, it must always already be eating, drinking, touching, and breathing it. This is why Chrétien (following Aristotle) says, "The most fundamental and universal of all senses is the sense of touch. . . . While touch is separable from other senses . . . the sense of touch is inseparable from life itself: no animal is deprived of touch without also being deprived of life."[22] Touch, in other words, is coextensive with a living body. Without touch, people would be deprived of their being and their potential for becoming, and they would forfeit their access to any world at all. "Touch is the perpetual place of exchange through which the nonidentical is identified, through which we are disclosed to the world and the forms of the world are disclosed to us. All particular forms of sensitivity only extend and develop this very first consent to being, a consent from before all initiative."[23] The unmistakable proof of this is that every human body carries a belly button that is the abiding physical reminder of one's birth in and dependence on a mother's womb. Skin is not a garment of containment that seals people off from our womb-like world but a permeable and highly sensitive membrane that opens them to it.

The touchiness of creaturely existence communicates that life proceeds along intertwining paths of intimacy that boggle the mind. This is why philosophers have, from the beginning, noted that we cannot comprehend fully the extent and the ways of touch.[24] Before people can think about it, and before they can make the effort to predict, freely choose, or fully control the social and material conditions of their living, they have needed to be in appropriate touch with others. We see this in the fact that a young child deprived of affectionate touch cannot develop properly. When the tactile experiences of being nursed, held, cuddled, bathed, and caressed are withheld, infants languish and eventually die, despite having received the calories they need. It isn't enough for them to see, hear, or smell others. They need to be lifted up and hugged. This is a need that carries well beyond the months of infancy and extends throughout a person's life. For people to flourish they need to know *and feel* that they are cherished, most basically by acts of compassionate touch. Each human life arises out of the physical intimacy of sexual union, develops through multiple umbilical connections, maintains itself in the digestion of flesh, and maximizes its potential in contexts of nurturing touch. This physiological fact indicates that touch is foundational, even a precondition for other senses to do their work. Though it is but one sense, it disperses throughout our bodies and is active in our capacities to taste, smell, hear, reproduce, and grow. "While we can close our eyes, our ears, our nostrils and our lips, we are always touching and being touched. Touch is a 'membrane' sensitive to what is not itself, a portal opening to a world that can never be shut."[25]

The primordial and abiding experience of touching and being touched indicates that human beings are *sensitive* beings that *feel* the world before they think it. This observation does not undermine the importance of reason or the value of disinterested observation and analysis of the world. Instead, it reminds us of the need to cultivate in each other the wisdom of gentleness and the virtue of empathy that together are attuned to the vulnerabilities of flesh. It reinforces the importance of compassionate touch in facilitating the processes of healing that our world so desperately needs. I stress *compassionate* touch, for as Richard Kearney has reminded us, not all forms of touch are nurturing. Though compassionate touch is well recognized as a powerful therapy in healing the traumas that beset human life, violent touch has long been the source of unspeakable harms: "If the tactile body possesses extraordinary powers of healing, it is also the barometer of past hurts. The body carries traces of our shame, guilt, childhood conditioning, repressed desires, and deepest fears. Hence the need for a highly sensitive approach to touch in the treatment of trauma victims in therapy."[26]

The intimacy of embodied touch teaches us that to exist at all is to be "exposed" to countless others and to find oneself caught up in movements that solicit a response. Not responding is not an option. When people believe themselves to be self-standing, autarchic, or autonomous, they deceive themselves and others because they think they can set the terms for their exposure or create a safe and controlled environment that is immune to suffering and pain. This cannot be done. It can certainly be a humiliating experience to find oneself somewhat helpless in face of the bewildering and overwhelming character of our entanglements with others, but it can also be a blessed experience in which the grace and goodness of life are felt. It can be frustrating, even the source of just rage, to know that bodies are susceptible to so much potential abuse and pain, but the knowledge of the intimacy of our need can also be a source of joy when mercy and compassion are the powers animating our movements with others. Humble people appreciate, as Chrétien notes, that thought and speech invariably fall short in the face of the vulnerability, unpredictability, and fragility that saturate creaturely life. We cannot make sense of all that we encounter, nor can we control it. The frailty of creaturely life teaches us that incomprehension is not a "contingent deficit nor a regrettable imperfection. . . . It is the very event of a wound by which our existence is altered and opened, and becomes itself the site of the manifestation of what it responds to."[27] Learning to live with wounds, both the wounds we experience and those that we (knowingly or not) inflict on others, is difficult to do, which is why it is so important to cultivate the gentleness and mercy that animate a humble heart.

Humble people recognize that life is a perpetual passion play, an unfathomably costly drama in which vitality, suffering, and death inform, close, and again open possibilities. The wounded character of our living, a wound we experience intimately and inescapably through our feeling bodies, is the mark of our finitude and our dependence upon others. Through the daily actions of touching, tasting, smelling, hearing, and seeing, people discover that they cannot bring about their own existence or the existence of the world in terms of which they live. Human experience is thus permeated and formed by a fundamental disproportion or incommensurability between itself and that which brings it about. "Our task is not to give an answer that would in some sense erase the initial provocation by corresponding to it, but to offer ourselves up as such in response, without assigning in advance any limit to the gift."[28]

CHRISTOLOGICAL TOUCH

My brief analysis of touch has shown us that "to be" is always already "to be in relation" with, and thus also susceptible to, others. There is no human life that is "out of touch" with soils, forests, watersheds, sunshine, rain, farm fields, worms, bees, homes, kitchens, families, friends, artisans, and teachers (to name a few). Those who are humble recognize their need of others to be the most basic truth about their living, and so do what they can to honor the relationships they live through. It is simply wrong to presume too much for oneself, not because of some infection of self-loathing, but because presumption misunderstands what human creatures *are* and what they should *do* in this world. When faced with the neediness and vulnerability of human flesh, how should people live?

As Christians considered the character of this created world and reflected on the means and ends of created life, they turned to Jesus as the one who, precisely through his ministries of touch, modeled what a life-giving way looks like and entails. They believed, as Graham Ward has put it, that Christ is the "archetype of relationships" because he is the one *through whom* and *for whom* all things are created, and the one *in whom* all things hold together (Colossians 1:15–17). Jesus, in other words, is to be followed because his modalities of living reveal life's point and purpose as a humble journey with others that serves their nurture, healing, and liberation. If people want to experience life's abundance and sanctity, they should participate in his attentive, loving, and touching ministries, since these ways of being coincide exactly with God's eternal way of life (Hebrews 1:3). "Christ, as second person of the Trinity, is the archetype of all relation. All relations, that is, participate in and aspire to their perfection in the Christological relation. Not only in him is all relation perfected, but the work and economy he is implicated in . . . the reconciliation of the world to God."[29] Love perfects humility because love best inspires and animates the practices that sustain and protect our vulnerable life together.

When we turn to specific examples of Jesus's ministry, the character of a humble life comes into focus. Consider the story of the woman who had been suffering from hemorrhages for twelve years. Though she had spent all she had on physicians, not only did she continue to suffer, but her condition grew worse. The power of life (which is what Jews understood blood to mean) was slowly draining out of her body. Mark's gospel describes the woman and what she experienced this way: "She had heard about Jesus, and came up behind him in the crowd and touched his cloak, for she said, 'If I but touch his clothes, I will be made well.' Immediately her hemorrhage stopped; and she felt in her body that she was healed of her disease" (Mark 5:27–29). This encounter is a testimony to the power of healing touch, but it is also a witness to the intimacy with others that a healed life presupposes. For this woman, there was no hope in being alone. To be whole and free from her suffering she needed to be in embodied touch with the power that heals life, which is why she touched Jesus. She went to Jesus because she believed his body to be a site through which the power of God's love fully flowed.

Jesus's response is also illuminating. Though he was in a crowd of people where contact was unavoidable, this woman's touch was different, which is why Jesus asked, "Who touched my clothes?" Mark explains his question by saying that Jesus was "immediately aware that power had gone forth from him" (Mark 5:30). The woman wasn't seeking mere contact with Jesus. She was looking for the personal touch that put her in intimate relationship with the divine power that creates, sustains, and liberates people into the fullness of their lives. Jesus felt her hand and her desire, and because his body was *open* to giving her the power she needed, the woman was healed. Jesus, we might say, understood himself to be a *conduit* through which the love of the Father could be extended and take root in the places and communities through which he moved. He did not believe that the divine power given to him was something to hold onto and keep for himself. It is meant to be shared with others, most basically in the service and skill we offer to improve others' lives. Mark's healing episode models what the divine way of being looks like in the flesh and then calls people to participate in a way of being that both *receives* the gift of life and *gives* it to others in the form of compassionate and hospitable touch. Luke described this dynamic succinctly when he spoke of the crowds that regularly came to be with Jesus. "They had come to hear him and to be healed of their diseases; and those who were troubled with unclean spirits were cured. And all in the crowd were trying to touch him, for power came out from him and healed all of them" (Luke 6:18–19).

The story of the hemorrhaging woman, along with many other stories of Jesus healing, feeding, befriending, forgiving, and reconciling people, indicates that the goal of a Christian life is not to escape from our entangled embodiment but to practice the divine touch that cherishes our life together. But for that to happen, people must participate, and in ways that are unique to each person's capacities and abilities, in the divine way of being here and now. Salvation is not what happens to people after they die. It is their ever-deeper immersion into God's life—what early church theologians described as *theosis*—in which embodiment is not left behind but transformed so that each human body can now be a vessel through which God's love freely flows. In Ward's formulation, "Human beings are not truly themselves, are not truly flesh, until they have become flesh as he [Jesus] became flesh. . . .

Touch is an orientation towards being incarnate and it finds its true self-understanding in love."[30]

It is easy to be mistaken about the kind of relationality Jesus calls us to, especially when we acknowledge how the power that animates many of our relationships is often a power that is *over* others. Monarchical conceptions of power are a mistake because they do not reflect or extend the hospitality that characterizes God's creating, sustaining, and liberating ways. As Rowan Williams has helped us to appreciate, so much of our thinking and acting goes wrong because we misunderstand the logic of creation. When thinking about creation—what it is, how it thrives, and what it is ultimately for—it is crucial to affirm that God does not create out of a divine lack or need. If that were the case, then the point of each creature's life would be to serve and meet God's need. Its identity would be wrapped up in making God (somehow) feel good or feel better about the divine self. In sharp contrast to this way of thinking, Christians have affirmed that God creates in complete freedom and without any external pressure or constraints. God creates *ex nihilo* and *ex amore*, from nothing and only out of love. The practical implication that follows is enormous, since it means that creatures are now *free to become themselves*. Put another way, God is glorified not at the expense of creatures, as when people believe they must become small and insignificant in order for God to be great, but when creatures live into the fullness of the lives they have been given. "With God alone, I am dealing with what does not need to construct or negotiate an identity, what is free to be itself without struggle. Properly understood, this is the most liberating message we could ever hear."[31]

The logic of creation teaches that God's creating and sustaining power is not a coercive or manipulating power *over* others. Jesus incarnated this logic in his embodied life and demonstrated that divine power is the kind of power that comes *alongside* others, *dwells with* them, *abides in* them, and *shares* in their pain and joy. Jesus did not jockey with others for position or prominence. Instead, he took up the humble role of a servant who seeks to further not his own interests but the interests of others. He emptied himself of all vestiges of the *self-serving* ego so that he could model a cruciform, *self-offering* life that is humble to the core (Philippians 2:4–8).

Christians believed that the noncoercive, noncompetitive power that Jesus incarnated in his ministries was the power that led to life's abundance, or to what the apostle Paul called "the life that really is life" (1 Timothy 6:19). But they also saw that this was a vulnerable power that could be put to death by Roman crucifixion, which was why they stressed that a Christian life is best realized in communities that were animated by Christ's love and that testified to the "fruit" of the Holy Spirit (enumerated in Galatians 5:22–23 as love, joy, peace, patience, kindness, generosity, faithfulness, gentleness, and self-control) being realized in their midst. Persons who commit to living a humble, self-offering life should not be left alone to serve on their own. They should be surrounded and supported by a community of persons who are each committed to coming to the aid of each other, rejoicing with those who rejoice, suffering with those who suffer, and helping when help is needed.

To understand the radical character of the power that is *with* others rather than *over* them, we are helped again if we consider the nature of touch as foundational to sensory perception. When we see two people come together, we also see that it is impossible for two people to be in the same space at the same time. We can get very close, even make contact, but each must remain in the space that is specific to each. The surface of each person is like a border that cannot be crossed. But if we make touch our focus, then the sense of a clear border dividing two people from each other is called into question, because in touching another I am also touched in return and at the same time. Put more precisely, in touching another I am also at the same time positioned to feel myself. As Chrétien puts it, "I feel myself only by the favor of the other. It is the other who gives me to myself insofar as the return to myself and my own actions or affections always supposes this other. . . . I never start by saying 'I.'"[32] Touch does not obliterate difference between two (or more). Instead, it reveals a dimension of intimacy in which another gets beneath my skin so as to become an inspiring, animating presence within me.[33] In other words, touch helps me appreciate that I am never simply myself, self-standing and alone. Since I must be in touch with others to be at all, what I call "I" is really plural in nature. I cannot be myself unless I am with others, since whatever path I choose to "come to myself" is a path that is always populated and propelled by others.

It is noteworthy that when Jesus called people to a life of love, he gave the image of himself as a vine onto which they were to be grafted. He told them, "Abide in me as I abide in you. Just as the branch cannot bear fruit by itself unless it abides in the vine, neither can you unless you abide in me. I am the vine, you are the branches" (John 15:4–5). This is striking imagery because it communicates the intensity of the intimacy that defines the co-abiding that ought to govern our life with others. A branch can be distinguished from a vine, but it is also clear that a branch does not and cannot exist as a separable thing. It must be deeply in touch with the vine if it is to grow and bear fruit. It must penetrate the vine and be penetrated by it if it is to receive the power of life, making it difficult to draw a precise line distinguishing the branch from the vine. This is how the power of love moves: by animating people from within rather than coercing them from without. It takes humility to affirm oneself as a branch, and to know that one is nothing apart from the vine.

A MUSICAL CODA

For many people, listening to music is a moving experience. It isn't simply that people enjoy the rhythms and sounds. More radically, and often in unsought and unbidden ways, they feel their bodies move spontaneously, or they feel emotions well up from deep inside as they are caught up within its sounding. The experience of music has the power to transport people to another dimension and to transform what they feel and how they feel it. Put another way, music has the ability to touch people without their thinking or intending it. It works its way into our being, not just our ears, and thus demonstrates that the human body is fundamentally a *listening body*.

But what if our bodies don't listen? Can we describe a humble life as a careful, courteous, and sympathetic life that listens?

In a journal entry dated October 26, 1851, Henry David Thoreau said, "The instant I awoke, methought I was a musical instrument. . . .

My body was the organ and channel of melody, as a flute is of the music that is breathed through it. My flesh sounded and vibrated still to the strain, and my nerves were the chords of the lyre." But the enthusiasm of the realization of himself as a musical, listening body was quickly dampened by "an infinite regret—to find myself, not the thoroughfare of glorious and world-stirring inspirations, but a scuttle full of dirt. . . . My regret arose from the consciousness how little like a musical instrument my body was now."[34] Thoreau's lament was over his inability to tune his body like a musical instrument, or even a tuning fork, through which the rhythms, pulses, and melodies of this world might sound and vibrate. As he characterized it, both he and his contemporaries were too much oriented away from this material world, focusing on heavenly or spiritual realities that were above and far away and could be accessed only through the mind. As a result, not nearly enough effort was being devoted to training and refining their bodily senses.

In *A Week on the Concord and Merrimack Rivers* he claimed that "our present senses are but the rudiments of what they are destined to become. We are comparatively deaf and dumb and blind, and without smell or taste or feeling."[35] The effect of this sensory deficit is that people can be in the world and not appreciate where they are by not being attuned to the creatures they are with. The world remains outside. Its people are unaffected, untouched, and unmoved.

It is possible to read in this journal entry one more exhibition of Thoreau's often cranky nature. But should we not also see in it a profound statement of our need to educate and train our senses so that we can live more attentively and harmoniously—more sensitively—in this world? As this chapter has argued, an articulation of the human body as like a musical instrument is true to our experience of the intimacy of the influences that move through us in the forms of nurture, growth, and healing. More than we can say, our bodies witness to the fact we are hosted and held by the bodies of countless others, which is why a true or authentic voice will witness, as Chrétien put it, to the many voices within it. It will acknowledge that "between my voice as it speaks and my voice as I hear it vibrates the whole thickness of the world whose meaning my voice attempts to say, meaning that has gripped it and swallowed it up, as it were, from time immemorial." The effect of that acknowledgment should be gratitude and praise, since these are the humble forms of speech that register that the gift has been received.

I have concluded with a turn to music because the listening body is also a *sounding body*. Though we clearly speak with our mouths, it is also the case that our whole body sounds and communicates. What sort of sound does it make?

The options are various, ranging from a loud discordant note that asserts itself among others to a softer sympathetic note that listens and tunes itself to the sounds of others. Of these two options, it is the latter that clearly strikes a humble note. But what is a humble sound, and what does it accomplish? In an essay entitled "Music Language Dwelling," Julian Johnson argues that our thinking about music is too much dominated by the idea that its primary aim is to signify or communicate a message. Round about the start of the nineteenth century, however, a different model of what music does was being explored. "By this model, music does not say; it takes place. It puts its participants into *communion*, in the sense of partaking in something shared, but it does not convey information or communicate any extraneous content; it does not pass messages, tell stories, express emotions, or represent things."[36] Put another way, this model argued that the power of music is its ability to create the conditions in which the world can come into presence in ways that do not claim to name, know, grasp, and control it. This is a form of music that asks of listeners that they desist from trying to comprehend what appears or sounds, and instead cultivate the attentive regard and respect that welcomes what comes. When characterized this way, "Music affords an openness to the world, a contemplative attitude of mind that allows 'what is' to come. Musical listening does not say, propose, argue, or assert; it listens, opens, and receives."[37]

What Johnson describes as happening in the forms of music popular in "high" European culture has roots that go much further back if one listens to traditional or folk music. The British singer Sam Lee, for instance, has devoted his life to recovering and recording the ancient tunes of Irish, Scottish, and English "travelers." These balladeers did not think of themselves as possessing or controlling the music they sang. Instead, they tried to achieve a quality of singing the Scots call *maizie* and the Irish call *coniach*. Here a singer opens him- or herself up to the ancestors and calls upon the music that they gave and that is all around. As Lee describes it, "The songs didn't exist inside you. They were outside you, and you breathe them in. You activated them. And when you had the *maizie* inside you, the ancestors would appear." But not just human ancestors. So much traditional music has the character of a conversation with wind and surf, howl and birdsong. Lee describes how the experience of singing with a nightingale was utterly transformative because the nightingales *sang back* to him. In their response they opened a connection to the nonhuman world that pierced and moved his soul. Speaking of nightingales, Lee says, "They have a particular way of opening you up. . . . They unlock you and rinse through you, because that's the power. . . . It's a quivering sensation as the frequencies kind of, you know, pass through you. That's a gift. Sometimes you have to work very hard to have those palpable experiences of cleansing, of communion with nature."[38] To listen to a nightingale and respond with one's own voice to the invitations their sounds and silences create is to come into the presence of the world in a profoundly sensuous and sonorous way.

This way of characterizing music does not render listeners passive. Instead, it positions them to engage their world in more resonant ways that do not block or control what one hears but come into sympathetic attunement with it. To see what I mean, consider the possibility of harmonious sound. Here, two (or more) notes do not simply come alongside each other, nor do they compete with each other or dissolve into each other. Rather, they enact the "sympathetic resonance" that is possible only because of listening attunement. Jeremy Begbie describes the phenomenon this way: "The tones we hear are not in competition, nor do they simply allow each other room. The lower sound establishes the upper, frees it to be itself, enhances it, without compromising its own integrity. Moreover, when certain other strings are opened alongside both these strings—for instance, to make an extended major chord—we will hear those other strings come to life."[39] Harmony is a phenomenon in which members are distinct yet interpenetrate and *sound through* each other so that something more is achieved without the diminishment of either.

Is it possible for people to live in such a harmonious manner with each other and in their places? Can people learn to orient their bodies in ways that enhance and free others to be themselves in ways they could not be on their own? Such a possibility would require that people work to make themselves the kind of presence that helps others *come to life*. Not the life we might choose for them, but the God-given life that is uniquely theirs to achieve. As this chapter has argued, humility is at the heart of this possibility because humble people understand themselves to be nothing in and of themselves. They know, as Weil says, that they do not have within themselves the energy they need to rise but are vessels that must constantly receive from others—and ultimately from God—the gifts of nurture and companionship they need to live. It is why they respond to their places and communities in modes of gentle and compassionate touch, for it is as the power of God's love moves ever more freely through them that the prospect of a harmonious and healed future emerges.[40]

CHAPTER EIGHT

Learning Generosity

I would like to speak of gratitude as a labor undertaken by the soul to effect the transformation after a gift has been received. Between the time a gift comes to us and the time we pass it along, we suffer gratitude. Moreover, with gifts that are agents of change, it is only when the gift has worked in us, only when we have come up to its level, as it were, that we can give it away again. Passing the gift along is the act of gratitude that finishes the labor. The transformation is not accomplished until we have the power to give the gift on our own terms.

—Lewis Hyde

Gratitude is good, even indispensable, but it isn't enough. More exactly, it is incomplete. It is like a spark that in failing to become a fire simply vanishes into thin air. For gratitude to be effective and take hold in the world, it has to touch kindling and catch fire. Generosity is the fire that is sparked by gratitude. Generosity is like an inviting hearth or campfire that brings warmth into the cold and light into the darkness. It is the power that transforms the raw into the cooked and the disparate into communion. This doesn't mean that gratitude doesn't matter. It surely does, but as the ignition that leads us on to the most important thing, and to the goal of our deepest yearning, which is to participate within the flows of the divine Generosity that gives to us and to others the many gifts of life. To live generously is to believe things are worth sharing and others worth sharing with.

It is important not to push the analogy with fire too far because, as we know, fire can be immensely destructive when it gets out of control. The best fire is the kind that warms, brightens, and feeds life. Its perfect realization, we might say, is the fire of God that, when revealed to Moses in the burning bush (Exodus 3), does not consume and destroy but magnifies and brightens whatever it touches. This is a theophanous, divine fire that attracts, amazes, and humbles us because it brings us into the presence of the holy Power that is the Source and Sustenance of all that is. Each creature is a sacred gift that embodies the divine, life-giving fire at work within it. What is required of us so that we can perceive our places and communities as suffused with such generosity? This would be a form of perception that opens to us a world aglow with the kindness of God. It would eventuate in social forms and economic policies that abound in love, joy, peace, patience, faithfulness, and gentleness because these are the fruits that grow when people realize that they live in a sacred world saturated with divine gifts.

The link between gratitude and generosity becomes apparent to anyone who has tried to teach a child to be grateful. Upon being given a gift, a child may simply run off in excitement, open it up, and start to play with it. This is usually the time when a parent follows after the child and says, "You have to go back to your grandparents and thank them." It isn't obvious to the child that saying, "Thank you!" is necessary because what they most want to do is enjoy the gift. After all, isn't the point of a gift to give enjoyment to its recipient? Let's say the parent succeeds in getting the child to say the words. Merely saying the words, however, isn't enough, especially when they have been said under duress. It's a good and important start but, like a spark, seems to vanish along with the child that has run off to play.

But then a moment (hopefully) comes when the spark of saying, "Thank you!" ignites into the generosity that is the mark of genuine and effective gratitude. In our family it happened when one of our kids was eating popcorn. You have to appreciate that to this child, popcorn is a big deal. Properly salted and buttered, it is much more than a source of nutrition. It is one of the simplest and most delicious proofs that God wants creatures to be happy. One evening we had gathered as a family to watch a movie with visiting grandparents. We all had our bowls of popcorn. Grandpa's was the first bowl to go empty. Then it happened. Without any prompting on our part, this child—about three years old at the time—noticed Grandpa's empty bowl and scooched over to share some of his own. "Do ya want some more, Appa?" he asked, as he began dumping sticky fistfuls of his popcorn into his grandpa's bowl.

It was a beautiful moment because it demonstrated that the popcorn our son had received wasn't only his to enjoy but was also *a gift to be shared with others*. His generosity bore witness to the authentic gratitude that lifts people out of themselves so they can participate in the receiving-giving dynamic that is the movement of life. Upon receiving the gift, he didn't vanish to consume it by himself but became a hospitable, sharing presence to those he was with instead.

To fail to share, or, more basically, to fail to appreciate why it is important to share, is to reflect the idea that the world is a realm to appropriate for ourselves. It is raw stuff that exists for people to take and use as needed or wanted. Depending on one's level of worry or ambition, and depending on how much one believes oneself to inhabit places of scarcity and competitive struggle, the world quickly turns into the sort of place that requires of people that they grasp and hoard as much of it for themselves as they can. Think here of how the fears and stresses of the Covid-19 pandemic compelled many people to stock up on supplies they really didn't need. So much of today's manufacturing and shopping suggests that if we don't seize, commodify, and take control of every square inch of the planet, others will get there first, and we will be the losers for it. This is why it is advisable to maximize one's earning and purchasing power. To be without money is to be without access to all the products and services people need to live. To be without money is to have to rely on, and thus be at the mercy of, others.

This is not a minor point, for as Peter Sloterdijk has argued, the modern money economy transformed how people relate to each other and to the earth itself. If at one time access to goods and services depended on personal and communal relationships—and the sharing that can happen within them—most people now depend on money to broker their access to the things they need. To live in "the universe of money" is to have all the decisive dimensions of existence mediated by monetary exchange. The use of land and a house, the consumption of food and energy, the benefits of teaching and counsel—these (and many more) now depend on whether one has the money to purchase them. It is hard to appreciate how pervasive this way of relating to things has become until one recognizes that in previous times "virtually all access to people and things depended on belonging to a group and its environment of things; before modernity, belonging was the price of the world."[1] Clearly, there are dangers associated with making *belonging* the price of access to the world's goods, because we know that people have regularly been ostracized or pushed to the margins by communities and thus made to suffer on their own. In cases like this, money can be a saving medium that reopens a world that has been closed. Even so, what we can describe as a person's feeling for life and what he or she believes about the things of this world changes dramatically because now things and services register *as commodities* rather than *as gifts*.

The shift from a world populated by gifts to a world populated by commodities reflects a profound transformation of the way people characterize the relationships they live through. What people think and feel, and thus *how they relate*, change decisively because the commodification of creatures signals a shift from a *covenantal* to a *contractual* sensibility. Covenantal ways of being are all about establishing sympathetic and nurturing relationships with others because people recognize their need of each other. Attention and attunement to others are hallmarks of a covenantal mind because one assumes that genuine flourishing is mutual and that the good of individuals is best realized in a community that nurtures them. As we know from experience, however, being with others in shared contexts of vulnerability and fallibility is often difficult, which is why God's way of relating to creatures is paradigmatic of what a covenant is and what it requires. Scripture reveals God as the one who commits to be with people, fellow creatures, and the whole of creation as a feeding, sustaining, healing, forgiving, reconciling, and liberating presence *no matter what happens.* God promises to remain in relationship with people when—perhaps even especially when—they fail, frustrate, and run away, because God knows that to turn away is to precipitate their death. To live in a covenant sensibility is to know there is no real life apart from the relationships people have with others. It is to know that the best life is a convivial life. This is why it is so important to nurture, heal, and celebrate the communal conditions of life.[2]

A contractual sensibility does not eliminate relationships. Instead, it changes their character decisively because it instrumentalizes them. People still enter into relationships with others, but their primary motivation is to derive some personal or financial benefit from it. This is why contracts are impersonal in their framing and execution. The anthropologist Marcel Hénaff describes the preference for contractual over covenantal ways of being as humanity's way of eliminating the idea of a priceless gift altogether.

> We may ask if the whole of the enormous movement of the modern economy—what is now a global production machine—might not be the last and most radical way to eliminate the gods, to do away with gift-giving and debt. It may be that we produce, exchange, and consume in order to reduce our relationship to the world and to each other to the management of visible and quantifiable goods, to prevent anything from escaping the calculus of prices and control by the marketplace, so that the very concept of the priceless would disappear. Then nothing would remain outside the realm of commerce. Material innocence would finally have been achieved: no more faults, sin, gift-giving, or forgiveness, nothing other than the mistakes in calculations, positive or negative balance sheets, and payments with agreed deadlines.[3]

This is not to suggest that a contractual mind is necessarily malicious. It is, instead, to note that contractual ways of being assume that

persons are first and foremost individuals who must negotiate and secure the world for themselves. Their aim, as Hénaff suggests, is to absolve people of the need to rely on and accept responsibility for each
other, which is why in situations of wrongdoing people do not seek
forgiveness from each other. When a contractual dispute arises they
turn to the law instead.[4]

Within a strictly contractual way of being, expressions of gratitude
and generosity all but evaporate because people are not positioned with
each other in ways that enable them to experience their lives as blessed
by gifts that continuously come their way. This isn't any one person's
fault because people increasingly find themselves in built environments
where reliance on each other is replaced by reliance on impersonal
networks.[5] When a financial need arises, people turn to banks. To miti-
gate life's risks, they turn to insurance companies. To secure their livelihood, they turn to stores and the Web. One of the hallmarks of
modernity is the growth of bureaucratic (and often alienating) institutions that increasingly take the place of personal networks of care and
support.[6] The result is that the meaning of the "stuff" of life changes.
A meal, for instance, rather than being a declaration of another's concern and love for you, now signifies as a package of calories or a unit
of fuel that reflects someone else's business interest in you. But a further
result is that the patterns and goals of our engagement with others also
change if the "voice" at the other end of the line is a robotic or machine-
generated voice. We should not be surprised that transactions are now
increasingly handled by computers and algorithms and are brokered
by the voices of Siri and Alexa because impersonality has been the
operating assumption of contractual ways of living from the beginning.
When you are shopping at a store, there is no reason to say, "Thank
you!" to the checkout machine on your way out the door.

The practical difference between a covenantal and a contractual
way of being became especially clear to me when I heard the story of
my two friends Fred and David. Fred is a major organic grower and
advocate of regenerative agriculture, while David is a member of an
Amish community. When Fred suffered a major fire on his farm that
wiped out buildings and equipment, David called him on the tele-
phone to see how he was doing. Fred noted the fire's many catastrophic

consequences but also assured David that he had an insurance policy that would enable him to rebuild and get back to work. David was glad for Fred but also expressed a measure of sadness because the road to recovery would be through a check rather than the support of his neighbors. In Amish culture, when a barn burns down, the community comes together to build a new one. Raising the barn, they also raise up and support the family that will use it. Though hardly a perfect society, Amish people live out of the conviction that life together is the best life and that people should turn to each other to address their need. They understand that they are the beneficiaries of gift upon gift and cannot possibly thrive alone, so they work to become a generous people who make their work and their neighborliness a practical demonstration of their gratitude to God.[7]

The covetous and ungrateful character of so much contemporary life is doing tremendous damage to our communities and neighborhoods. It isn't only that so many places and creatures are being abused, wasted, or abandoned. It is that we increasingly feel ourselves to be living in a cold, stingy, and lonely world where there is less and less occasion for the cherishing of things and each other. This is why it is so important to cultivate in each other the capacities for gratitude and generosity that testify to the conviction that this world is beloved and blessed by God. To be generous with oneself and with what one has is to communicate that love is the fundamental power animating this life.

THE POWER OF GRATITUDE

In a remarkable set of reflections on the Eucharist, the Orthodox theologian Alexander Schmemann said, "Thanksgiving is the experience of paradise." It is the experience of paradise, not because it places people in pretty places, but because it opens and orients them so they can more fully sense the life-giving presence of God in their midst. "*Thanksgiving* is the 'sign,' or better still, the presence, joy, fullness, of knowledge of God, i.e., knowledge as meeting, knowledge as communion, knowledge as unity. . . . Knowing God transforms our life into thanksgiving."[8] Paradise is not a special somewhere-other-than-this-earth place that awaits people after they die but the deep communion with and knowledge of God that John described as "eternal life" (*aionios zoe*) or, more exactly, the kingdom-of-God life that occurs in the age when the power of God's love is the only power animating what people do and experience: "And this is eternal life, that they may know you, the only true God, and Jesus Christ whom you have sent" (John 17:3).[9]

Life with God is the experience of paradise, and the experience of paradise is saturated with thanksgiving because people feel themselves to be touched and moved by the divine, creative, life-generating power that is continuously active in the sun and the rain, the bees and the butterflies, and the friends and family that nurture our lives. God is not far removed but is working within and through our neighborhoods and communities, and within and through our bodies, as the generous and lavish power that provides for our every need. Can there be anything more valuable in one's experience than to touch and be touched by the love of God? The seventeenth-century poet Thomas Traherne didn't think so, which is why he said, "Lov is the true Means by which the World is Enjoyed. Our Lov to others, and Others Lov to us. We ought therfore above all Things to get acquainted with the Nature of Lov · for Lov is the Root and Foundation of Nature: Lov is the Soul of Life, and Crown of Rewards. If we cannot be satisfied in the Nature of Lov we can never be satisfied at all."[10]

As we saw in the last chapter, it is a humbling experience to believe that we each live by our need for the gifts that others provide. This is why it is important to say that gratitude, as Hyde suggested, is something people *suffer* or undergo as they feel themselves inspired, animated, and nurtured by powers that are not their own. But the needy contexts that inspire our gratitude can also be discomforting and distressing, especially when we recognize that not every creature or place is made for our particular happiness. To say that our world and all its life are sacred gifts does not mean that everything exists as a gift to be used and enjoyed by us. This is one of the primary lessons that God had to teach his servant Job, who had come to believe that God's world was more or less well tailored to satisfy his needs and wants. God reminds Job (in Job 38–41) that this world and the great diversity of its creatures, though all pleasing to God, may not be pleasing to him. In fact, God delights in creatures that Job knows nothing about (like mountain goats and lions), even creatures (like Behemoth and Leviathan) that would destroy him if he came near them. What Job needs to learn is that it is presumptuous on his part to claim to understand all that exists or to know what every life is ultimately for. What he needs to do is learn how to receive his life gratefully without claiming to comprehend or control the terms of his receiving. This, too, is a kind of suffering because it positions people before others as more or less beggar-like, and without the calculus or ledger sheet that keeps a tally of life's credits and debits. This is hard to do, especially if one thinks of such a ledger as a way of keeping score and justifying one's actions before others.

The impossibility of keeping a precise ledger that keeps a comprehensive score on life's receiving-giving dynamic does not mean that people should abstain from making the effort to "count their blessings." In large part, this is because the recalling and naming of gifts regularly received reminds people that they live in a given world that is blessed and beloved by God. Precisely *as given*, people acknowledge that they do not inhabit a random or pointless world. Instead, they live in neighborhoods and communities that are the material, embodied manifestations of the love of God. This is why the nation of Israel was instructed over and over again to *remember* the mighty acts of God as made manifest in their deliverance from Egypt and in the provisioning of a promised land. This is why the earliest Christian communities were instructed to eat the Lord's Supper in *remembrance* of the many ministries of Jesus. To remember God isn't to recall some ideas that one may have about God. It is to keep in mind and heart the specific and manifold ways that God is practically *involved* in one's day-to-day life, present and active to make it ever-fresh, beautiful, and abundant. To remember the gifts of God, and to know that one's own life is also a gift, is thus also to feel oneself moving within the currents of divine love.

According to older forms of speaking, thanking and thinking go together. The connection isn't merely etymological, as when scholars note that the Old English word *thanc* meant a thought of, even a gesture of goodwill toward, another. It is also logical because to be a genuinely thoughtful person is to take the time to study and honor what one is thinking about. Thoughtful people don't assume that others are easily or quickly known. To rush one's thinking is invariably to miss details and to miss the stories of how creatures and things came to be the beings that they are. Memory is crucial for this work, but so too are habits of patient attention and personal devotion that keep our minds and hearts fixed on the uniqueness, even sanctity, of others. Thoughtfulness is essential because by its exercise people come to see how any particular thing can be the thing it is only because of the many influences of others that intersect with it, inspire it, and enable it to be the thing that it is. Thoughtful people understand that no life equals a snapshot representation of it. They know to give thanks for the places, things, and fellow creatures that enable each life to become the unique life that it is.

To see what I mean, consider what a thoughtful and thankful relationship to food might entail. There are many reasons to lament today's industrial, commodifying, convenience- and cheapness-obsessed fast-food culture, but one of its major degradations is to deprive its eaters of a thoughtful relationship to food. When food simply (and seemingly miraculously) shows up at a grocery store or on a website, it registers as a product that is shorn of its complex and far-reaching history. The stories of a loaf of bread's coming-to-be, for instance, are unknown and often masked by the packaging and sales pitch that marketers have devised to entice you to buy it. Shoppers, many of them stressed and in a hurry, do not have the time or patience to appreciate that each loaf requires the coming together of sunshine and rain, soils and roots, microbiomes and worms, seeds and compost, farmers and bakers, bankers and equipment manufacturers, farm communities and food distribution networks, and the staff who stock and sell the loaves on the shelves. Embedded within and all along the way there are the many geo-bio-chemical processes ranging from germination to photosynthesis to fermentation to digestion, and then also and fundamentally the divine creativity that inspires and animates whatever life there is to begin with. Not a single element or process is to be taken for granted if one's aim is to be mind-full of what a loaf of bread *is* and how it comes to be. Each member and each step along the way manifests this world's potential delectability, but also its contingency and vulnerability.

Clearly, this is a lot to attend to. But this is what a thoughtful understanding of food entails. When people become thoughtful about the food they eat, they can also be genuinely thankful for it because they now know that there is nothing obvious about a loaf of bread—who would have thought that a few handfuls of grain could be transformed into something so delicious?—or that its availability is guaranteed. They can express their gratitude to bakers who use their intelligence and skill to make, for instance, a soft and crusty baguette or a savory focaccia bread, and to the farmers who cultivate the fields that grow the grain that is made into dough. Above all, they can thank God for creating and sustaining a world that not only tastes so good but also is conducive of creating opportunities for fellowship and companionship precisely through the eating of it. The gift of food ought to continually call forth gratitude in us because it puts us in intimate, flavorful, fragrant, gustatory, digestive *touch* with the provisioning, hospitable love of God. It should also put us into more grateful, gracious, and embodied *touch* with the earth—the watersheds and fields, the forests and orchards, the farming and baking communities, and the places of distribution and fellowship—*through which* God nourishes and blesses creatures.

A great deal is at stake in our ability to be thoughtful or not. As C. S. Lewis already observed in a June 22, 1930, letter to Arthur Greeves, at issue is our ability to understand ourselves as rooted beings that through their eating are intimately joined to the land and to each other.

> There is certainly something attractive about living as far as may be on the produce of the land about you: to see in every walk the pastures where your mutton grazed when it was sheep, the gardens where your vegetables grew, the mill where your flour was ground, and the workshop where your chairs were sawn—and to feel that bit of country actually and literally in your veins. Tolkien once

remarked to me that the feeling about home must have been quite different in the days when a family had fed on the produce of the same few miles of country for six generations, and that perhaps this was why they saw nymphs in the fountains and dryads in the wood—they were not mistaken for there was in a sense a *real* (not metaphorical) connection between them and the countryside. What had been earth and air & later corn, and later still bread, really was in them. We of course who live on a standardized international diet (you may have had Canadian flour, English meat, Scotch oatmeal, African oranges, & Australian wine today) are really artificial beings and have no connection (save in sentiment) with any place on earth. We are synthetic men, uprooted. The strength of the hills is not ours.[11]

As I have already indicated, it isn't easy for people to come into a thoughtful relationship to food, especially if their eating happens within an anonymous economy. In an anonymous economy people do not know where products come from or the practical conditions through which it came to be. Thinking again of a loaf of bread, they do not often know if the soil is being eroded by excessive or inappropriate tilling, if soils and waters are being poisoned by undue pesticide and fertilizer applications, if farmers and bakers are being properly compensated for their work, or if the loaves themselves are being laced with chemical preservatives and flavorings that adversely affect human health, because the loaf comes from far away and its production is far from any eater's sight. As a result, eaters of a loaf do not always know if they should pronounce an "Amen—Lord let it be so" over it. If the goal is to be able to "say grace" over a meal, and really mean it, then people must take the time and the effort to know the stories of their food's coming-to-be. They might, perhaps as the Shakers once did, start each meal with two minutes (or so) of silence in which they calm themselves so as to come more gently and courteously into the presence of what they are about to eat. Saying grace is so much more than a pious gesture. It is also a political and economic act because when people come more fully into the presence of the creatures they eat they are also better positioned to advocate for their gentle and just treatment.

ACTIVATING GENEROSITY

It would not be much of an exaggeration to say that the dominant economies of the modern world have premised their success on violating each of the Ten Commandments. The worship of money, steadfast allegiance to so-called free markets (no matter how violent their mechanisms and destructive their effects), the endorsement of obscene levels of income inequality, the plundering of lands for their agricultural, mineral, timber, and fossil-fuel wealth, the theft of land from indigenous and peasant communities, the murder of untold numbers of slaves and conscripted workers, the dishonoring of ancestors in the abuse or abandonment of the places and creatures they loved, the coveting of what the (however conceived) "competition" has, the violating of Sabbath rest and delight, and the elevation of greed as the motor that propels innovation and growth—these are now so well enshrined in our thinking and our habits of being that many people take Fredric Jameson's much-quoted claim that "it is easier for people to imagine the end of the world than to imagine the end of capitalism" to be a cliché.[12] Moral protestations notwithstanding, many people now inhabit built environments and depend on institutions that commit them to economic ways of life that they might not otherwise choose. Few people, for instance, feel they have much say or control over their work choices and schedules, budgeting priorities, modes of transport, food and energy production, or home and neighborhood design. Those who do are often considered to be living a privileged life.

These economies, as Wendell Berry has observed, depend on limitless acquisition and consumption, limitless growth, limitless wants, limitless wealth, limitless natural resources, limitless energy, and limitless debt. And though these economies have created standards of living unimaginable to people of previous generations, many feel the stress of not having enough or are anxious that what they have will be taken away or rendered obsolescent. In contexts like these, it is hard for gratitude and generosity to take root and grow. What has grown instead Berry calls a "moral minimalism," which is the "minimization of neighborliness, respect, reverence, responsibility, accountability, and self-subordination."[13] If we are to evaluate an economy by how well it treats the land and its inhabitants, and furthermore utilize the fruit of the Spirit—love, joy, peace, patience, kindness, generosity, faithfulness, gentleness, and self-control (Galatians 5:22–23)—as definitive markers by which to determine wellness and flourishing, then it is clear that a radical revisioning and reorienting of our economic priorities and practices are in order.

This is not a simple matter. Multiple corrections and adjustments need to be made with respect to what people think life *is* and what it is ultimately *for*, what our earth *is* and what it is *for*. Given what I have said so far, the cultivation of gratitude will be an essential component in this effort, since it will remind us that we live in a sacred world populated by the gifts of God. It will be equally important, however, to cultivate a capacity for generosity, since generosity is not only gratitude's logical and practical fulfillment but also the capacity that reorients people in the world so that they can be a nourishing, healing, communion-building, and celebratory presence in the world.

To appreciate why the cultivation of generosity is so important, we should recall that after giving the Ten Commandments to the Israelites, God instructs Moses to instruct the people to make an altar upon which they should offer their sacrifices to God: "You shall not make gods of silver alongside me, nor shall you make for yourselves gods of gold. You need only make for me an altar of earth and sacrifice on it your burnt offerings and your offerings of well-being, your sheep and your oxen; in every place where I cause my name to be remembered I will come to you and bless you" (Exodus 20:23–24). It is as though this practical task—building an altar and regularly offering gifts to God on it—distills and focuses what the Ten Commandments together are meant to accomplish. As we now have to see, cultivating a sacrificial sensibility is crucial to a community's well-being because it fosters the economies that by honoring God also properly engage the world God loves.

The practice of sacrifice and the cultivation of generosity go together because the authentic realization of sacrifice presupposes that people have learned to receive the many sources of their livelihood as gifts from God. Because they understand their dependence on a giving

God, they also know not to hold too tightly or treat as private possessions the many gifts that nourish their life. The proof that they have
learned to hold lightly and handle gently the gifts of God is that they
are prepared to offer them back to God as the expression of their gratitude. In the offering at the altar, people do not simply or in the manner
of an occasional transaction give a few elements from their stock. Sacrifice goes much deeper, because what God most desires is for people
to learn to offer *themselves* in the giving that honors God. The logic
goes something like this: one cannot honor God if one does not honor
the creation that God loves; and the way to honor creation is to be the
sort of person who lives gently, graciously, and generously within his
or her community by giving him- or herself to its good.

For people to live generously they must first be convinced that
they do not live by their own cunning and strength but by receiving
the gifts of life.[14] Being people who live by receiving, they must also
come to the realization that the hoarding of gifts is a violation that
impedes their free flow to others. They must understand that the desire
to acquire and privately possess represents a blockage of the flow of
gifts and thus undermines the work of God in the world. This is why
the fundamental work of generosity is to learn to open oneself up, like
a seed that opens itself to the soil (John 12:24–25), and to make oneself
into a *conduit* so that the gifts of God can move *through* oneself and
onto others in a self-offering life of sharing *with* others. It is impossible
to be generous if one does not first recognize that what one has is not
finally one's own but is given to us to enjoy and share with others.

The phenomenon of sacrifice is regularly misunderstood and, as a
result, has become the justification for the abuse of others.[15] In large
part, this is because people do not understand that the heart of the
sacrificial act is not the immolation of an animal or the burning of flesh
and grain. The purpose of sacrifice is not to put on a show or to (ab)use
others for the purposes of self-advancement or self-glorification.[16] It
isn't even to please God, as if God needed us to fulfill some divine lack
or need. It is, instead, to cultivate the kind of people who learn to *give
themselves* to the care of others, for it is in acts of care that people live
out the covenant sensibility that people need each other (and their
lands and animals) and so must offer their attention, skill, and energy

to them if they are to live well. In every sacrifice there are two offerings: the offering of what is given to God, and the offering of oneself in the act of giving. Of the two, the latter is the most important because the cultivation of a self-offering mode of life prepares a person to live more gently and generously in the world. Recall that the ancient Israelites were not to bring sickly animals to the altar or leftovers from their food supply. They were to bring healthy animals and the first fruits from their harvest—the very elements that were crucial to a family's livelihood and that had been the focus of their daily work. To offer anything less to God would be an insult to God as the giver of gifts. It would also reflect badly on the farmer or shepherd, since it would communicate that one did not really cherish what God provided. To offer a healthy animal and the first fruits of the harvest was to communicate that one cherished *through one's daily work* what God cherished. Insofar as one lived out of a self-offering sensibility, one's attention, skills, and energy would be devoted to promoting the good of others.

The sacrificial sensibility that God sought to cultivate in his Israelite followers did not come to an end in a Christian context. Instead, it was reframed in light of the life and ministries of Jesus Christ. In the acts of feeding, healing, exorcising, and befriending people, Jesus is the inspiration and model for what a sacrificial, self-offering life looks like and what it entails. Recall that the apostle Paul instructed those who would be followers of Jesus to "present your bodies as a living sacrifice, holy and acceptable to God" (Romans 12:1). What he meant by this phrase was that people were to learn to give themselves to the care of their communities. Though Christians were no longer required to go to the temple in Jerusalem to offer sacrifices, they were—in what is one of the more striking affirmations of embodiment in scripture—to understand their own bodies as temples of the Holy Spirit (1 Corinthians 6:19) that incarnated and exercised the eternal life of God in their communities. Put another way, Christians were asked to make their bodies a practical site through which God's giving and self-offering ways were extended to others.

It is important to underscore that a sacrificial sensibility, along with the generosity it activates, is not confined to its occasional ritual performance. The goal of sacrificial practice is to transform one's daily

life. This is not to say that rituals are unimportant. Rituals matter because they regularly instruct people about how they should focus their
attention and direct their intention. As such they serve the larger purpose of changing a person's overall way of being in the world. This
means that the authenticity of a ritual depends on whether it produces
a more just social and economic order. As the prophet Isaiah put it, it
is futile to bring offerings to God if people do not cease to do evil. In
fact, God despises burnt offerings if they do not grow out of the self-
offering sensibility that—as its logical and practical entailment—issues
in doing good, seeking justice, rescuing the oppressed, defending the
orphan, and pleading for the widow (Isaiah 1:2–17). The best way to
know that a sacrificial sensibility has taken hold is that it will create
people who make the flourishing of their communities and lands the
first and abiding priority.

Early Christian communities witnessed a similar dynamic. When
the Holy Spirit entered into the lives of Christ-followers, it transformed them from within and reoriented their bodies so that they
could now live in a self-offering manner with each other. The distances
that separated people from each other—like linguistic barriers or the
Jewish prohibition of eating with Gentiles—were overcome so that
they could genuinely be and grow together. Practical and economic
ways of relating were transformed in that people no longer claimed
possessions for themselves but brought them to the community to be
distributed to those who were in need. "All who believed were together
and had all things in common; they would sell their possessions and
goods and distribute the proceeds to all, as any had need. Day by day,
as they spent much time together in the temple, they broke bread at
homes and ate their food with glad and generous hearts, praising God
and having the goodwill of all the people" (Acts 2:44–47). As these
people came under the influence of the Holy Spirit, and thus were
empowered to participate more fully in the flows of God's generous,
giving life, an astounding economic reality was born: "There was not
a needy person among them" (Acts 4:34).[17]

It is important to pause over the fact that as people welcomed the
Holy Spirit into their lives they were also transformed to become
self-offering and generous people who shared with others what they

had. These people understood that no possession is to be held onto tightly because a tight hold communicates that one does not believe what one has to be a gift. Moreover, it leads, practically speaking, to the hoarding that blocks the divine giving of gifts that is meant to flow through people and unto others. To deny that what one has is a divine gift is not only to refuse gratitude. It is also to refuse to participate in God's generous ways of being with others, and thus to forfeit the experience of touching/being touched by the love that makes life meaningful and potentially a joy. The point of living a sacrificial life is to create individuals, communities, institutions, and economies that have been transformed by the generous love of God. As Willie Jennings has observed, for this new God-inspired reality to appear, the first and fundamental priority is for people to learn to offer themselves: "A new kind of giving is exposed at this moment, one that binds bodies together as the first reciprocal donation where the followers will give themselves to one another. The possessions will follow. What was at stake here was not the giving up of all possessions but the giving up of each one, one by one as the Spirit gave direction, and as the ministry of Jesus made demand."[18]

It is no accident that the practical context that generated this self-offering sensibility was the ritual act of eating together in the name of Jesus. By eating together, these early Christians came into the presence of each other and so could learn about each other's needs, identify where the sources of help were, and thus grow into a covenantal community. And because their eating was done in remembrance of Jesus, they were asking to be inspired by the ministries of service he modeled. By eating Jesus as the "bread of life," they were asking to be nurtured in such a way that they could, in turn, become sources of nurture to others.

The power that turned people to each other was clearly an unsettling power because it confronted people with their own selfishness and the many strategies people put in place to hide or justify what they had. Moreover, when people are committed to living face to face with each other, they will invariably also have to face the untruths people like to think about themselves. Opening oneself up to the perceptions and insights of others can be a terrifying thing because, eventually, they will confront you with the truths you do not want to see. James Baldwin made this point clearly when he observed: "if you love somebody . . . you try to correct the person whom you love. Now that's a two-way street. You've also got to be corrected. . . . If I love you, I have to make you conscious of the things you don't see. . . . I will not see without you, and vice versa, you will not see without me. No one wants to see more than he sees. You have to be driven to see what you see. The only way you can get through it is to accept that two-way street which I call love."[19]

Love is the crucial power not only because it keeps people committed to each other despite histories of wrongdoing, but also because it drives out the fear that compels people to think they need (at best) to make it on their own or (at worst) secure their living in opposition to others. The two-way street Baldwin had in mind is not a street we can control from outside. We know it by participating in the flows of a (sometimes painful) receiving-giving life.

The experience of Israel and Christian communities is that rituals will play an important role in cultivating a generous sensibility. Insofar as people feel themselves to be caught within built environments and economic systems that keep them fearful, stressed, and anxious, rituals play the important countercultural role of focusing attention and intention in a different direction. What altars do we need to erect in our homes, neighborhood parks, and business districts that remind us that this world and its life are gifts from God? What regular ritual performances and liturgies do we need that loosen our grip on things so that we can learn to offer generously to others what we have received?

No doubt, there is considerable room for creativity here as people assess the potential latent within their communities and places. What works for one person or group may not work for another. I suggest the following as a start:

1. Make regular eating together a priority. Make the procurement, cooking, eating, and cleanup of food occasions for learning, sharing, and celebration. Do it all in remembrance of Jesus so that your life becomes a participation in God's hospitable ways with others.

2. Practice the Sabbath. Find regular ways to stop your normal flows of activity so that you can come into the presence of the world as the place that brings God delight. Refuse the (often market-driven) paths of restlessness and ingratitude that keep you wanting more, doing more, and trying to be more. Find your rest instead in the cherishing of the creatures that God cherishes.

3. Establish a routine in which you regularly give something to others. Put up an altar in your home that reminds you to give your focus, talents, energy, help, and money to others. Don't assume that self-offering service will just happen. Plan for it by committing to groups and projects that can benefit from what you have to give.

4. Practice celebration. On a regular basis, identify someone you know who will benefit by being celebrated by you and your community. Help them know that they are cherished and that the world is blessed by their presence. This will be a source of encouragement to them, and it will help them know they belong and are needed.

5. Grow some food. The point is not to grow everything you eat. It is, instead, to learn something of your own impotence, ignorance, and impatience in the face of a living, productive, delectable, wounded, and vulnerable world. It is to learn in a visceral way that we live by receiving and are blessed by submitting humbly to processes beyond our control.

6. Practice neighborliness. Get out of your house and into your neighborhood. Get to know where you are and who you are with. Get to know the history of how your neighborhood came to be, for it is in knowing its history of pain that you can be an agent in its healing. It is in knowing the potential of what and who is there that you can be a trusted advocate for the goodness that is yet to come.

7. Punctuate each day with a time of thanksgiving. Make the time to remember and thank God for the gifts that have come your way. Speak to others about the gifts you have received. Help them to discern the gifts that populate their living.

8. Develop useful skills that can be a benefit to others. Learn the various arts of making—growing, cooking, building, mending, creating, repairing—that can be shared with others. A kind word to others surely matters. A helpful, practical hand matters too. Pattern your life on Jesus's ministries of touch.

9. Support local economies and financial institutions, since these create opportunities for consumers and producers to learn from each other about shared needs, potential, and responsibilities. Shortening the distance between production and consumption also makes it more likely that people will understand the history of things coming to be.

CHAPTER NINE

Learning to Hope

Whoever is joined with all the living has hope.
—Ecclesiastes 9:4

We want a healing, I think, a cure for anguish, a remedy that
will heal the wound between us and the world that contains
our broken histories.

—Linda Hogan

When I talk to people about climate change, soil degradation and erosion, fresh water contamination and depletion, species
extinctions, confinement animal feeding operations, the exploitation
of agricultural workers and manual laborers, the commodification and
mining of lands and oceans, ongoing hunger and food insecurity, or
the abandonment of rural and urban communities, I now know that I
risk inducing the symptoms of what some mental health professionals
are calling *Pre*-Traumatic Distress Syndrome. This form of PTSD happens when people are bombarded, as with so many concussive blows,
by an unrelenting stream of bad news. They recognize that multiple
disasters are here and more are on the way, but they also feel powerless
to extricate themselves from the impending doom. It is too much to
bear, so they retreat, detach emotionally, and look for ways to shield

themselves from yet one more eco-social catastrophe. They don't often want a detailed exposition of the injustices that are happening all around them. They want, instead, to get straight to the heart of the matter: Are there grounds for hope in a world that is being steadily degraded and becoming increasingly uninhabitable? Young people routinely ask me if they should still plan on having children. Some ask if I have any tips for surviving the coming eco-apocalypse.

In this chapter, I explore some of the grounds for hope and offer a response to people who are earnest in their searching for hope but also suspicious of the vague assurances and hypocritical posturing that often frame invocations to be hopeful. If, as Wendell Berry suggests, "Hope lives in the means, not the ends," then hope does not depend on having figured out what the future will be.[1] To focus on means is not to suggest that the future doesn't matter or that we should dismiss scientific forecasts on rising sea levels or cataclysmic weather events. Rather, the cultivation of hope depends on inspiring the commitment and developing the practices that can position people to live *now* in ways that affirm, nurture, and heal life, ways that draw people more sympathetically into relationships with others and their shared places. Insofar as people feel themselves to be orphans of time—seeing in the past a world of ruins they did not make and do not want to inherit, and anticipating a future in which the prospects for a good life have been greatly diminished—the practices of hope work to *place* people in time by giving them reasons to believe that a commendable future is possible and worthy of their present dedication.[2] We do not owe people of the future an accurate prediction of what their life will be. What we owe them is our commitment to do now the good work that will lessen the prospects of a future nightmare.

Put another way, when people ask me about the grounds for hope, I often ask them to think about the grounds for love. What do you love, why do you love it, and what do you need to sustain your love? Insofar as you can find it in yourself to love a place, a community, or another human being, the question of hope turns to the very practical matter of what your particular love requires of you. To love your family or community requires you to work for the flourishing of each of its members by making sure their varying needs are met. To love your neighborhood is to work for the maintenance and repair of its streets, homes, and parks and to commit to making it a place where justice and belonging happen. To love food is to commit to honoring farmers, gardeners, cooks, servers, and eaters, and it is to advocate for the health of agricultural lands, the just distribution of food, and the transparency of supply lines. The love that activates hope certainly has an interior and personal dimension that transforms you into becoming a nurturing and healing presence wherever you are and whomever you are with. But its inspiration comes from without as people respond to the loveliness and love-worthiness that is always already operating in the world. Hopeful people do not have it all figured out. What they have is the (sometimes unclear) desire and (sometimes unsteady) commitment to join their love with the divine loving going on around them. The ways of hope come down to people learning to participate in the sacred power that creates, nourishes, heals, and reconciles life.

As I develop my account of hope, I will be taking my cue from Quoheleth, the Sage of Ecclesiastes, who said, "Whoever is joined with all the living has hope" (Ecclesiastes 9:4). If you have read the whole of this text, you know this is not a simple or naive hope. Pain, suffering, vanity, frustration, bewilderment, loss, and death—these all feature prominently in the picture of life he portrays. We need this picture, not only because of its unflinching honesty, but also because it alerts us to the central role that vital relationships with fellow creatures and deep connections with places play in the cultivation of hope. Hope is an existential need because it creates in people a desire to join with others in the performance of a shared life. The work of joining may be difficult and beset with all manner of frustrations, but hopeful people believe the effort is worth it because this life, despite its many ruins, is precious, even sacred. If hope resides and manifests itself in a commitment to honor and nurture life with others, then it is clear that the stress, anxiety, and depression that many people feel undermine hope. How can people be hopeful in the time of the Eremocene, the time described by E. O. Wilson as the Age of Loneliness? Hope withers when people detach and withdraw from others. Hope grows when people discover and commit themselves to furthering the goodness, beauty, and love they believe to animate this world.

As researchers and writers have addressed the hopelessness that people often feel in our Anthropocene epoch, they have, quite rightly, made grief a focal concern. The loss of life and the enormity of Earth's destruction are so great that people should feel grief. Feeling grief, however, is hard to do in cultures that are relentless in their emphasis on being positive and feeling good. Avoidance and denial have thus become key default coping strategies. But there is value in learning, as Lesley Head has suggested, to have "grief as a companion."[3] Expressing grief can help humanize the hard, scientific facts that climate and earth scientists give us and can thus provide a more resonant understanding of the plight we are in. Acquaintance with grief can alert people to how the more-than-human world is vital to personal and communal well-being and can thus arouse greater sympathy for it. And the experience of collective grief can bring people together, make apparent their shared love and anger, and thus, as Judith Butler and Kathryn Yusoff argue, inspire political action.[4]

I affirm this turn to grief as a response to ecological destruction and loss. But is it not equally important to learn to confess, repent, and seek forgiveness, especially when we know that so much of the damage is anthropogenic? Ecological destruction didn't/doesn't just happen. It is the effect of social/political priorities and economic practices that violate land, water, air, and fellow creatures alike. Clearly, not all people are directly implicated in these practices, and those that are, are not necessarily implicated in the same way or to the same degree. Some have been intentional in their desire to mine and appropriate the world for their own benefit. Others have simply been the nonmalicious, indirect beneficiaries of economies that, upon even minimal investigation, reveal histories of violation and wrongdoing. To raise the need for practices of forgiveness in our Anthropocene time is to note that we do not simply have to take our place in a wounded world. We must also take our place in a world that continues to be under assault by us.

It is hard to be in the presence of another's pain and suffering. It is even harder if you know yourself to be the cause of that suffering. A strong temptation is to look away and walk on. Why? Because the recognition of one's hurtful behavior to another induces shame before the other, and shame puts in motion various strategies of denial and avoidance. To appreciate what I mean, simply observe how difficult it is to say directly, and without qualification, "I am sorry for the pain I caused you." From an early age people resist this practice, which is why it takes so much adult effort to convince a child to say it. Why this resistance? I don't think there is a simple or single answer to this question. Maybe we want to believe ourselves to be innocent. Maybe we think that if the whole history of wrongdoing comes to light, we will be crushed. Maybe we worry that we won't, or perhaps can't, be forgiven for the wrongs we have done.

I believe that a desire for forgiveness is vital to the cultivation of hope because practices like confession and repentance communicate an earnest desire to be in right, or at least agreeable, relationship with each other. The aim of forgiveness should not be to enable the guilty to live with impunity, since it would be a great injustice to claim that the guilty party did nothing wrong. Nor should it attempt to erase or evade the wrongs that have been done to another, because it is precisely the history of wrongs that needs to be kept in view so that a less violating future can be imagined.[5] This makes forgiveness an uncommon effort. Following Paul Ricoeur, it is important to understand that both the seeking and the granting of forgiveness do not operate on a contractual level, because there is a gulf between the avowal of fault and the bestowal of forgiveness.[6] Forgiveness assumes a covenantal sensibility in which people acknowledge their need of each other. Even so, forgiveness cannot be demanded. If it comes at all, it will be as a gift beyond deserving, much like the experience of unconditional love. This keeps the practices of forgiveness at the level of a desire, or in the optative grammatical mood expressing a wish and a hope: "If only . . ."

A desire for what? Not for erasure or closure. Not even for dissonant-free harmony or wholeness. As I will argue, the desire to be forgiven is fundamentally a desire for the kind of personal and communal transformation in which people are enabled to be in meaningful relationship with others. When people lament histories of wrongdoing, and then commit their efforts to being a helping and healing presence going forward, they also begin to shed the defensive or self-justifying strategies that keep them from being in a respectful relationship with the wounded. They shed the illusion that they are innocent and exempt from a need to change. Confession and repentance signal the commitment to name and be instructed by the pain and suffering of the past so that people can work together for a better future. A desire for forgiveness, in other words, places people in time by making possible a more honest and educative relationship to the past. The granting of forgiveness, in turn, liberates people into a future, because they now know that even in the face of error and wrongdoing, they can begin again. They can partner with others, including those wronged, in the healing of a wounded world.

Descriptions of forgiveness normally center on personal and social realms. Helpful as these descriptions are, I do not think they go far enough. If the harms people do extend to the land, water, and air, along with the many creatures that inhabit them, then we should also seek forgiveness from them. But can the land forgive? What might it look like to seek forgiveness from fellow creatures?

I believe that the witness of Don and Marie Ruzicka, specifically the story of how they came to farm differently, can be of significant help as we consider these questions. In telling their story, I do not mean to suggest that they have forgiveness "all figured out." Both Don and Marie would resist such a characterization. I tell it because I think it opens and illuminates some of the complexities of forgiveness that are crucial to the cultivation of hope in our Anthropocene time.[7]

DON AND MARIE'S STORY

Ruzicka Sunrise Farm, located north and west of Killam, Alberta, was founded by Don's maternal grandparents in 1910. Like so many European immigrants, they had moved west in pursuit of greater opportunity and a good life. They built a barn first (in 1913), and then a house (in 1916). The farm prospered. Some of the family stayed on to do the work. When Don and Marie bought the farm from Don's uncle in 1983, they delighted in the knowledge that they were building on a family history and commitment to this particular piece of land. But as Don recalls it, they were also excited to know that as owners they could now realize their dreams on the land.

During the 1980s, the push in agriculture from bankers, government officials, and agricultural experts was to industrialize production and maximize yield by mining the land.[8] All across the Canadian West, wetlands and sloughs were drained, bush and woodlots were cut down, and native prairie was plowed up, all so that as many acres as possible could be planted in grain. Don was no different from other farmers. He grew grain and raised as many cattle as he could for the commodities markets. Every year the pressure to increase yield in the face of dwindling profit margins mounted. To keep the farm going, operating loans for bigger, new machinery and (seed and fertilizer) inputs had to increase at the same time. It didn't take long for an enormous debt load to accrue. The stress of it all went straight into Don's body. In March of 1986 he was diagnosed with Crohn's disease.

An industrial, mechanized logic has no patience with personal illness. The work simply had to continue, even accelerate. But by the fall of 1995, the year's grain harvest now completed, Don and Marie could no longer avoid the question: "Should we continue on this stressful journey of uncontrollable debt, should we sell and move, or should we try another way of farming?" The first option didn't look very promising since it was, quite literally, destroying their lives and the fertility of the land. The second option was attractive because it represented a release from all the pressure. The third option was a bit unnerving. What would a different way of farming look like, and what would it require of them?

When Don went to pick up the mail the next day, an answer was waiting for them in the form of a one-page flyer whose caption read: "Would you like to get off the agribusiness treadmill?" It was an invitation to attend an information meeting to learn about Holistic Management. Don went to the meeting and discovered that Holistic Management is about farming in ways that restore land to health, while also affording farmers and ranchers a sustainable and decent way of life. Together, Don and Marie signed up for the eight-day course. In it they learned about ecosystem services, the value of riparian zones and native species, the dangers of pesticides and herbicides, and the importance of species diversity. In it they were also beginning to understand their complicity in histories that were systematically degrading and destroying the land. A crucial insight was dawning in their minds: as farmers, they did not simply live *on* the land, but *from* it and *through* it as members of one vast community of life.

The following spring Don and Marie saw their farm with fresh eyes. They now understood that they were going to have to change their lives. The patterns of their daily work, the range of their affections and sympathies, the metrics that measured success and failure, and what they imagined a good human life to be—all these needed to change if they were going to farm in this new way. It was not going to be easy. Twelve years of industrial methods had to be unlearned, and the pressure of banks and neighbors to continue in well-established and officially sanctioned ways had to be resisted. It was an enormous risk. How would they pay their bills? Would they still be accepted by their community? The farm, a family history, and inherited ways of knowing, feeling, and working—all were on the line.

The following year, 1997, Don and Marie sold all of their grain equipment and 320 acres of cultivated land. The 600 remaining acres of cultivated land were converted to pasture, and the 200 acres of native prairie, wetlands, and woods were going to be treated with new-found respect. A system of rotational grazing was put in place for the broilers, turkeys, laying hens, and hogs that were now a base of the farm operation. And cattle would be regularly moved through fenced-in paddocks so as not to overgraze pastureland or contaminate riparian zones. The method moving forward was going to be organic. The goal was to restore the land to vitality and health by giving it regular times to rest and replenish. By May of 1999, Don and Marie had paid down all of their debt. As Don puts it, "I am unable to clearly explain and do justice to how this removal of debt affected me. I felt as though I had been held hostage by the banking system, and now I was free!"

The freedom Don now felt was wholly unlike the freedom he had felt upon first purchasing the farm. In 1983 it was a freedom to do with the land whatever he wanted, a freedom to work out his dreams of personal and family success by making the land produce. In 1999 it was a freedom to serve the land and to nurture it to health, a freedom to give himself to the land (rather than to bankers) in practices of work that facilitated multispecies flourishing. To realize this new form of freedom, Don knew he was going to need a lot of help. A lot of it came in the form of teachers—biologists, riparian and agro-forestry specialists, ornithologists, entomologists, ecologists, and range and wetland specialists—who gently and graciously offered their expertise. They helped him understand the damage that industrial methods had done to the land, and they showed him a better way. What followed was a complex, intensive management program that prioritized the protection of riparian zones, the replanting of roughly one hundred thousand trees, the reintroduction of native grasses and pollinator-friendly plants, and the creation of habitat for diverse wildlife species, all while raising domestic livestock in a humane and species-honoring manner.

Don traces his experience of being forgiven by the land to May 21, 2000, at approximately 6 a.m. He was out in a pasture moving his chicken shelters to fresh grass when he heard the unmistakable song of a Western meadowlark. Don considers this birdsong to be among the most beautiful sounds on the prairie. He had not heard it since the spring of 1989, when, for some reason, the birds stopped showing up at his farm. He had missed their presence and their song terribly. And now, here it was. As Don remembers it, the first song made him stand up. Could it be that the meadowlarks had returned? The second song hit him like a trumpet blast. It reverberated through his body and sent him to the ground. In its song, he heard the land say, "I forgive you."

In our conversation Don speaks to how this experience happened as part of a journey of personal transformation. He doesn't claim to comprehend all of it. What he recognizes is that his commitment to stop mining and abusing the land went hand in hand with a growing appreciation for the land and its creatures as kin. Over time, and with much newfound attention and effort, Don came into the presence of what he calls "the spirit of the land," the sense that the land wasn't simply a piece of private property but a being with integrity and sanctity. It had a life of its own that called forth wonder and respect. It could be harmed and violated, and it had a moral, even personal, claim upon his life. One could say, the land came to have a face and a voice that communicated to those who had learned to humble and open themselves to its presence. Insofar as Don was committed, like fellow farmers, to "making the land pay," the land was mute and reduced to a commodifiable object that had lost any spiritual or moral resonance.[9]

To hear the voice of the land does not require that one be a mystic. What is required is that one learn to come into the presence of the land *as it is* rather than *as one wishes it to be*. This takes time, focused attention, and patient listening. Rather than asking, "How much can I get out of the land?" Don now asked the questions he had learned from Wendell Berry: What is here? What will nature allow me to do here? What will nature help me to do here? As Don describes it, he needed to slow down so he could meditate on the life moving around him. The crucial effort was to shift from making his life an imposition on the land to making his life a conversation and a joining with the land. With the help of teachers, Don was learning what the land would be doing in his place if he wasn't forcing it to do what he wanted, and then learning to bring his labor into alignment with it. In effect, what Don needed to do was to dedicate himself to the land's flourishing and thereby rethink all his work as a form of husbandry, a difficult matrimony that must continually work out the demands of fidelity in contexts of ignorance and surprise, but also negligence and hurt.

Thinking about his earlier farming practices, Don observes how easy it is to damage the land and harm one's livestock without even seeing the problem. The pressure to pay the bills by meeting production quotas is so intense that one can see the land only in terms of its ability to yield. But when land and animals are reduced to "units of production," they cease to register as creatures with integrity and sanctity that merit reverence, perhaps even repentance. This is why the idea of ecosystem services, and the recommendation to participate in the land's regenerative capacities, are nonstarters for many farmers. Don acknowledges that some of his neighbors respect what he is doing, even feel morally convicted, but many more want no part in it. Understandably, they don't want to work that hard or be tied to the land. They want time off and time away. Moreover, how will they pay off their bank loans? Rather than learn to be in listening, resonant relationships with the land, calibrating their expectations with the possibilities and limits of the land, they have put their hope in expensive technologies that will "solve" the problems of soil erosion, water contamination, species extinctions, and declining yields.

Over months and years, Don and Marie were developing new habits of work that enabled deep resonance and fidelity with their land.

Rather than being objects upon which to project their ambition, land and creatures became conversation partners that communicated in the modes of their health and vitality. One way to characterize these new habits of work is to note how Don and Marie transformed their work into a complex set of practices and skills that communicated *hospitality*. What I mean is this. The industrial methods of farming that mine and exploit the land are fundamentally inhospitable because they push native plant, animal, and bird species out. Their homes are destroyed or poisoned, so they either die or go away. But as Don and Marie eliminated the use of poisons, repaired their water systems, and replanted native grasses, flowers, bushes, and trees, they also created a welcoming, hospitable habitat for microbes and insects, bees and butterflies, and birds and mammals to come back. Along with the meadowlarks that sent Don to the ground, Swainson's hawks, Sprague's pipits, pileated woodpeckers, kingfishers, beavers, badgers, deer, and moose (to name just a few) have all returned to the farm. Their growing presence and population are material evidence that the Ruzickas have made their farm a welcoming, nurturing, hospitable place, a place where a multitude of creatures can feed, reproduce, and thrive. We can interpret Don and Marie's new farming practices as acts of confession and repentance, and we can interpret the meadowlark's song as the bird's declaration of forgiveness. Why? Because the return of the meadowlark communicates that it welcomes Don's welcome, that it does not see Don's presence as a threat, and that it is prepared to carry on its life with his. The offering of forgiveness communicates that a life-giving relationship is now possible, and thus also a hopeful life.

Don is learning what it takes to be attentive and listen to the land. That so many creatures are now content to remain and thrive in Don's presence and on his land is a clear communication to Don that he is doing rightly with his fellow creatures, and that he is at least on the right track of action and need not let a history of shame prevent him from continuing in his new way of farming. In this listening, Don has heard that the land not only *forgives* him. It also *loves* him by providing for his needs.[10] The land does not simply belong to him. He also belongs to it and is accepted by it as one who grows out of the ground and is nurtured by its life. The hope that Don now feels is not the result of what he has done. It isn't something he has generated from out of himself. Instead, hope has grown in him as he has learned to make his love—his attention, energy, and skill—a participation in the divine love that creates and sustains the land and its many creatures.

The love and acceptance Don feels are not sentimental or romantic, because they are framed by the memory of so many wounds. The experience of it was prepared by Don learning to slow down and humbly open himself to, and express gratitude for, the sanctity of life going on around him. He needed to confess when he saw that his action precipitated harm, and he needed to repent by learning the science that informs the hard work of restoring riparian zones and reintroducing native species. When speaking to guests and audiences of the new mission of Sunrise Farm, Don often shows pictures of a seventeen-acre area that was once home to several sharp-tailed grouse nests. It was a lek, or breeding ground, where mating occurred. In 1987 he cleared the area to grow more grain and make more money. He has never seen a grouse since, because once a lek is destroyed, it is highly unlikely that grouse will ever return. But Don has not given up. He describes his recent efforts to reintroduce native grass and tree species as making "reparation for his sins." He says, "I may never create the habitat required for the sharp-tails to return, but hopefully other species will appear, and they have. Again, forgiveness is evolving by doing the best I can to make things right with the land." He proposes that we may need a new organization like "Ecological Sinners Anonymous," where people can tell their stories of mistakes made, but also of the repair work attempted, so that solutions for healing and right living can be shared with as many people as possible. The time is overdue, Don thinks, for those embroiled within the ways of industrial agriculture to engage in practices of confession and lament.

CONDITIONS FOR HOPE

When we attend to the histories of agriculture, it is clear that there is a lot to confess: the dispossession of indigenous peoples from ancestral lands; the enslavement of people to perform agricultural work; wars between people over access to water and land; the seizure and consolidation of land and food by powerful elites; a long-standing disdain for and abuse of peasants and agricultural workers; the xenophobia and sexism of agricultural communities; global trade agreements that destroy agricultural communities and undermine food democracy; and racist policies in lending and land tenure. This is an incomplete list. Moreover, its focus is primarily on the harms people do to each other. What about the harms people inflict on the land itself, and upon its many plant and animal creatures? So many places have either been degraded, exhausted, or destroyed. So many wild creatures have been made to go extinct, and so many domestic animals have been consigned to lives of misery. To explore this history, and to want to understand it in its details, is to risk being overwhelmed by the enormity of the suffering, violation, and loss it represents. Who can bear to face it all? It makes a lot of sense, both emotionally and practically speaking, to look away and move on.

But Don and Marie did not move on. Though selling was clearly an option, they stayed, and committed to facing and correcting (as much as they were able) the wrongs they had inflicted on the land. They decided they wanted to redeem at least a part of the history of abuse to which their land bore witness by committing to work for its healing and repair. At first, they did not think of their work in terms of practicing repentance and seeking forgiveness—this way of speaking is highly unusual in farming circles—but that is how they came to think about the process of living in right relationship with the land. In taking this path, Don and Marie learned that their efforts might not be enough or even appropriate and that forgiveness might not be offered.[11] For instance, their work to repair the lek after its destruction displaced the sharp-tailed grouse has not resulted in their return. They might never return, which is to say that if forgiveness comes at all, it will be as a gift. In the remainder of this chapter, I want to explore why their decision matters and what it means for our thinking about hope.

It is important to underscore that there was not much in Don's formation as a farmer to induce a desire for forgiveness from the land. Though raised in the Roman Catholic faith where practices of confession and prayers for healing are common, it was not assumed that these practices applied directly to farming. Don knew something about St. Francis's love of nature, but he was not often a topic of serious conversation in church. When Pope Francis in 2015 issued the encyclical *Laudato Si'*, Don could not find many who wanted to talk about its condemnation of environmental abuses and its recommendations to heal society and creation. Though personal study eventually taught Don that Christian faith had important things to say about living rightly on the land, personal experience taught him that church leaders and parishioners were not much interested.

Similarly, the conventions of farming did not provide Don with the tools to understand why forgiveness from the land mattered or was needed. To appreciate why this was the case, it helps to place agricultural life within a larger cultural and economic context. Don speaks often of the oppressive weight that financial debt placed upon him and his family. The pressure to pay back mounting loans was destroying both his life and his farm. For some farmers, the pressure is so great that they commit suicide. What Don came to understand is that the financial system that compels farmers to maximize yield at whatever cost doesn't simply damage families, soils, watersheds, woodlots, and wild and domestic animal life. It also renders farmers blind and numb to where they are and whom they are with, because commodities markets shape how and what they see. An acre of land, rather than being *home* to a bewildering array of life that extends from the soil microbiome to the Canada geese that fly overhead, is reduced to a *unit of production* that must be maximally mined to produce income. Land and creatures cannot be themselves. They cannot present in all their complexity, fragility, mystery, and sanctity. What they are, how they signify, and how they are valued, along with how they are to be used, are features of the roles they play in satisfying the production- and profit-maximizing demands of the market.

As a number of historians have argued, the market logic driving much of today's farming represents a profound rupture in the ways people traditionally related to their lands. Ellen Wood, for instance, shows how the pressure within capitalist enterprises to constantly accumulate, search out new markets, render production more efficient, reduce costs, eliminate competition, and above all grow in size and output resulted in "a complete transformation in the most basic human relations and practices, a rupture in age-old patterns of human interaction with nature."[12] Jason Moore has made a similar argument, saying that the development of capitalist markets had the effect of reconceiving the entire web of life in such a way that nature could be reduced to a stockpile of objects to be explored, mapped, mined, and appropriated.[13] Insofar as today's farmers are bound up in this capitalist web, compelled to serve the demands of bankers and commodities markets, they will also be compelled to treat soils, ponds, prairie grasses, butterflies, beavers, chickens, or cows as either assets or liabilities in someone's stock portfolio. Though farmers may feel affection for their farms and animals, the hard reality of paying the bills eclipses and often renders that affection inoperable.

The capitalist web that has shaped decisively the way farmers do their work has also profoundly affected the way urbanites perceive and understand the land. The widespread deployment of the language of "natural resources," even among environmentalists, signals that a commodification logic has become pervasive. Insofar as people primarily shop (whether in stores or online) for the food they eat, how the food is understood depends on how it has been packaged, marketed, and displayed. Today's dominant food economy is an anonymous economy, which means that many people do not know where their food comes from or the conditions under which it was produced. This economy renders food as an abstraction, cut off from the stories of its coming to be. Food simply appears, shorn of any trace of its history with soil, disease, sweat, blood, sunshine, or death. It is also a friction-free economy, which means that people lack the embodied experience of laboring to nurture fields and care for livestock. They do not know what it means to be ignorant and powerless in the face of inclement weather, obstinate animal behavior, plant sickness, and animal suffering. They do not know the difficulty and struggle inherent in things coming to be. The result is a food imagination in which it is assumed that food will almost always be available, attractive, convenient, and cheap.[14] Insofar as food signifies primarily as a product or commodity, it is very difficult for consumers to appreciate how the land and creatures are fragile and can be violated. Being so far removed from the

sources of their eating, and being mostly unaware of how their consumer choices are affecting the land, it is hard for them to think that
they might need to seek forgiveness from it.

My point is not to suggest that farmers and shoppers are malicious.
It is, rather, to note that the financial pressures of farm work and the
everyday practices of a shopping life do not encourage what we might
call sympathetic relationships with the land, relationships that make it
possible to encounter what Don calls the "spirit of the land." For Don
to realize that he needed to seek forgiveness from the land required that
he first perceive his land in ways that acknowledged its integrity and
sanctity. He needed to engage his land, not as an object upon which to
impose his dreams, but as a living, fragile, surprising reality that invited
care and respect. He needed to understand that he does not simply live
on the land but *from* it and *through* it, and that with other creatures
they all together form a community of life. To damage the land is not
only to harm one's interest or financial investment in the land. It is to
harm the land itself, because land is a living reality that can be frustrated and violated, and it is to harm oneself, because the power of life
that moves through the land also moves through each person touching
it. The "spirit of the land" is not something mystical or ethereal that
people add to the land. It is, instead, the mysterious power of life that
is working itself out in places and in bodies in the various forms of
fertility, germination, growth, flowering, decomposition, digestion,
reproduction, death, and birth.

Why this emphasis on Don discovering the "spirit of the land,"
and what does it mean for our thinking about hope? To start, one way
to interpret his discovery is to note that it was not simply about encountering new information about the land. It was also about discovering how deeply intertwined his own life was with the processes of life
and death that circulated through it. To acknowledge the "spirit of the
land" is to recognize one's own participation in and reliance on communal kin-creating, life-promoting processes that join us to each other
in shared places. To affirm this spirit is to understand that people do
not stand apart from the land, but are always already entangled within
it, responding to it, and benefiting from its complex, life-nurturing
movements of co-becoming. We could say that Don's relationships to
the land and to its creatures had become *resonant*.

Resonance is an acoustic phenomenon in which a body vibrates in sympathetic response to the vibration of another body, as when one tuning fork hums in response to another. The response is not simply mechanical or entirely passive. It is also creative, since each responding body vibrates in ways that are unique to the kind of being that it is. Resonance is inwardly transformative because it reorients how one perceives and engages what one meets. To be in resonant relationship with the land and to sense its spirit is, therefore, to feel the wide range of its powers and potential moving through one's own body. Land is no longer encountered as an object out there. Instead, one has become sympathetic to the land in such a way that one feels its vitality and its sufferings within oneself.[15] Insofar as a farmer's relationships are resonant, the birth of a healthy calf or the bloom of a pasture will evoke profound joy and delight, while the sight of a damaged field or an abused animal will evoke visceral feelings of shame and regret.

This brings us to a crucial realization: practices like confession and repentance presuppose resonant relationships that acknowledge the sanctity of others. Why? Because a desire to be forgiven communicates that one values highly the lives of the ones wronged and believes that life without them constitutes an overall diminishment. Resonant relationships, in other words, position people so they can appreciate that another *can be violated* and that such violation stands in the way of a praiseworthy future life together. Having been thus positioned, they can also appreciate how the gift of forgiveness can open new possibilities for a shared, ongoing life. Put another way, insofar as one relates to another as an object or commodity, it is hard to see how the practices of forgiveness can even be imagined as pertinent.[16] Learning to come into resonant relationships with fellow creatures and with the places of one's life is key because the best way to *carry on* with others is in the modes of sympathetic attunement to them. This is why hope and resonant relationships go together.

The habits of being and the forms of life that enable people to come into resonant relationship with each other and with places have become increasingly difficult to cultivate. In his wide-ranging and insightful analysis of the concept of resonance and its erosion in modern societies, Hartmut Rosa observes that "institutions and interactions that are systematically geared toward calculation and accounting as such leave no room for forgiveness. In a society whose dominant mode of interaction is competition, and whose subjects consequently are subjected to pressures of optimization in nearly all aspects of life, the concept of forgiveness (along with the possibility of a *new beginning*) tends to lose all meaning."[17] We see this especially in the neoliberal philosophy that has come to dominate contemporary politics and economics. Neoliberalism denies the communality of being. It teaches that people are individuals (they "bowl alone," as Robert Putnam famously put it), should not rely on social institutions or communal networks (which is why politicians like Ronald Reagan and Margaret Thatcher worked to dismantle these), and are on their own in their pursuits of a successful life. Couching personal success and failure in terms of individual effort has been enormously damaging because it means that if you are one of the many who do not "make it," it is your own fault. The isolation, loneliness, anxiety, and guilt that result enable us to characterize neoliberalism as essentially a philosophy and a politics of antihope.[18]

In addition to the economic forces I have already mentioned, it bears noting that practical trends within modernity like mass urbanization, bureaucratic governance, liquid employment, widespread mobility, and the rapid acceleration of the pace of life have also made the development of resonant relationships more difficult. Reference to the "Great Acceleration" as a descriptor of our Anthropocene moment does not apply only to the rapid production and consumption of products across the globe.[19] It also applies to patterns of daily life that propel people through places so that they barely have the time to notice, let alone deeply engage with, where they are and whom they are with.[20] How can people encounter the "spirit of the land" if they are moving quickly past places rather than settling into them? How will they develop the attention, patience, and commitment required to open themselves to a place, and thus come to an appreciation of how that place intersects, supports, and nurtures their own being, if they do not experience Sabbath rest?

People who live in hope believe that being joined to others is a necessary and fundamental good because in being so joined they are also put in touch with the divine power that has been creating, nurturing, and healing life from the beginning. There is no hope in being alone in a mute, commodified world. There is no hope in an unsympathetic existence. A hopeful life is founded upon resonant relationships in which confession and care, and repentance and a commitment to healing are primary practices. It depends on cultivating what Jed Purdy has called a "commonwealth politics" that turns people to each other and to the places of their shared life so they can create the economies and built environments that promote mutual flourishing.[21]

If hope presupposes an abiding affirmation of the goodness of this world and its life, and manifests itself practically in a dedication to join with all the living in the work of nurture and support, then it is clear that the damaging and the breaking of relationships that punctuate so many of our histories must be noted, confessed, lamented, and repented. Insofar as people want, as Linda Hogan suggests, "a healing . . . a cure for anguish, [and] a remedy that will heal the wound between us and the world that contains our broken histories," then grief over the pain and loss people cause is not enough. We should also seek forgiveness by committing to repent and work for repair, because the desire for forgiveness registers as the commitment to be in life-affirming relationship with others.

To seek forgiveness from others is to acknowledge that they and the relationships we have with them are vital to the maintenance of a meaningful and praiseworthy life. To seek forgiveness from the land is to affirm that our lives cannot be healthy apart from the fertility and vigor of the places, creatures, and communities that nurture us. A desire for forgiveness, however, is not a guarantee. Nor does the search for pardon ever come to a decisive conclusion. What remains is an unending desire for the kind of transformation that brings people into ever more resonant, affirming, and healing relationships with the places and creatures they live with.

NOTES

ONE. On Not Losing Creation

The Simone Weil epigraph is from "Last Thoughts," in *Waiting for God* (New York: Harper and Row, 1951), 97.

1. Maximus the Confessor, "Ambiguum 7," in *On the Cosmic Mystery of Jesus*, trans. Paul M. Blowers and Robert Wilken (Crestwood, NY: St. Vladimir's Seminary Press, 2003), 60.

2. I have developed the logic of creation in *This Sacred Life: Humanity's Place in a Wounded World* (New York: Cambridge University Press, 2021).

3. I have found Pierre Hadot's description of "spiritual exercises" especially clarifying. In his account of ancient philosophical and Christian life he argues that spiritual exercises were not about indoctrination but about cultivating in people an *art* for living that repositioned and reoriented them in their places and communities so that a particular vision of life's flourishing could be achieved. The aim was to create "a concrete attitude and determinative life-style, which engages the whole of existence. The philosophical act is not situated merely on the cognitive level, but on that of the self and of being. It is a progress which causes us to *be* more fully, and make us better. It is a conversion which turns our entire life upside down, changing the life of the person who goes through it. It raises the individual from an inauthentic condition of life . . . to an authentic state of life, in which he attains self-consciousness, an exact vision of the world, inner peace, and freedom" (*Philosophy as a Way of Life: Spiritual Exercises from Socrates to Foucault* [Oxford: Blackwell, 1995], 83).

TWO.   Why Agrarian?

1. For a clear description of global demographic trends, see the multiple publications of Our World in Data based at the University of Oxford, but especially its report by Hannah Ritchie and Max Roser, "Urbanization," last revised September 2019, Our World in Data, https://ourworldindata.org/urbanization.

2. I have put "nostalgia" in quotation marks because for many people this term refers to a romanticized or sanitized version of the past that disregards its unseemly or lamentable elements. As such, nostalgia prevents a truthful relationship to a past that is often injurious and unjust and thereby also prevents the sort of reckoning—confession and repentance, for instance—that is prerequisite to a more just and praiseworthy future. It is right to express concern about nostalgia so conceived. But when the term was first coined by doctors in the late eighteenth century, it referred to the acute, often incapacitating, physical and emotional symptoms people felt being far away from home. It may well be that this form of attachment to and affection for specific places and communities is precisely what we need to cultivate in today's world, characterized as it is by (physical and metaphysical) homelessness, displacement, forced migrations, and detention centers and refugee camps. For a lucid and brief meditation on the value and pitfalls of nostalgia, see Barbara Cassin's *Nostalgia: When Are We Ever at Home?* (New York: Fordham University Press, 2016).

3. Glenn Adamson, *Fewer, Better Things: The Hidden Wisdom of Objects* (New York: Bloomsbury, 2018), 4.

4. My aim is not to reduce the world and its creatures to what people can make of them. It is, instead, to highlight that we live in a world brimming with possibility that, in many instances, passes us by as unknown and unrealized. Sometimes the possibilities within creatures enhance human life, but sometimes they do not. The larger point is that the realization of creaturely possibilities gives glory to God as their maker, and it gives people further reason to honor and cherish their being.

5. I am thinking here of how Richard Powers opens his novel *The Overstory* (New York: Norton, 2018):

> *That's the trouble with people, their root problem. Life runs alongside them, unseen. Right here, right next. Creating the soil. Cycling water. Trading in nutrients. Making weather. Building atmosphere. Feeding and curing and sheltering more kinds of creatures than people know how to count.*

A chorus of living wood sings to the woman: If your mind were only a slightly greener thing, we'd drown you in meaning.

The pine she leans against says: Listen. There's something you need to hear. (4)

6. Simone Weil, "Forms of the Implicit Love of God," in *Waiting for God* (New York: Harper and Row, 1951), 170. As Weil goes on to say, "The suitability of things, beings, and events consists only in this, that they exist and that we should not wish that they did not exist or that they had been different. Such a wish would be an impiety toward our universal country, a lack of the love of the Stoics" (176). Christianity, in Weil's view, takes a major misstep when it rejects Stoic forms of love that teach acceptance for the world as it is. "Christianity will not be incarnated so long as there is not joined to it the Stoic's ideal of filial piety for the city of the world, for the country here below which is the universe" (175). To accept the world "as it is" is not necessarily to accept the injustices that people instantiate within it.

7. In *Making: Anthropology, Archaeology, Art and Architecture* (London: Routledge, 2013) Tim Ingold says, "I want to think of making . . . as a process of *growth*. This is to place the maker from the outset as a participant in amongst a world of active materials. These materials are what he has to work with, and in the process he 'joins forces' with them, bringing them together or splitting them apart, synthesizing and distilling, in anticipation of what might emerge. . . . Far from standing aloof, imposing his designs on a world that is ready and waiting to receive them, the most he can do is intervene in worldly process that are already going on, and which give rise to the forms of the living world we see all around us—in plants and animals, in waves of water, snow and sand, in rocks and clouds—adding his own impetus to the forces and energies in play" (21).

8. James C. Scott, *Against the Grain: A Deep History of the Earliest States* (New Haven, CT: Yale University Press, 2017), 29. Scott notes that the earliest states were inherently fragile from an epidemiological and political standpoint. Mobile and free people who hunted and gathered did not appreciate their confinement, nor did their bodies respond well to densely populated living quarters and a much-restricted diet. One of the merits of *Against the Grain* is to show that the exercises of plant and animal domestication were much more varied and complex than traditionally thought.

9. Sven Beckert, *Empire of Cotton: A Global History* (New York: Vintage Books, 2014), 38.

10. W. E. B. Du Bois, "The Souls of White Folk," in *Writings*, ed. Nathan Huggins (New York: Library of America, 1986), 933.

11. See Nancy Isenberg's *White Trash: The 400-Year Untold History of Class in America* (New York: Viking, 2016) for a description of the derision in which many of the white settlers of America's first colonies were held.

12. Du Bois, "Souls of White Folk," 924.

13. Pete Daniel, "The Last Plantation: The USDA's Racist Operating System," in *We Are Each Other's Harvest: Celebrating African American Farmers, Land, and Legacy*, ed. Natalie Baszile (New York: Amistad, 2021), 78. Daniel gives a more detailed treatment in *Dispossession: Discrimination against African American Farmers in the Age of Civil Rights* (Chapel Hill: University of North Carolina Press, 2013).

14. Analena Hope Hassberg, introduction to Baszile, *We Are Each Other's Harvest*, 11. Hassberg observes that a growing number of oppressed people are "returning to agrarian identities that have been suffused with stigma and trauma, and [are] reimbuing them with honor and pride. In cities, they are reclaiming urban space and developing new relationships to food and farming. They are rediscovering land where there seemingly was none: in the parkway dirt between the sidewalk and the street, in pots on porches, and in the tracts of empty, blighted lots. There are also the stirrings of a reverse migration from the city back to the countryside, where a new generation of Black farmers are reclaiming traditions and relearning lost skills to survive the end of the (modern) world" (10).

15. Monica M. White, *Freedom Farmers: Agricultural Resistance and the Black Freedom Movement* (Chapel Hill: University of North Carolina Press, 2018), 5.

16. Michael Twitty, "Everyone beneath Their Own Vine and Fig Tree: A Remembering in Seven Parts," in Baszile, *We Are Each Other's Harvest*, 20. In *The Cooking Gene: A Journey through African American Culinary History in the Old South* (New York: Amistad, 2017), Twitty acknowledges that we are the inheritors of a history saturated with many sins. But the possibility of "ten times the redemption" exists if people commit to learning from this sinful past (xvii). In "Black to the Land," Leah Penniman describes how her own farming journey required her to "uncover the truth that our twelve-thousand-year history of noble, autonomous, and dignified relationship to land as Black people far surpassed the 246 years of enslavement and the seventy-five years of sharecropping in the United States. As Black farmer Chris Bolden-Newsome explains, 'The land was the scene of the crime.' I would add, 'She was never the criminal'" (Baszile, *We Are Each Other's Harvest*, 64).

17. The work of the architect Christopher Alexander, especially *A Pattern Language: Towns, Buildings, Construction* (New York: Oxford University Press, 1977), which he cowrote with Sara Ishikawa, Murray Silverstein, Max Jacobson, Ingrid Fiksdahl-King, and Shlomo Angel, is of enduring significance in this regard. Alexander and his team traveled the globe to learn the design elements that have produced flourishing communities and healthier, happier inhabitants. In *A Pattern Language* they distill them to 253 in number. They include things like the incorporation of green space and agricultural land within urban settings; the optimal size and configuration of neighborhoods; how to best mix work, shopping, and residential spaces; the importance and location of health centers; the construction of roads, sidewalks, and bike paths; the importance of sacred spaces and community-gathering centers; the placement and design of schools; the architecture of homes (including the design of kitchens, living spaces, bedrooms, and welcoming porches); and the importance of windows and color. The design elements Alexander develops are not his ideas of what to do with a place. Instead, they are based on what people have themselves built over many centuries of work, and thus they reflect what is known to produce a higher quality of life.

THREE.   Placing the Soul

The Henry Bugbee epigraph is from *The Inward Morning: A Philosophical Exploration in Journal Form* (Athens: University of Georgia Press, 1999), 159.

1. Wendell Berry, *The Unsettling of America: Culture and Agriculture* (1977; repr., San Francisco: Sierra Club Books, 1996), 3.

2. Michio Kaku, *The Future of Humanity: Terraforming Mars, Interstellar Travel, Immortality, and Our Destiny beyond Earth* (New York: Doubleday, 2018), 3. Kaku, a professor of physics at the City University of New York, acknowledges that many of the threats to humanity's long-term survival on Earth are self-inflicted. Even so, it is only a matter of time before a catastrophic event of some kind (a massive volcanic blast or a meteor strike, for instance) comes our way.

3. For a current description of the varying future scenarios societies across the planet can expect to face, see David Wallace-Wells's *The Uninhabitable Earth: Life after Warming* (New York: Tim Duggan Books, 2019). Wells notes that it is impossible to make precise predictions and that it is not the whole planet, all at once, that will become uninhabitable. "But if we do nothing about carbon emissions, if the next thirty years of industrial activity trace

the same arc upward as the last thirty years have, whole regions will become unlivable by any standard we have today as soon as the end of this century" (15).

4. Plato, *Five Dialogues: Euthyphro, Apology, Crito, Meno, Phaedo*, trans. G. M. A. Grube (Indianapolis: Hackett, 1981), 102–3.

5. Henry Staten, *Eros in Mourning: Homer to Lacan* (Baltimore: Johns Hopkins University Press, 1995). Staten defines eros expansively as follows: "Eros is another name for life, vitality, or soul; I privilege this term because it brings to a focus the principle of motivation, the *voluptas* that draws the self toward an object of desire, and which animates life or soul as its innermost essence" (8).

6. Ibid., 10. It is important to underscore that the otherworldly impulse here described as mourning in the face of limit and loss does not capture the entirety of Augustine's, let alone all of Christian, thought. For a discussion of what Christian love for this created world looks like, see my *From Nature to Creation: A Christian Vision for Understanding and Loving Our World* (Grand Rapids, MI: Baker Academic, 2015). Staten is also clear that the incarnation of the Christian God in the body of Jesus Christ calls into question the logic of mourning that underwrites a desire for otherworldly escape. Jesus calls his followers to love each other even though they will mourn his loss and the loss of each other. He asks them to trust that their integrity and value as God's beloved are not destroyed by imperfection and death.

7. In ancient philosophy, Parmenides argued that according to rational principles the world of becoming, which is also a world governed by change, is fundamentally unreal. What is, is, and cannot not be. True reality is in the realm of unchanging being, where things eternally "are," rather than the realm of becoming, where things move from "is" to "is not." This Parmenidean logic has been highly influential in Western thought and is reflected in the idea that perfection does not admit change of any kind.

8. In *From Nature to Creation* I describe the power of bestowing meaning and value upon others in terms of an idolatrous posture. Idolatry, rather than simply being the worship of other gods, is first and foremost the effort to establish oneself as a god determining the meaning and value of others. The being of others, what we might also call their integrity and sanctity, is decided by a meaning-giving subject that assigns value and purpose. A creature, rather than being an icon opening up a sacred dimension within things calling forth respect and reverence, becomes an idol that confirms the gaze of an imperious self.

9. One way to characterize the difference between intrinsic and extrinsic value is to note that while you might be upset with injury or damage

done to your computer, the offense would be in the injury done to your *interest in* the computer. The offense would not be that the computer itself has somehow been violated. It can be replaced. Whatever value machines have is extrinsic to them and is maintained by persons who have bestowed the value upon them from outside.

10. In her classic book *The Death of Nature: Women, Ecology and the Scientific Revolution* (New York: Harper and Row, 1980), Carolyn Merchant described the new "man of science" as an inquisitor: "Nature must be 'bound into service' and made a 'slave,' put 'in constraint' and 'molded' by the mechanical arts. The 'searchers and spies of nature' are to discover her plots and secrets" (169).

11. As Louis Dupré has observed in *Passage to Modernity: An Essay on the Hermeneutics of Nature and Culture* (New Haven, CT: Yale University Press, 1993), it would be only a matter of time before people realized that they should not put too much confidence in the human ability to bestow meaning and value on things. As products of a meaningless, valueless, and accidental world, should we not conclude that we ourselves, and whatever judgments we make, are similarly meaningless, valueless, and accidental, and that all human endeavors are finally absurd and futile?

12. The literature on the Anthropocene is now vast. For summary treatments, see Erle C. Ellis's *Anthropocene: A Very Short Introduction* (Oxford: Oxford University Press, 2018) and Simon L. Lewis and Mark A. Maslin's *The Human Planet: How We Created the Anthropocene* (New Haven, CT: Yale University Press, 2018).

13. For a description of the "technosphere" as decisive for our thinking about Earth (alongside categories like the biosphere and ecosphere), see Peter Haff's "Being Human in the Anthropocene," *Anthropocene Review* 4, no. 2 (2017): 103–9. For a description of the built environment as it relates to the Anthropocene, see Jedediah Britton-Purdy's "The World We Have Built," *Dissent*, July 3, 2018, www.dissentmagazine.org/online_articles/world-we -built-sovereign-nature-infrastructure-leviathan.

14. The thought that engineers might redesign another planet to support human life shows a stupendous ignorance of the trillions of organisms that have grown alongside (and inside) human bodies over millions of years of evolutionary codevelopment. It indicates a dramatic and naive simplification of human life to presuppose that one can transport a human body to another place without also transporting the billions of geophysical/organic/microbial relationships that make such a life possible.

15. Berry, *Unsettling of America*, 22.

16. Aristotle, *Physics*, bk. 4 (209b1), in *The Basic Works of Aristotle*, ed. Richard McKeon (New York: Random House, 1941), 271.

17. It is worth noting that this view is not shared by indigenous peoples. For many tribes, land and identity are inseparable, which is why the forced removal of tribes from their ancient lands was described as an existential catastrophe. Linda Hogan gives a succinct articulation of this view when she writes, "The face of the land is our face, and that of all its creatures. . . . What grows here and what grows within us is the same" (*Dwellings: A Spiritual History of the Living World* [New York: Norton, 1995], 97).

18. Thomas Merton, though himself (especially in his earlier years) sometimes falling prey to a dualistic impulse, came to see that "there is no evil in anything created by God, nor can anything of His become an obstacle to our union with Him. The obstacle is in our 'self,' that is to say in the tenacious need to maintain our separate, external, egotistic will" (*New Seeds for Contemplation* [New York: New Directions, 1961], 21). For a feminist critique of body-despising forms of spiritual discipline, see Janet Martin Soskice's *The Kindness of God: Metaphor, Gender, and Religious Language* (Oxford: Oxford University Press, 2007) and Sarah Coakley's *The New Asceticism: Sexuality, Gender, and the Quest for God* (London: Bloomsbury, 2015).

19. In the introductory chapter "Who Is the You That Eats?" to *Food and Faith: A Theology of Eating*, 2nd ed. (New York: Cambridge University Press, 2019), I argue that our thinking about persons changes fairly dramatically if eating and touching, as compared to hearing and looking, are the primary sensory points of departure for self-understanding. For a description of how attention to the sense of touch radically reframes the character of a human life, see Richard Kearney's *Touch: Recovering Our Most Vital Sense* (New York: Columbia University Press, 2021). In an age of "excarnation" and profound loneliness, Kearney advocates for the possibility of "tactile communion" with the world and with fellow creatures.

20. Tim Ingold, *The Life of Lines* (London: Routledge, 2015), 11.

21. In *Vibrant Matter: A Political Ecology of Things* (Durham, NC: Duke University Press, 2010), Jane Bennett argues that the range of bodies affecting human development must not be confined to animate beings. Bodies are more than objects. Material things, ranging from food and garbage to buildings and electrical grids, inform, resist, and inspire us because they are characterized by a *vitality* that is not the expression of some external force operating upon things but is intrinsic to things as such.

22. Tim Ingold, *Being Alive: Essays on Movement, Knowledge and Description* (London: Routledge, 2011), 117.

23. The Italian philosopher Roberto Esposito has described modernity as activating "a process of immunization" in which individuals, through a variety of economic and political forms, work to protect themselves from "a risky contiguity with the other, relieving them of every obligation toward the other and enclosing them once again in the shell of their own subjectivity. . . . *Immunitas* returns individuals to themselves, encloses them once again in their own skin" (*Terms of the Political: Community, Immunity, Biopolitics* [New York: Fordham University Press, 2013], 49).

24. Ingold, *Being Alive*, 168.

25. See Scott F. Gilbert, Jan Sapp, and Alfred I. Tauber's "A Symbiotic View of Life: We Have Never Been Individuals," *Quarterly Review of Biology* 87, no. 4 (December 2012): 325–41, for an account of how research on the human microbiome fundamentally challenges the idea of human beings as single, self-contained organisms.

26. Lynn Margulis, *Symbiotic Planet: A New Look at Evolution* (New York: Basic Books, 1998), 9. Donna Haraway echoes this characterization by saying, "Critters do not precede their relatings. . . . I use *holobiont* to mean symbiotic assemblages, at whatever scale of space or time, which are more like knots of diverse intra-active relatings in dynamic complex systems, than like the entities of a biology made up of preexisting bounded units (genes, cells, organisms, etc.) in interactions that can only be conceived as competitive or cooperative." Donna Haraway, *Staying with the Trouble: Making Kin in the Chthulucene* (Durham, NC: Duke University Press, 2016), 60.

27. David R. Montgomery and Anne Biklé, *The Hidden Half of Nature: The Microbial Roots of Life and Health* (New York: Norton, 2016), 126.

28. Ingold, *Life of Lines*, 14.

29. See Jane Bennett's *Influx and Efflux: Writing Up with Walt Whitman* (Durham, NC: Duke University Press, 2020) for a description of the self's susceptibility to the multiple influences of others.

30. Ingold, *Life of Lines,* 141.

31. Berry, *Unsettling of America*, 106.

32. E. O. Wilson. "Beware the Age of Loneliness," in *The Economist*, November 18, 2013, www.economist.com/news/2013/11/18/beware-the-age -of-loneliness.

33. Wendell Berry, *Life Is a Miracle: An Essay against Modern Superstition* (Washington, DC: Counterpoint, 2000), 48–49. Earlier in this essay Berry says, "The uniqueness of an individual creature is inherent, not in its physical or behavioral anomalies, but in its *life*. . . . Its life is all that happens to it in its place. Its wholeness is inherent in its life, not in its physiology or biology.

This wholeness of creatures and places together is never going to be apparent to an intelligence coldly determined to be empirical or objective. It shows itself to affection and familiarity" (40).

34. In *The Enchantments of Mammon: How Capitalism Became the Religion of Modernity* (Cambridge, MA: Belknap Press of Harvard University Press, 2019), Eugene McCarraher develops in great detail the thesis that capitalism is a spirituality that is replete with its own distinct priests (economists), power (money), sacred texts (economics textbooks), moral code (management theory), iconography (advertising), and beatific vision (a life of wealth).

35. The lyrics and music for both songs are readily available in songbooks and websites.

36. The "masters of suspicion"—Karl Marx, Friedrich Nietzsche, and Sigmund Freud—focused their critiques of religion precisely on this quietist retreat from the world. Christianity and its priests came under withering, and I would suggest often rightful, critique for counseling Christian followers to cast their hope and their home in an afterlife. As a result, some Christians felt little need to change an unjust world or work to know its depths and beauties. It is instructive that the "liberation theologies" first developed by Gustavo Guttierez, Jon Sobrino, and Leonardo Boff, theologies that were resolute in their commitment to the flourishing of people in the here and now, were inspired by Jesus's commitment to the poor and informed by the critiques of Marx, Nietzsche, and Freud.

37. Wendell Berry, "Christianity and the Survival of Creation," in *The Art of the Commonplace: The Agrarian Essays of Wendell Berry*, ed. Norman Wirzba (Washington, DC: Counterpoint, 2002), 306.

38. In *The Paradise of God: Renewing Religion in an Ecological Age* (New York: Oxford University Press, 2003), I argue that the doctrine of creation has often been misunderstood, and thus also easily dismissed, because it has been taken to describe the mechanics of the origins of the universe. This framing is theologically confused because God is not a being, however powerfully conceived, that exists in a mechanical or causal relationship with creatures. For succinct, further treatment on this topic, see Kathryn Tanner's *Jesus, Humanity and the Trinity: A Brief Systematic Theology* (Minneapolis: Fortress Press, 2001) and Herbert McCabe's *God Matters* (London: Continuum, 2005).

39. In *Eccentric Existence: A Theological Anthropology* (Louisville, KY: Westminster John Knox, 2009), David Kelsey describes creaturely life as breathing a "borrowed breath," thereby communicating creaturely need and dependence on God and fellow creatures.

40. Berry, "Christianity," 313. The biblical scholar Ed Noort agrees: "Breath and body are not conflicting principles. Neither the breath, nor the body are the 'better' parts of a human being, they need each other. For the Hebrew Bible, from Genesis via Ezekiel to Ecclesiastes, the use of 'dualism' is not suitable." Ed Noort, "Taken from the Soil, Gifted with the Breath of Life: The Anthropology of Gen. 2:7 in Context," in *Dust of the Ground and Breath of Life (Gen. 2:7): The Problem of Dualistic Anthropology in Early Judaism and Christianity*, ed. Jacques T. A. G. M. van Ruiten and George H. van Kooten (Leiden: Brill, 2016), 15.

41. In *Believing Three Ways in One God: A Reading of the Apostles' Creed* (Notre Dame, IN: University of Notre Dame Press, 1992), Nicholas Lash describes God's investment in and commitment to creation in the most succinct formulation I know: "Life is God, given" (104).

42. The idea that people may be possessed by evil spirits or demons will be especially off-putting to people committed to an individualistic account of persons. New Testament writers do not share this individualized conception. People are social beings, which is why they are understood to live the best life possible to the extent that they are vibrant members of an ecclesial community that is animated by the love of God. Moreover, the scope of the powers that influence and animate personal lives is not confined to the social realm. As Paul says to his followers in Ephesus, Christians struggle against powers that are both political and cosmic in their reach (Ephesians 6:12). As Susan Eastman has argued in her book *Paul and the Person: Reframing Paul's Anthropology* (Grand Rapids, MI: Eerdmans, 2017), this way of speaking is not mythical but is instead confirmed by recent neuroscientific research that stresses a person's participation in vast networks of association that extend well beyond an individual body. Paul "displays a functional understanding of human beings as relationally constituted agents who are both embodied and embedded in their world" (2). A person's identity is constituted by its wide and deep participation in the world in which it moves.

43. Readers of this story are often puzzled and dismayed that Jesus allows the demons (at their own request) to enter a large herd of swine that numbered around two thousand. Upon entering the swine, the whole herd ran down a steep bank and into the sea (or lake), where they drowned. Why did Jesus allow this? Did Jesus really hate pigs? It is, of course, difficult to know exactly what Jesus was thinking at this moment, but one plausible interpretation would suggest that the death of the herd was Jesus's indictment of a form of agriculture that was abusive and degrading to life. To raise a herd that large meant that one could no longer properly care for or fully respect the integrity

of each pig. In a herd that size, the best that a pig could do would be to register as a "unit of production" in a system that was exploitive (recall here that the agriculture of the Roman Empire was founded upon the abuse and exploitation of land, water, creatures, and slaves). It is also important to note that Jesus did not send the demons into the pigs. The demons asked to be located there, perhaps sensing in the pigs' abusive condition a place where their violent, demonic ways could feel at home. If this interpretation is correct, then this story can be read to expand the scope of Jesus's concern for the value of creaturely life beyond humans to include pigs as well. Jesus, in other words, worked to undo the powers that degraded people and pigs alike.

44. N. T. Wright is one among several biblical scholars who have shown that spirit/flesh is not another version of ancient dualism and that creation/new creation are decisive categories for thinking about the meaning of the world. For an accessible examination of these themes, see *Surprised by Hope: Rethinking Heaven, the Resurrection, and the Mission of the Church* (New York: HarperOne, 2008).

45. For an extensive and detailed account of Paul's understanding of the work of the Holy Spirit, see Gordon Fee's *God's Empowering Presence: The Holy Spirit in the Letters of Paul* (Grand Rapids, MI: Baker Academic, 2009). It should be noted that in subsequent exegesis and theological reflection, the Holy Spirit is frequently described as the power that constitutes, animates, sanctifies, beautifies, and consummates the whole of creation. See Paul M. Blowers's *Drama of the Divine Economy: Creator and Creation in Early Christian Theology and Piety* (Oxford: Oxford University Press, 2012) for detailed treatment and Sigurd Bergman's *Creation Set Free: The Spirit as Liberator of Nature* (Grand Rapids, MI: Eerdmans, 2005).

46. For further scholarly treatment, see Ellen Davis's *Scripture, Culture, and Agriculture: An Agrarian Reading of the Bible* (New York: Cambridge University Press, 2009) and Sean McDonough's *Creation and New Creation: Understanding God's Creation Project* (Bletchley, UK: Paternoster, 2016).

47. This chapter is a greatly revised and extended version of the essay "Placing the Soul: An Agrarian Philosophical Principle," which first appeared in *The Essential Agrarian Reader: The Future of Culture, Community, and the Land*, ed. Norman Wirzba (Lexington: University Press of Kentucky, 2003).

FOUR.   Learning to Pray

The Simone Weil epigraph is from *Gravity and Grace* (London: Routledge, 1963), 106.

1. Aristotle argued, "Every sentence is not a proposition; only such are propositions as have in them either truth or falsity. Thus a prayer is a sentence, but is neither true nor false." Aristotle, *On Interpretation* 17, A 4–5, in *The Basic Works of Aristotle*, ed. Richard McKeon (New York: Random House, 1941), 42.

2. The Orthodox archbishop Anthony Bloom addresses this matter when he says, "Unless the prayer which you intend to offer to God is important and meaningful to you first, you will not be able to present it to the Lord. If you are inattentive to the words you pronounce, if your heart does not respond to them, or if your life is not turned in the same direction as your prayer, it will not reach out Godwards. So the first thing is . . . to choose a prayer which you can say with all your mind, with all your heart and with all your will." Anthony Bloom, *Beginning to Pray* (New York: Paulist Press, 1970), 55.

3. Simone Weil, *Gravity and Grace* (London: Routledge, 1963), 105–6.

4. Evagrius, *On Prayer*, in *The Philokalia: The Complete Text*, vol. 1, trans. and ed. G. E. H. Palmer, Philip Sherard, and Kallistos Ware (London: Faber and Faber, 1979), 71.

5. Iris Murdoch, *The Sovereignty of Good* (London: Routledge, 1970), 47. Murdoch does not use this term, but her description of the desire to live in a fantasy world tailored to a person's satisfaction maps fairly precisely onto the practice of idolatry. The essence of idolatry is replacing God with oneself as the object of worship. For further development of how idolatry deforms our perception of and engagement with the world, see my *From Nature to Creation: A Christian Vision for Understanding and Loving Our World* (Grand Rapids, MI: Baker Academic, 2015).

6. Murdoch, *Sovereignty of Good*, 64–65.

7. Rainer Maria Rilke to Lou Andreas-Salomé, August 8, 1903, in *Letters of Rainer Maria Rilke: 1892–1910*, trans. Jane Bannard Greene and M. D. Herter Norton (New York: Norton, 1945), 118.

8. Rainer Maria Rilke to Arthur Holitscher, December 13, 1905, in ibid., 196–97.

9. Murdoch, *Sovereignty of Good*, 66–67. "Freedom is not strictly the exercise of the will, but rather the experience of accurate vision which, when it becomes appropriate, occasions action. It is what lies behind and in between actions and prompts them that is important, and it is this area which should be purified. By the time the moment of choice has arrived the quality of attention has probably determined the nature of the act" (67).

10. Alexis Wright, "The Inward Migration in Apocalyptic Times," in *Emergence Magazine*, January 2021, https://emergencemagazine.org/story

/the-inward-migration-in-apocalyptic-times/. Wright goes on to say that individuals will need to call on the insights of ancestors who have the accrued wisdom that perceives reality in detail and with the depth that appreciates things in terms of their interrelatedness and their coming-to-be. This will be the work of storytellers who name and narrate the world with an appreciation for the wondrous and sacred character of life.

11. Weil, *Gravity and Grace*, 107.

12. Simone Weil, *Waiting for God* (New York: Harper and Row, 1951), 111.

13. For a description (one among many) of the significance of historical consciousness for self-understanding, see Pierre Manent's *The City of Man* (Princeton, NJ: Princeton University Press, 1998). For Manent the uniquely modern inspiration finds its fulfillment in Immanuel Kant's moral philosophy. Speaking of the quintessential modern individual, Manent writes: "He can now think that he is neither a creature of God nor a part of Nature, that he is in short born of himself, the child of his own liberty" (189).

14. Harvard economist Shoshana Zuboff calls this the age of "surveillance capitalism" because the thing to be mined and marketed is no longer nature but human nature. See *The Age of Surveillance Capitalism: The Fight for a Human Future at the New Frontier of Power* (New York: PublicAffairs, 2019).

15. Yves Citton, *The Ecology of Attention*, trans. Barnaby Norman (Cambridge: Polity Press, 2017), 9.

16. Jonathan Crary, *Suspensions of Perception: Attention, Spectacle, and Modern Culture* (Cambridge, MA: MIT Press, 2001), 13–14.

17. Bloom observes that "if we cannot find the kingdom of God within us, if we cannot find God within, in the very depth of ourselves, our chances of meeting Him outside ourselves are very remote" (*Beginning to Pray*, 45).

18. In *After Whiteness: An Education in Belonging* (Grand Rapids, MI: Eerdmans, 2020), Willie James Jennings describes how the imaginaries of Christians have been deformed by the legacy of white, imperialist power that degrades, abuses, and enslaves life. This legacy casts the white, self-sufficient, mastering, controlling, possessing male as the ideal for people to aspire to. It leads to modes of life that deny vulnerability and foreclose the possibility of genuine sharing and togetherness. The goal of education and of formation—I would add the goal of prayer—ought to be to activate the eros that leads to communion. "By communion, I mean the deepest sense of God-drenched life attuned to life together, not with people in general but with the people that comprise the place of one's concrete living and the places (the landscapes, the animals, and the built environments) that constitute the actual conditions of one's life" (13–14).

19. In *Scripture, Culture, and Agriculture: An Agrarian Reading of the Bible* (New York: Cambridge University Press, 2009), Ellen Davis argues that one of the central tasks of the prophets was to help people see and feel the world as they should. What the Israelites needed was a "tragic imagination" (16) that enabled them to see their violation of the world for what it was—an affront to God's love of all creatures—and that enabled them to live in their places and communities with mercy and justice. "The prophets instruct our weak religious imagination by means of 'visual enhancement'; they enable us to see the present moment of history in divine perspective. . . . Prophets see the world as God sees it, with a wide-angle lens" (10).

20. In *Christ the Heart of Creation* (London: Bloomsbury Continuum, 2018), Rowan Williams makes the important qualification that being for others must be without coercion and conditions: "Christ's essential identity lies in being *pro nobis* and *pro me*; Christ is who he is as the one who exists for my and our sake. If Christ for a moment sought to coerce my response, that would mean that he ceased to be 'for me' in this radical sense; he would be seeking to implement his will as a rival to mine, *and this is precisely what he has forgone in becoming human*" (190).

21. Mary Zournazi and Rowan Williams, *Justice and Love: A Philosophical Dialogue* (London: Bloomsbury Academic, 2021), 99.

22. Ibid., 43. Paul gave a memorable description of God's unconditional love when he said, "I am convinced that neither death, nor life, nor angels, nor rulers, nor things present, nor things to come, nor powers, nor height, nor depth, nor anything else in all creation, will be able to separate us from the love of God in Christ Jesus our Lord" (Romans 8:38–39).

23. In *Believing Three Ways in One God: A Reading of the Apostles' Creed* (Notre Dame, IN: University of Notre Dame Press, 1992), Nicholas Lash says that in creating the world God "lovingly gives life; gives all life, all unfading freshness; gives only life, and peace, and beauty, harmony and joy. And the life God gives is nothing other, nothing less, than God's own self. Life is God, given" (104).

24. The experience of the ancient Israelites is instructive in this regard. To be a nation that resisted the violating, enslaving ways of Egypt, they needed a long period—forty years in the wilderness—of re-formation in which they learned to trust in God rather than the cunning of their own might. Learning to receive manna was central to this effort. Insofar as the Israelites learned to receive life from God, they also became better prepared to construct an economy that was just and life-giving.

25. Lewis Hyde, *The Gift: Creativity and the Artist in the Modern World* (New York: Vintage Books, 2007), 60.

26. It is important to recall that the command to observe the Sabbath applied to all people, domestic animals, and the land itself. The aim of Sabbath rest isn't simply to offer an occasional escape or reprieve from life but to draw people more deeply into the enjoyment and delight of a good and beautiful world created by God. As such, Sabbath rest puts an end to the *restlessness* that damages both land and life. Jubilee is the extension of this Sabbath principle by putting a halt to anxious acquisitiveness and by restoring people to the land where they can experience God's provision and care. For further treatment of this theme, see my *This Sacred Life: Humanity's Place in a Wounded World* (New York: Cambridge University Press, 2021). The acquisitive drive is a hallmark of a restless life, which is why the prophet Isaiah warned: "Ah, you who join house to house, who add field to field, until there is room for no one but you, and you are left to live alone in the midst of the land! The Lord of hosts has sworn in my hearing: "Surely many houses shall be desolate, large and beautiful houses, without inhabitant" (Isaiah 5:8–9). His concern was not simply that dispossessed people are thereby deprived of the sources of life and livelihood. It was also that a possessive grasp of the land leads to practices that make the land and its inhabitants languish. As Isaiah 24 frames it, the earth is spoiled and laid to waste because people have broken "the everlasting covenant" (24:5) that joins people, land, fellow creatures, and God together through bonds of respect and responsibility. Systems that depend on indebtedness, in other words, lead to the degradation of the whole creation.

27. My understanding of debt, what it is and how it works, is informed by David Graeber's erudite treatment of it in *Debt: The First 5000 Years*, new and expanded ed. (Brooklyn, NY: Melville House, 2014). The observation about ancient revolutionary movements was made by the renowned classical historian Moses I. Finley.

28. Jesus signaled the futility of a calculus in the Parable of the Unforgiving Servant who owed 10,000 talents to the king (Matthew 18:23–35). A single talent was roughly equivalent to fifteen years of wages for a laborer, suggesting that the debt this servant owed was incalculable and could never be repaid. Even so, the king forgave (*aphes*) the debt. This parable clearly means to say that forgiveness is fundamentally a gift that moves within a covenantal sensibility inspired by love rather than a contractual sensibility bound to ledgers and precisely kept accounts.

29. Almost every religious and spiritual tradition was outspoken in its rejection of the charging of interest. In large part this is because usury seeks

to profit from another person's need or misfortune. It also locates "wealth" in the machinations of money rather than in God's gifts.

30. Graeber, *Debt*, 14. Numerous examples of the troublesome effects of cost-benefit analysis can be given: the incarceration of people as a profit-seeking endeavor; the calculating of disease and disaster as positives for GDP growth; the exclusion of poor communities and communities of color from essential services and infrastructure (health, education, grocery stores, green space) because these are deemed economically unprofitable; the denuding of soils and the poisoning of waters to maximize agricultural yields; and the political protection of financial institutions that prey on people's desperation and need.

31. Anthony Bash, *Forgiveness and Christian Ethics* (Cambridge: Cambridge University Press, 2007), 99. In this book Bash covers a variety of themes relating to the role of forgiveness in Christian, but also public, life. He addresses the role of forgiveness in restoring wrongdoers to communities, the gift character of forgiveness, and the relation between forgiveness and justice.

FIVE.   Learning to See

The Simone Weil epigraph is from *Waiting for God* (New York: Harper and Row, 1951), 212.

1. Though I employ sight in this essay as the metaphor for understanding the world, it should be clear that other senses, like touch and smell and taste, should not be ignored, particularly since they often lead to a more embodied, practical, and intimate relationship with the world. In *Food and Faith: A Theology of Eating*, 2nd ed. (New York: Cambridge University Press, 2019), I argue that taste, along with the embodied practices of food's production and consumption, open fresh lines of inquiry and sympathy as we move to understand where we are. See also the important collection of essays *Carnal Hermeneutics*, ed. Richard Kearney and Brian Treanor (New York: Fordham University Press, 2015), on the body as site of interpretation. The hegemony of sight in philosophical traditions of inquiry, and the distancing of self and world it often presupposes, are well described by Martin Jay in *Downcast Eyes: The Denigration of Vision in Twentieth-Century French Thought* (Berkeley: University of California Press, 1994) and the collection *Modernity and the Hegemony of Vision* (Berkeley: University of California Press, 1993), edited by David Michael Levin.

2. Hermeneutics "denotes the basic being-in-motion of Dasein that constitutes its finitude and historicity, and hence embraces the whole of its

experience of the world" (Hans-Georg Gadamer, *Truth and Method*, 2nd ed. [New York: Crossroad, 1991], xxx). For a wide-ranging discussion of the implications of hermeneutics for our understanding of the natural world, see *Interpreting Nature: The Emerging Field of Environmental Hermeneutics*, ed. Forrest Clingerman, Brian Treanor, Martin Drenthen, and David Utsler (New York: Fordham University Press, 2014).

3. Pierre Hadot, *What Is Ancient Philosophy?* (Cambridge, MA: Harvard University Press, 2002), 172–233. Put succinctly, "In antiquity it was the philosopher's choice of a way of life which conditioned and determined the fundamental tendencies of his philosophical discourse" (272–73).

4. Ibid., 260. In *We Built Reality: How Social Science Infiltrated Culture, Politics, and Power* (New York: Oxford University Press, 2020), Jason Blakely gives a lucid account of how social scientists like economists, political theorists, and psychologists regularly confuse scientific investigation with "scientism" (as when they confuse *description* and *interpretation* of the world) in their attempts to influence how people make meaning in their worlds, assess the significance of events, and decide between various behaviors.

5. For a rigorous and wide-ranging examination of the various modes whereby truth conditions are established and legitimated, see Bruno Latour's *An Inquiry into Modes of Existence: An Anthropology of the Moderns* (Cambridge, MA: Harvard University Press, 2013). Latour delineates the many values and modalities people have employed to experience and understand "reality" and shows how the scientific, social, and economic framings of "experience" overlap and come apart to make possible the regional ontologies that make our worlds meaningful.

6. Quoted in Conor Cunningham's *Darwin's Pious Idea: Why the Ultra-Darwinists and Creationists Both Get It Wrong* (Grand Rapids, MI: Eerdmans, 2010), 9–10.

7. Ibid., 10.

8. It is important to stress that Darwin made room for concepts of cooperation and community in his work and that more recent evolutionary theory has developed these themes in very important ways (see especially *Evolution, Games, and God: The Principle of Cooperation*, ed. Martin A. Nowak and Sarah Coakley [Cambridge, MA: Harvard University Press, 2013] for an excellent overview and development of these themes). I focus here on the themes of struggle and survival because these are the ones that have most captured the imaginations of lay people.

9. In *Nature's Economy: A History of Ecological Ideas*, 2nd ed. (New York: Cambridge University Press, 1994), Donald Worster details how differing

schools of ecological thought reflected in their dominant, organizing concepts trends that were at play in the broader culture of the time. Ecologists from the 1980s that stressed individual competition (as compared with those from an earlier generation that stressed community and cooperation) reflected the competitive individualism of neoliberal politics that asserted, in the famous words of Margaret Thatcher, that there is no such thing as society.

10. Marilynne Robinson, "Darwinism," in *The Death of Adam: Essays on Modern Thought* (New York: Picador, 1998), 46–47.

11. Robinson develops this theme in *Absence of Mind: The Dispelling of Inwardness from the Modern Myth of the Self* (New Haven, CT: Yale University Press, 2010). Here Robinson defends the human mind as more than a material mechanism and as having the ability to, among other things, reflect morally about the world. We need to be able to affirm that "the strangeness of reality consistently exceeds the expectation of science, and that the assumptions of science, however tried and rational, are very inclined to encourage false expectations" (124).

12. I develop the character of idolatrous seeing in *From Nature to Creation: A Christian Vision for Understanding and Loving Our World* (Grand Rapids, MI: Baker Academic, 2015).

13. The philosopher of science Jean-Pierre Dupuy addresses misplaced faith in science in *The Mark of the Sacred* (Stanford, CA: Stanford University Press, 2013) and argues that a rediscovery of the sacred character of the world, and along with that an acknowledgment of the limits of human reasoning and the need for self-limitation, are essential to a viable future. I develop this theme in *This Sacred Life: Humanity's Place in a Wounded World* (New York: Cambridge University Press, 2021).

14. See the work of Rob Nixon in *Slow Violence and the Environmentalism of the Poor* (Cambridge, MA: Harvard University Press, 2011).

15. In *Hiroshima ist überall* (*Hiroshima Is Everywhere*), Günther Anders says, "The fantastic character of the situation quite simply takes one's breath away. At the very moment when the world becomes apocalyptic, and this owing to our own fault, it presents the image . . . of a paradise inhabited by murderers without malice and victims without hatred. Nowhere is there any trace of malice, there is only rubble. . . . No war in history will have been more devoid of hatred than the war by tele-murder that is to come. . . . This absence of hatred will be the most inhuman absence of hatred that has ever existed; absence of hatred and absence of scruples will henceforth be one and the same" (quoted in Dupuy, *Mark of the Sacred*, 194).

16. Paul M. Blowers makes this point in a magisterial way in *Drama of the Divine Economy: Creator and Creation in Early Christian Theology and Piety* (Oxford: Oxford University Press, 2012). See also Denis Edwards's essay "Where on Earth Is God? Exploring an Ecological Theology of the Trinity in the Tradition of Athanasius," in *Christian Faith and the Earth: Current Paths and Emerging Horizons in Ecotheology*, ed. Ernst M. Conradie, Sigurd Bergmann, Celia Deane-Drummond, and Denis Edwards (London: Bloomsbury T. and T. Clark, 2014).

17. I developed this position in *The Paradise of God: Renewing Religion in an Ecological Age* (New York: Oxford University Press, 2003).

18. It was a general principle among ancient Greek philosophers that the task of thought was to bring the thinker into union with what is. A properly ordered soul is at its best when it is in harmonious alignment with the order of the world. Joshua Lollar describes Greek *theoria physike* in detail in Part I of *To See into the Life of Things: The Contemplation of Nature in Maximus the Confessor* (Turnhout, Belgium: Brepols, 2013).

19. Richard Bauckham has developed this theme in a detailed way in *Jesus and the God of Israel: God Crucified and Other Studies on the New Testament's Christology of Divine Identity* (Grand Rapids, MI: Eerdmans, 2008).

20. Sean M. McDonough, *Christ as Creator: Origins of a New Testament Doctrine* (Oxford: Oxford University Press, 2009), 2.

21. St. Maximus the Confessor, *Ambigua 7*, in *On the Cosmic Mystery of Jesus Christ*, trans. Paul M. Blowers and Robert Louis Wilken (Crestwood, NY: St. Vladimir's Seminary Press, 2003), 70.

22. Lollar, *To See*, 262.

23. Lars Thunberg, *Microcosm and Mediator: The Theological Anthropology of Maximus the Confessor*, 2nd ed. (Chicago: Open Court, 1995), 30.

24. In *Quaestiones ad Thalassium 2*, in *On the Cosmic Mystery*, trans. Blowers and Wilken, Maximus describes God's creative, sustaining, and redeeming presence as follows: "God, as he alone knew how, completed the primary principles [*logoi*] of creatures and the universal essences of beings once for all. Yet he is still at work, not only preserving these creatures in their very existence [*to einai*] but effecting the formation, progress, and sustenance of the individual parts that are potential within them. Even now in his providence he is bringing about the assimilation of particulars to universals until he might unite creatures' own voluntary inclination to the more universal natural principle of rational being through the movement of these particular creatures toward well-being [*to eu einai*], and make them harmonious and uniformly moving in relation to one another and to the whole universe. In

this way there shall be no intentional divergence between universals and particulars. Rather, one and the same principle shall be observable throughout the universe, admitting of no differentiation by the individual modes according to which created beings are predicated, and displaying the grace of God effective to deify the universe. . . . The Father approves this work, the Son properly carries out, and the Holy Spirit essentially completes both the Father's approval of it and the Son's execution of it, in order that the God in Trinity might be *through all and in all things* (Eph 4:6), contemplated as the whole reality proportionately in each individual creature as it is deemed worthy by grace, and in the universe altogether, just as the soul naturally indwells both the whole of the body and each individual part without diminishing itself" (99–101).

25. Lollar gives beautiful expression to this vision when he says, "God is moved by His love for creation and this motion is realized in the Dionysian outpouring of Goodness to beings and Its return, which is the very outpouring and return of God from Himself to Himself; hence the language of 'self-motion (*autokinesis*).' Everything that exists just is the 'motion' of God proceeding from Himself and returning to Himself" (*To See*, 283–84).

26. Maximus, *Ambigua 7*, in *On the Cosmic Mystery*, trans. Blowers and Wilken, 60.

27. Wendell Berry, "People, Land, and Community," in *The Art of the Commonplace: The Agrarian Essays of Wendell Berry*, ed. Norman Wirzba (Washington, DC: Counterpoint, 2002), 187. In *The Sunflower Forest: Ecological Restoration and the New Communion with Nature* (Berkeley: University of California Press, 2003), William R. Jordan III speaks similarly about the work of habitat restoration going hand in hand with a transformed vision: "Restoring a landscape is like grinding a corrective lens. . . . The restorationist is forced to refine her ideas about how that landscape has changed, and about her species's role in causing those changes. . . . Restoration also has value as a means of discovering the beauty of a historic landscape, or of ecosystems or processes that had been considered ugly or repellant" (86).

28. Thunberg, *Microcosm and Mediator*, 76.

29. C. A. Tsakiridou, *Icons in Time, Persons in Eternity: Orthodox Theology and the Aesthetics of the Christian Image* (Burlington, VT: Ashgate, 2013), 176.

30. Ibid., 57.

31. Ibid., 182.

32. Simone Weil, *Waiting for God* (New York: Harper and Row, 1951), 210.

33. Maximus believes that in the paradise of the Garden of Eden something like a proper *theoria physike* obtained. With the Fall humans lost the ability to see each thing in terms of its reference and grounding in God. Adam's great mistake was to try to know the world by sensation alone rather than in terms of the divine love at work within it.

34. Maximus, *Ambigua* 42, in *On the Cosmic Mystery*, trans. Blowers and Wilken, 82.

35. Ibid., 90.

36. William Blake, "The Marriage of Heaven and Hell," in *The Complete Poetry and Prose of William Blake*, rev. ed., ed. David V. Erdman (New York: Doubleday, 1988), 39.

37. Dumitru Staniloae, one of the last century's leading interpreters of Maximus, gives a useful account of the passions in *Orthodox Spirituality: A Practical Guide for the Faithful and a Definitive Manual for the Scholar* (South Canaan, PA: St. Tikhon's Seminary Press, 2003).

38. Tsakiridou gives the following helpful summary: "When creatures are perceived spiritually or in a God-loving manner (*theophilos*), they are seen in their true nature and subsistence, as his living (incarnating) works. When, by contrast, they are perceived from the standpoint of desire or self-love (*philautia*), this vital, animating reality in them disappears and the mind imposes its own self-serving and distorted reasons . . . on things. . . . The passions obscure the inherent divinity and sanctity of creation and it is therefore in their activities rather than in the things themselves that evil arises" (*Icons in Time*, 183).

39. Pavel Florensky, *The Pillar and Ground of Truth: An Essay in Orthodox Theodicy in Twelve Letters* (Princeton, NJ: Princeton University Press, 2004), 35–36.

40. Quoted by Bruce Foltz in *The Noetics of Nature: Environmental Philosophy and the Holy Beauty of the Visible* (New York: Fordham University Press, 2014), 163. For a magisterial treatment of how monastic ascetic traditions can aid in the healing of earth, see Douglas E. Christie's *The Blue Sapphire of the Mind: Notes for a Contemplative Ecology* (New York: Oxford University Press, 2013). In this book Christie puts the wisdom of the ancient desert spiritual traditions, above all Evagrius of Pontus, in conversation with more recent environmental writers to yield a deeply compelling account of *theoria physike*.

41. Here following the translation of Maximus by Blowers in *Drama of the Divine Economy*, 362.

42. This chapter is a revised version of my essay "Christian *Theoria Physike*: On Learning to See Creation," *Modern Theology* 32, no. 2 (April 2016): 211–30.

SIX.   Learning Descent

The first epigraph, by Pseudo-Dionysius, is from *The Divine Names* 1.5, in *The Complete Works* (Mahwah, NJ: Paulist Press, 1987). The second epigraph, from Wendell Berry's "In Rain," was first published in Berry's *The Wheel* (1982) and is included in his *Collected Poems: 1957–1982* (San Francisco: North Point Press, 1984), 268. All quotations from *Collected Poems* are used with the permission of Counterpoint Press.

1. Wendell Berry, *The Long-Legged House* (Washington, DC: Shoemaker and Hoard, 2004), 141.

2. Ibid., 150.

3. Wendell Berry, "A Native Hill," in *The Art of the Commonplace: The Agrarian Essays of Wendell Berry*, ed. Norman Wirzba (Washington, DC: Counterpoint, 2002), 7.

4. William James, *The Varieties of Religious Experience* (New York: New American Library, 1958), Lectures XVI and XVII. These were the 1901–2 Gifford Lectures.

5. An excellent place to begin, one that submits James's version to sustained analysis and critique, is Nicholas Lash's *Easter in Ordinary: Reflections on Human Experience and the Knowledge of God* (Notre Dame, IN: University of Notre Dame Press, 1988). I have also benefited greatly from Bernard McGinn's magisterial, multivolume history of Western Christian mysticism, especially volume 1, *The Foundations of Mysticism: Origins to the Fifth Century* (New York: Crossroad, 1991), for these general remarks on mysticism.

6. Olivier Clément, *The Roots of Christian Mysticism: Texts from the Patristic Era with Commentary* (New York: New City Press, 1993), 26–35.

7. Quoted in Reiner Schürmann's *Wandering Joy: Meister Eckhart's Mystical Philosophy* (Great Barrington, MA: Lindisfarne Books, 2001), 209.

8. This is another way of saying that God's transcendence is ontological rather than spatial. John of Damascus, an early church father considered to be the "Doctor of the Church" by many Christians, put this point succinctly when he said, "All things are far from God: not in place, but in nature" (*An Exact Exposition of the Christian Faith*, 1.13, in *Saint John of Damascus:*

Writings, trans. Frederic H. Chase [Washington, DC: Catholic University Press of America, 1958], 199).

9. I have developed the "logic of creation" in Part III of *This Sacred Life: Humanity's Place in a Wounded World* (New York: Cambridge University Press, 2021).

10. *The Cloud of Unknowing V* (New York: Doubleday, 1973), 53. The Eckhart quotation is from *Meister Eckhart: From Whom God Hid Nothing: Sermons, Writings, and Sayings*, ed. David O'Neal (Boston: Shambhala, 1996), 108.

11. Thomas Merton, *New Seeds of Contemplation* (New York: New Directions, 1961), 21.

12. Nicholas Lash, "Creation, Courtesy and Contemplation," in *The Beginning and the End of "Religion"* (Cambridge: Cambridge University Press, 1996), 173.

13. Pseudo-Dionysius, *The Divine Names* 4.7, in *The Complete Works* (Mahwah, NJ: Paulist Press, 1987), 77–78. Basil the Great speaks similarly in *Homelia Hexameron* (2.2): "God has united the entire world, which is composed of many different parts, by the law of indissoluble friendship, in communion and harmony, so that the most distant things seem to be joined together by one and the same sympathy."

14. Marcia Bjornerud, *Timefulness: How Thinking Like a Geologist Can Help Save the World* (Princeton, NJ: Princeton University Press, 2018), 7, 15.

15. Tim Ingold, *Correspondences* (Cambridge: Polity Press, 2021), 7. Ingold argues that "for life to carry on, and to flourish, we need to learn to attend to the world around us, and to respond with sensitivity and judgment" (3).

16. Ibid., 11. Ingold says correspondences have three distinguishing properties: "First, every correspondence is a *process*: it carries on. Secondly, correspondence is *open-ended*: it aims for no fixed destination or final conclusion, for everything that might be said or done invites a follow-on. Thirdly, correspondences are *dialogical*. They are not solitary but go on between and among participants" (11).

17. In *The Kindness of God* (Oxford: Oxford University Press, 2008), Janet Martin Soskice shows how the images used to describe the soul's ascent to God can differ dramatically. Whereas Julian of Norwich used metaphors that come from ordinary, daily life (birth, gestation, and domestic life), Augustine of Hippo used mentalist images like willing, remembering, and understanding that give one's ascent a distinctly disembodied feel. Soskice notes that, "in this loss of the body, the female body was particularly at risk, being mired in birth and child-rearing and far from the soaring life of the soul. . . .

Augustine consistently privileged mind over body, sometimes identifying the self with mind alone, and sometimes speaking of the mind as *using* the body" (133). In the history of spirituality, Augustine's approach has been the dominant one.

18. Rowan Williams, "On Being Creatures," in *On Christian Theology* (Oxford: Blackwell, 2000), 76.

19. Rowan Williams, *Teresa of Avila* (Harrisburg, PA: Morehouse, 1991), 145–46.

20. Berry, "Native Hill," 18–19.

21. Wendell Berry, *A Timbered Choir: The Sabbath Poems, 1979–1997* (Washington, DC: Counterpoint, 1998) (hereafter *TC*), 29. All quotations from *A Timbered Choir* are used with the permission of Counterpoint Press.

22. In *Island Zombie: Iceland Writings* (Princeton, NJ: Princeton University Press, 2020), artist Roni Horn echoes Berry when he says, "When you're on a path, you're in the place you're in. There's no distinction between the path and the place itself. The path's a minor clearing, a simple parting. But it's a complex thing because it takes the shape of each place, intimately. . . . A road is not a place. A road is a platonic surface homogenizing with velocity and predictability. A road takes you from here to there and what's in between is merely in between. . . . The road clears everything out of the way, gets you there no nonsense. You're nowhere but on the road when you're on a road; you're not where it is. It's the nature of the road, it takes you out of the place you're in and makes the road the where you are. . . . Roads lack dedication" (27). Horn is making the observation that the culture of Iceland changed significantly when it moved from being a land of paths to a land of roads.

23. James B. Nardi, *Life in the Soil: A Guide for Naturalists and Gardeners* (Chicago: University of Chicago Press, 2007), 18.

24. Among botanists, Suzanne Simard is one of the pioneer foresters to draw our attention to the complex underground life of a tree. Far from being solitary organisms confined to a discrete plot of land, trees share life with others through root systems that in their entanglements defy comprehension. Trees are social, cooperative beings that live through root meshworks that share nutrients and communicate vitality and vulnerability. See *Finding the Mother Tree: Discovering the Wisdom of the Forest* (New York: Alfred A. Knopf, 2021).

25. David George Haskell, *The Forest Unseen: A Year's Watch in Nature* (New York: Penguin Books, 2012), 229 (my emphasis).

26. I have developed this insight in chapter 3 of *This Sacred Life*.

27. Berry, "Native Hill," 29.

28. "It is the creation that has attracted me, its perfect interfusion of life and design. I have made myself its follower and apprentice" (ibid., 24).

29. Ibid., 27.

30. Ibid., 24–25.

31. For further information, see "Durham Pilgrimage of Pain and Hope," DurhamCares, https://durhamcares.org/pilgrimage/.

32. It is important to note that the nurturing movement that roots embody is not one-directional. As plants draw nutrition from their soil environments, they also transform the energy of the sun into sugars that are sent down to the roots to feed the soil's micro-organismic life. In other words, plants contribute to the soil fertility that nurtures them. They are conduits that give and receive nurture. In this respect, they serve as powerful models of how people can act as conduits that are constantly receiving and extending the life-giving power of God.

33. In *The Ascent of Mount Carmel*, St. John of the Cross alludes to the dark night when he says that divine truth exceeds every natural light and all human understanding. He writes: "The excessive light of faith bestowed on man is darkness for him, because a brighter light will eclipse and suppress a dimmer one. The sun so obscures all other lights that they do not seem to be lights at all when it is shining, and instead of affording vision to the eyes it overwhelms, blinds, and deprives them of vision, since its light is excessive and unproportioned to the visual faculty. Similarly the light of faith in its abundance suppresses and overwhelms that of the intellect" (*The Ascent of Mount Carmel* 2.3, in *The Collected Works of St. John of the Cross*, trans. Kieran Kavanaugh, O.C.D., and Otilio Rodriguez, O.C.D. [Washington, DC: ICS Publications, 1979], 110). Pseudo-Dionysius reminds us that it is even improper to stay with the image of darkness. In *The Mystical Theology* (bk. 5), he says, "There is no speaking of it, nor name nor knowledge of it. Darkness and light, error and truth—it is none of these. It is beyond assertion and denial" (in *Complete Works*, 141).

34. Augustine argues that in turning our backs to the divine light that sustains all things we also darken our minds and the world and thus bring destruction to each (*Confessions* 4.30).

35. In this respect, Berry is in agreement with Augustine about the priority of love in the order of knowing. In his *Homilies on the Psalms* Augustine notes that we become fully conscious of God only insofar as love grows in us, because God is love. "Before you had the experience [of love], you used to think you could speak of God. You begin to have the experience, and there

you experience that you cannot say what you experience" (quoted in Mc-Ginn's *Foundations of Mysticism*, 241).

36. Here Berry joins hands with other "traditionalist" critics of modernity like Ananda Coomaraswamy, Kathleen Raine, and Philip Sherrard. In a tribute to Kathleen Raine he describes the nihilism of modernity as the desecration of humanity, once thought to be made in the image of God but now reduced to being little more than a "higher" animal. With this desecration came "the implied permission to be more bewildered, violent, self-deluded, destructive, and self-destructive than any of the animals" (Wendell Berry, "Against the Nihil of the Age," *Temenos Academy Review*, 2004, 82).

37. Berry observes that even our best attempts to heal are not without damage and pain. "An art that heals and protects its subject is a geography of scars" (*What Are People For?* [New York: North Point Press, 1990], 7). In this short text "Damage," Berry reflects on his effort to repair the destruction caused by his desire to have a pond midway up a slope in one of his fields.

38. Wendell Berry, *Collected Poems: 1957–1982* (San Francisco: North Point Press, 1984), 110, hereafter cited as *CP* with page numbers to this edition.

39. Agrarian practices that work the soil, sow the seed, and harvest the fruit are ideal for the cultivation of this understanding. As Berry observes of a farmer who grows food, he "enters into death / yearly, and comes back rejoicing. He has seen the light lie down / in the dung heap, and rise again in the corn" (*CP*, 103). Cf. also "The seed is in the ground. / Now may we rest in hope / While darkness does its work" (*TC*, 131). But as Berry also knows, this is a difficult hope, since crop failure is an ever-present reality.

40. This chapter is a revised version of my essay "The Dark Night of the Soil: An Agrarian Approach to Mystical Life," *Christianity and Literature* 56, no. 2 (Winter 2007).

SEVEN.   Learning Humility

The epigraph by Simone Weil is from *Gravity and Grace* (New York: Routledge, 1963), 27.

1. Erinn Gilson, *The Ethics of Vulnerability: A Feminist Analysis of Social Life and Practice* (London: Taylor and Francis Group, 2014), 9.

2. Anne Dufourmantelle, *Power of Gentleness: Meditations on the Risk of Living*, trans. Katherine Payne and Vincent Sallé (New York: Fordham University Press, 2018), 14.

3. Jean-Louis Chrétien, *The Call and the Response*, trans. Anne A. Davenport (New York: Fordham University Press, 2004), 123.

4. Ibid., 1.

5. Ibid., 14.

6. Simone Weil, *Gravity and Grace* (New York: Routledge, 1963), 29 and 27.

7. Bernard of Clairvaux defined humility as "the virtue by which a man recognizes his own unworthiness because he really knows himself" ("On the Steps of Humility and Pride," in *Bernard of Clairvaux: Selected Works*, trans. G. R. Evans [New York: Paulist Press, 1987], 103). Bernard, who is here following Augustine in his definition, reflects a common view within spiritual literature.

8. Consider here the sobering observations of Pascal (*Pensées*, trans. A. J. Krailsheimer [Harmondsworth: Penguin, 1966]): "When I consider the brief span of my life absorbed into the eternity which comes before and after . . . the small space I occupy and which I see swallowed up in the infinite immensity of spaces of which I know nothing and which know nothing of me, I take fright and am amazed to see myself here rather than there: there is no reason for me to be here rather than there, now rather than then. Who put me here?" (48), and "Man is only a reed, the weakest in nature, but he is a thinking reed. There is no need for the whole universe to take up arms to crush him: a vapour, a drop of water is enough to kill him" (95).

9. Norvin Richards, "Is Humility a Virtue?," *American Philosophical Quarterly* 25, no. 3 (July 1988): 253 (italics in the original). Richards uses as his example Bernard of Clairvaux, who says (in Sermon 42 on Canticle 6), "If you examine yourself inwardly by the light of truth and without dissimulation, and judge yourself without flattery; no doubt you will be humbled in your eyes, becoming contemptible in your own sight as a result of this true knowledge of yourself." Richards observes that, outside of an allegiance to the archaic belief in original sin, this "depressing view is not obviously correct. In fact, it is difficult to see a reason to hold it" (253). As we will see, Richards has failed to consider what it means to be a creature.

10. For a profound and detailed account of John's depiction of Jesus's ministries and instruction as ways of leading people into a "life of love," see David F. Ford's *The Gospel of John: A Theological Commentary* (Grand Rapids, MI: Baker Academic, 2021). The meaning and the goal of the whole of reality are for it to participate in the divine love that exists between the Son and the Father and that has been made incarnate in the life of Jesus.

11. Weil, *Gravity and Grace*, 35, 30, 35.

12. One aspect of human vulnerability is that people do not get to choose the soil they are planted in. Denuded or toxic soils either impair or deny proper growth and development. This is why care of the soil, understood as an ecological and a social reality, is an essential human task.

13. Ibid., 36.

14. For an excellent treatment of creation *ex nihilo*, how it developed and why it matters, see Ian A. McFarland's *From Nothing: A Theology of Creation* (Louisville, KY: Westminster John Knox, 2015), and chapter 6 in my book *This Sacred Life: Humanity's Place in a Wounded World* (New York: Cambridge University Press, 2021).

15. Christopher Cullen argues that for Bonaventure "The summary of the whole of Christian perfection consists in humility" (*Bonaventure* [Oxford: Oxford University Press, 2006], 13).

16. Ibid.

17. The story of how technology became the new sacred is worked out clearly in Bronislaw Szerszynski's *Nature, Technology and the Sacred* (Oxford: Blackwell, 2005). See also David Noble's less technical rendering in *The Religion of Technology: The Divinity of Man and the Spirit of Invention* (New York: Penguin Books, 1997). In certain respects, humanity's love affair with technology can be described as the attempt to install human beings as the new gods of the earth and thus to remove the Creator who makes the logic of humility intelligible.

18. Insofar as we engage others in terms of what they can do for us, they cannot be understood on their own terms. This is why humility is an essential epistemological virtue. To know others we must first attend to them as they are rather than as we want them to be. This is why Iris Murdoch says, "The humble man, because he sees himself as nothing, can see other things as they are" (*The Sovereignty of Good* [London: Routledge, 1970], 103–4). Earlier in the text she elaborates by saying humility is a "selfless respect for reality and one of the most difficult and central of all virtues" (95). Weil is in agreement with this epistemological insight when she says, "In the intellectual order, the virtue of humility is nothing more nor less than the power of attention" (*Gravity and Grace*, 116).

19. Jean-Louis Chrétien, "Retrospection," in *The Unforgettable and the Unhoped For*, trans. Jeffrey Bloechl (New York: Fordham University Press, 2002), 119.

20. Jean-Yves Lacoste, *Experience and the Absolute: Disputed Questions on the Humanity of Man* (New York: Fordham University Press, 2004), 8.

21. In *Touch: Recovering Our Most Vital Sense* (New York: Columbia University Press, 2021), Richard Kearney describes how Plato bequeathed a picture of humans as spectators of existence who "stand apart" from the world they live within so as to examine it and who "look upwards" and away from this world to discern the truth about it. "For Plato the eye is sovereign. The tactile body is a beast of burden and contagion to be kept in place" (33). For a more detailed description of the history of the dominance of sight in Western philosophical traditions, see *Modernity and the Hegemony of Vision*, ed. David Michael Levin (Berkeley: University of California Press, 1993).

22. Chrétien, *Call and the Response*, 85.

23. Ibid., 117.

24. Jacques Derrida wonders if touch is not best understood as "unrepresentable presence." See *On Touching—Jean-Luc Nancy*, trans. Christine Irizarry (Stanford, CA: Stanford University Press, 2005), 250. Chrétien agrees, saying, "Touch veils itself" (*Call and the Response*, 87).

25. Kearney, *Touch*, 44–45.

26. Ibid., 90. Kearney gives a helpful guide to recent research that emphasizes the role of the "emotional brain" (as compared to brains characterized in cognitivist terms) in healing therapies. This emotional brain is closely tied to the experiences of a feeling body.

27. Chrétien, "Retrospection," 122.

28. Chrétien, *Call and the Response*, 13.

29. Graham Ward, *Christ and Culture* (Oxford: Blackwell, 2005), 1.

30. Ibid., 76.

31. Rowan Williams, *On Christian Theology* (Oxford: Blackwell, 2000), 72.

32. Chrétien, *Call and the Response*, 120.

33. In Christian ritual and liturgical life it is the Lord's Supper where this dynamic is presented again and again. Disciples consume Jesus as the "bread of life," and by taking his flesh into their own flesh they ask to be transformed to live the embodied life that his ministries model. For further treatment of this theme, see chapter 6 of my *Food and Faith: A Theology of Eating*, 2nd ed. (New York: Cambridge University Press, 2019).

34. Henry David Thoreau, *The Journal, 1837–1861*, ed. Damion Searls (New York: New York Review Books, 2009), 90–91.

35. As quoted in Branka Arsic's *Bird Relics: Grief and Vitalism in Thoreau* (Cambridge, MA: Harvard University Press, 2016), 42. Arsic is clear that Thoreau wants to resist spiritual pursuits that call people to look upward to a divine realm beyond this material world. He wants them to search here below

for whatever heaven there might be. Where I part with Thoreau is when he sometimes collapses the divine into matter itself. Though I affirm God's intimate presence in creatures as the breath of life moving within every creaturely breath, I also believe it is important to affirm God's transcendence as the one who creates life and loves it as a sacred gift.

36. Julian Johnson, "Music Language Dwelling," in *Theology, Music, and Modernity*, ed. Jeremy Begbie, Daniel K. L. Chua, and Markus Rathey (Oxford: Oxford University Press, 2021), 309.

37. Ibid., 313.

38. "The Nightingale's Song: An Interview with Sam Lee," *Emergence Magazine*, June 7, 2021, https://emergencemagazine.org/interview/the-nightingales-song/.

39. Jeremy Begbie, *Music, Modernity, and God: Essays in Listening* (Oxford: Oxford University Press, 2013), 161.

40. This chapter is a much-revised version of my essay "The Touch of Humility: An Invitation to Creatureliness," *Modern Theology* 24, no. 2 (April 2008): 225–44.

EIGHT.   Learning Generosity

The Hyde epigraph is from *The Gift: Creativity and the Artist in the Modern World* (New York: Vintage Books, 2007), 60.

1. Peter Sloterdijk, *In the World Interior of Capital: For a Philosophical Theory of Globalization*, trans. Wieland Hoban (Cambridge: Polity Press, 2013), 208. Though money has circulated in economies for a very long time, it is with the imperial and colonial ambitions that define modern Europe that money becomes an earth and life-altering force. "The primary fact of the Modern Age was not that the earth goes around the sun, but that money goes around the earth" (46).

2. The metaphysical implications of a covenantal sensibility are enormous because what is at issue is what people believe the nature of reality to be. Reality is not impersonal, nor is it made up of individuals. It is personal and communal, with a personal God constantly facing creatures as they face each other. As early Christian theologians reflected on the nature of reality in light of the triune, social character of God's life as revealed in scripture and as made incarnate in Jesus and the power of the Holy Spirit, they rejected the substance metaphysics of Greek philosophy and argued that being is social. For a lucid description of this crucial insight, see John Zizioulas's *Being*

as Communion: Studies in Personhood and the Church (Crestwood, NY: St. Vladimir's Seminary Press, 1997).

3. Marcel Hénaff, *The Price of Truth: Gift, Money, and Philosophy* (Stanford, CA: Stanford University Press, 2010), 20–21.

4. In *The Dismal Science: How Thinking Like an Economist Undermines Community* (Cambridge, MA: Harvard University Press, 2008), Stephen Marglin agrees with Hénaff and argues that mainstream economic theory assumes that people are self-interested, calculating individuals who turn to markets to satisfy self-chosen aims. "By promoting market relationships, economics undermines reciprocity, altruism, and mutual obligation, and therewith the necessity of community" (27).

5. In the landmark essay "The Metropolis and Mental Life," published in 1903, the sociologist and philosopher Georg Simmel described how at the dawn of the twentieth century the migration of people from villages to cities—along with the new forms of labor, the intensification of one's reliance on money and impersonal forms of exchange, and the development of new forms of housing this migration entailed—had the effect of creating a "blasé outlook" in people. This outlook developed as a coping strategy in response to the speed, stimulation, and anonymity of urban spaces. Rather than turning outward, people retreated and turned inward. This new form of life changed in fundamental ways how people perceived and related to each other.

> The essence of the blasé attitude is an indifference toward the distinctions between things. Not in the sense that they are not perceived, as in the case of mental dullness, but rather that the meaning and value of the distinctions between things, and therewith of the things themselves, are experienced as meaningless. They appear to the blasé person in a homogenous, flat and gray color with no one of them worthy of being preferred to another. This psychic mood is the correct subjective reflection of a complete money economy to the extent that money takes the place of all the manifoldness of things and expresses all qualitative distinctions between them in the distinction of "how much." To the extent that money, with its colorlessness and its indifferent quality, can become a common denominator of all values it becomes the frightful leveler—it hollows out the core of things, their peculiarities, their specific values and their uniqueness and incomparability in a way which is beyond repair.

In *Georg Simmel on Individuality and Social Forms*, ed. Donald N. Levine (Chicago: University of Chicago Press, 1971), 329–30. Simmel saw that the development of an environment-induced blasé outlook was of the greatest social significance because it created in people attitudes of indifference, aversion, strangeness, and even repulsion. The freedoms promised by modern urban life were thus premised on people extricating themselves from communal bonds. As Simmel noted, "The metropolis places emphasis on striving for the most individual forms of personal existence" (337).

6. In multiple stories Franz Kafka explored, often in harrowing detail, what it feels like to live in a bureaucratic world where personal care and responsibility have been evacuated. This is a world in which people are reducible to being cogs in a brutalizing machine, losers in a pointless game, even vermin best suited for eradication.

7. It is telling that Amish communities have understood better than most how various technological devices can work to undermine a covenantal sensibility. Modes of transport and communication, but also certain kinds of agricultural machinery, have been rejected because they erode and weaken the bonds that join people to each other and the land. By contrast, Hutterite communities have embraced the latest, biggest, and most sophisticated machines as a way of boosting agricultural productivity. Though they espouse communal values, the use of these technologies has instrumentalized and contractualized their relationships to the land and their farm animals.

8. Alexander Schmemann, *The Eucharist: Sacrament of the Kingdom*, trans. Paul Kachur (Crestwood, NY: St. Vladimir's Seminary Press, 1987), 176.

9. It is important to stress, again, that the idea of *life with God* is fundamentally about this life's *transformation* rather than its *transportation* to another place. Moreover, "eternal life" should not be characterized simply as "unending" or "everlasting" life, since that is hardly good news to people if the life they currently experience is not inspired and animated by love. The overall aim of John's gospel is to bring people into the loving way of being that exists between Jesus the Son and God the Father. For a masterful articulation of how followers of Jesus learn to participate in the divine way of being, see David F. Ford's *The Gospel of John: A Theological Commentary* (Grand Rapids, MI: Baker Academic, 2021).

10. Thomas Traherne, *Centuries of Meditations* 2.62, in *Poems, Centuries, and Three Thanksgivings*, ed. Anne Ridler (Oxford: Oxford University Press, 1966).

11. C. S. Lewis, *The Collected Letters of C. S. Lewis*, vol. 1, *Family Letters, 1905–1931*, ed. Walter Hooper (New York: Harper San Francisco, 2004), 909. For an insightful discussion of Lewis on these matters, see Matthew Dickerson

and David O'Hara's *Narnia and the Fields of Arbol: The Environmental Vision of C. S. Lewis* (Lexington: University Press of Kentucky, 2009).

12. Fredric Jameson first made the claim in *The Seeds of Time* (New York: Columbia University Press, 1994), and then again in the article "Future City" (*New Left Review* 21 [May/June 2003]: 76). The latter article clarifies that Jameson was commenting on an observation by H. Bruce Franklin that some people might mistake the end of capitalism for the end of the world. That so many people have quoted this saying indicates its resonant power.

13. Wendell Berry, "Faustian Economics," in *Wendell Berry: Essays, 1993–2017*, ed. Jack Shoemaker (New York: Library of America, 2019), 452.

14. This is why God says (in Exodus 20:25) that any altars made of stone must use unhewn stone, that is, stone with no chisel marks. The point of coming to an altar is to commune with God by acknowledging God as the generous source of one's life. Chisel marks would distract by turning one's attention to one's own efforts. This way of thinking follows directly from the declaration that the Promised Land belongs to and is watched over and provided for by God. Israelite land is not Egyptian land that is managed and irrigated by people to maximize yield and thereby draw attention to a farmer's abilities. No, "The land that you are crossing over to occupy is a land of hills and valleys, watered by rain from the sky, a land that the Lord your God looks after. The eyes of the Lord your God are always on it, from the beginning of the year to the end of the year" (Deuteronomy 11:10–12). The overarching point is that ultimately it is God who feeds his people. Though people clearly play an important role in growing food, even learn crucial lessons in the growing of it, the moment they think food is something they create and control is also the moment that food is likely to be hoarded or weaponized.

15. In chapter 5 of my book *Food and Faith: A Theology of Eating*, 2nd ed. (New York: Cambridge University Press, 2019), I give a more detailed description of sacrifice as it developed in ancient Israel and of the theo-logic that governs its authentic practice.

16. It is important to note that the prophets issued a denunciation of sacrifice not because it was bad but because it had been perverted. Hosea (6:6) proclaimed that what God wants is not burnt offerings but hearts of steadfast love, while Isaiah (1:10–17) pointed to the incongruity of people who offer "sacrifices" while forsaking the oppressed, the widows, and orphans. The nation of Israel had become sick and unjust, with people using sacrifice to establish and publicize their standing in society. The heart of the prophetic critique focused on people confusing self-assertion with self-offering. If people were committed to offering themselves they would love those around them and oppression of others would cease. This means that the idea of sacrifice

should never be used as the basis or justification for the degradation of any person, creature, or place. That political leaders, economists, and power mongers regularly call on citizens, workers, and women to sacrifice themselves for another's ambition is a degradation of the term. That regions are turned into "sacrifice zones" in which places and communities are exploited for their wealth and then abandoned signals a perverse inversion of what sacrifice is and what it is meant to accomplish.

17. In *Christianity's Surprise: A Sure and Certain Hope* (Nashville, TN: Abingdon Press, 2020), C. Kavin Rowe reminds us about how surprising and transformative these Christian practices were, especially when understood in light of a Roman world that functioned according to very different assumptions about what a human being is and how people should live.

18. Willie James Jennings, *Acts* (Louisville, KY: Westminster John Knox Press, 2017), 39.

19. James Baldwin, *"The Black Scholar* Interviews James Baldwin," in *Conversations with James Baldwin,* ed. Fred L. Standley and Louis H. Pratt (Jackson: University Press of Mississippi, 1989). Baldwin was well aware that Christian churches regularly failed in the correcting power of love. The desires for privilege and prestige, but also a mischaracterization of the power of God as modeled on the white man's control and domination of (especially black) others, meant that church life was often not the performance of the Spirit-inspired participation of people in God's generous, giving ways. People did not truly face each other or learn to see the things they most needed to see because they kept looking at mirrors that reflected back whatever they wanted to see. Baldwin insisted that love "takes off the masks that we fear we cannot live without and know we cannot live within" (in "Down at the Crossroads," originally published in *The Fire Next Time* and reprinted in *Collected Essays,* ed. Toni Morrison [New York: Library of America, 1998], 341).

NINE.   Learning to Hope

The second epigraph is from Linda Hogan's *Dwellings: A Spiritual History of the Living World* (New York: Norton, 1995), 76.

1. Wendell Berry. "Discipline and Hope," in *A Continuous Harmony: Essays Cultural and Agricultural* (New York: Harcourt Brace Jovanovich, 1972), 131.

2. In *Juvenescence: A Cultural History of Our Age* (Chicago: University of Chicago Press, 2014), Robert Pogue Harrison argues that "the greatest blessing a society can confer on its young is to turn them into the heirs, rather than

the orphans, of history. It is also the greatest blessing a society can confer upon itself, for heirs rejuvenate the heritage by creatively renewing its legacies. Orphans, by contrast, relate to the past as an alien, unapproachable continent—if they relate to it all" (xi–xii). Becoming an heir, however, is anything but simple, especially if one's inheritance is saturated with violence and injustice. As Zadie Smith has shown, if people turn to the past, it is not obvious what they expect history to do for them. Will it be to confirm the rightness of their own position, or condemn the position of others? To seek revenge? Looking back, we soon discover "an unholy mix of the true and the false." Reflecting on the artist Kara Walker's efforts to present America's racist past, Smith writes: "Walker operates on the premise that when you make history truly visible, both your own and that of your people or nation, there exists a challenge to show all of it, the unholy mix, the conscious knowledge and subconscious reaction, the traumatic history and the trauma it has created, the unprocessed and the unprocessable. If you manage this it will be, by definition, *de trop*. But then again, too much for whom?" ("What Do We Want History to Do to Us?," *New York Review of Books*, February 27, 2020, 12). It is anything but simple to determine what an appropriate response to a ruinous history looks like. As I will argue in this essay, practices of confession and repentance should be central to this effort.

3. Lesley Head, *Hope and Grief in the Anthropocene: Re-conceptualizing Human-Nature Relations* (London: Routledge, 2016). See also *Mourning Nature: Hope at the Heart of Ecological Loss and Grief,* ed. Ashlee Cunsolo and Karen Landman (Montreal: McGill-Queen's University Press, 2017), for a collection of essays exploring the varied dimensions of grief in the face of ecological loss.

4. Kathryn Yusoff, "Aesthetics of Loss: Biodiversity, Banal Violence and Biotic Subjects," *Transactions of the Institute of British Geographers* 37 (2012): 578–92.

5. In *A Human Being Died That Night: A South African Woman Confronts the Legacy of Apartheid* (Boston: Houghton Mifflin, 2003), Pumla Gobodo-Madikizela gives an insightful and nuanced account of the relationship between justice and forgiveness as these are worked out in personal and political contexts. She argues that forgiveness "does not necessarily bring finality because it does not erase the past" (132). It works to bring about the transformation of persons and systems that is central to a hopeful life and to the creation of communities in which people commit to ongoing life together.

6. Paul Ricoeur, "Difficult Forgiveness," in *Memory, History, Forgetting*, trans. Kathleen Blamey and David Pellauer (Chicago: University of Chicago

Press, 2006), 457–506. To offer forgiveness makes as little rational sense as the idea of loving an enemy and believing that through such love the enemy will become a friend. To be forgiven, in turn, is to be bewildered by a mercy one does not deserve.

7. I am immensely grateful to Don and Marie Ruzicka for sharing their story with me, and to Don for his willingness to share some of his unpublished writing with me and for responding to multiple questions. A website for the farm can be found at www.sunrisefarm.ca.

8. This new push did not arise in a historical vacuum. It was preceded and informed by decades of economic and political policies that prepared the way for industrial agricultural development. Jim Selby observes: "Beginning in 1897, the pace of westward migration had accelerated. Lured by the promise of free homesteads, the rising international price of wheat, and government propaganda, tens of thousands of would-be farmers from central and eastern Canada and from Europe moved to the Canadian prairies" ("One Step Forward: Alberta Workers, 1885–1914," in *Working People in Alberta: A History*, ed. Alvin Finkel [Edmonton: Athabasca University Press, 2014], 71). In the decades following, volatile grain prices, unfavorable weather, and increasing mechanization led to ever-larger farms controlled by a smaller number of people, while ever-smaller profit margins for farmers necessitated maximization of yield. Smaller profit margins for farmers also went hand in hand with increased costs for machinery and farm inputs like fertilizers and herbicides.

9. In *Sources of the Self: The Making of the Modern Identity* (Cambridge, MA: Harvard University Press, 1992), Charles Taylor describes the modern scientific pursuit of objectivity as a desire to reduce the world's moral hold on people.

10. In *Braiding Sweetgrass* (Minneapolis, MN: Milkweed, 2020), Robin Kimmerer notes that the transformation of land into private property has rendered settlers incapable of feeling this love. Indigenous people have long known that the land and its many plant and animal creatures are medicine and food for everyone. The fundamental task is to learn to be good medicine to the land in return.

11. In *Wilding: Returning Nature to Our Farm* (New York: New York Review of Books, 2018), Isabella Tree describes how difficult it is for anyone to know what forms of life are appropriate for a place. She recounts the words of the Dutch ecologist Frans Vera, who says, "We've become trapped by our own observations. We forget, in a world completely transformed by man, that what we're looking at is not necessarily the environment wildlife prefer, but the depleted remnant that wildlife is having to cope with: what it has is not

necessarily what it wants. Species may be surviving at the very limits of their range, clinging on in conditions that don't necessarily suit them. Open up the box, allow natural processes to develop, give species a wider scope to express themselves, and you get a very different picture. . . . Minimal intervention. Letting nature reveal herself. And the result is an environment we know nothing about" (58).

12. Ellen Meiksins Wood, *The Origin of Capitalism: A Longer View* (London: Verso, 2017), 95. Wood argues that there is nothing natural or inevitable about the modern capitalist logic. It came to be in the specific context of English agrarian economies that were driven to "improve" land to maximize production for profit. Once this market imperative was put in place, "All economic actors . . . [were] subject to the demands of competition, increasing productivity, capital accumulation, and the intense exploitation of labor" (195). When farms and farmers are required to serve market demands for profit, their exploitation is practically guaranteed.

13. In *Capitalism in the Web of Life: Ecology and the Accumulation of Capital* (London: Verso, 2015), Jason Moore argues that capitalism is much more than an economic system operating in the same world as previously understood. It is fundamentally "a way of organizing nature" (2), which is to say that in the reorganizing of nature according to a new capitalist value structure, all relations, including the economic and social, are transformed with it.

14. It is also important to note that farmers work within an agricultural aesthetic that makes it difficult to imagine a different way to farm. Tree describes how in Britain the aesthetic embraced by farmers and urbanites alike is a manicured land, a "patchwork of neatly hedged fields dotted with mature trees and small copses, framed by bare rolling hills and slow-flowing rivers," all populated, we might add, by a shepherd and his sheep. As folks encountered the rewilding efforts that Tree was undertaking at her farm, their response was visceral in its disdain. Rather than seeing nature expressing itself in all sorts of fertile and fecund ways, they saw "quite a mess," a "foreign land," a place that looked "totally abandoned, like nobody cares for it anymore." Efforts to rewild the land "smacked of laziness, irresponsibility, even immorality. It was uncivilized, a 'backward step.' To some it was 'wanton vandalism'" (*Wilding*, 129–30).

15. In *Influx and Efflux: Writing Up with Walt Whitman* (Durham, NC: Duke University Press, 2020), Jane Bennett traces several ways in which people are susceptible to the influences of nonhuman actors and argues for the cultivation of capacities for sympathy for a world that is open to human habitation. In *The Sympathy of Things: Ruskin and the Ecology of Design* (Lon-

don: Bloomsbury, 2016), Lars Spuybroek shows how the multiple dimensions of sympathy transform our thinking about the human place in the world and make possible a radical reconceiving of the work of designing built environments in response to a given world.

16. My point is not to deny that one can be in a resonant relationship with *things*. To understand why, consider the relationship a musician has with his or her instrument, or a chef with his or her kitchen utensils. Both the musician and the chef have learned through years of practice how best to handle their devices, and in their handling they produce beautiful music and delicious dishes. Instruments and utensils become, in a sense, extensions of their bodies in such a way that their personalities communicate through their use. Not just any guitar or knife will do because each instrument or utensil has better and worse qualities and thus embodies different possibilities for their use. This is why musicians and chefs often express affection for the instruments and utensils they use and voice considerable sadness over their loss. Their use of things isn't simply instrumental or utilitarian. It is also governed by the sort of affection that communicates resonance.

17. Hartmut Rosa, *Resonance: A Sociology of Our Relationship to the World*, trans. James C. Wagner (Cambridge: Polity Press, 2019), 214. Rosa provides a detailed treatment of the many ways resonance has been eroded in modernity and how these developments have rendered the world mute and selves alienated and alone. Deploying the terms of Martin Buber, he argues that the cultivating of resonant relationships depends on people rejecting the commodifying, instrumentalizing, reifying procedures that reduce the world to an "it" and making themselves open to and vulnerable before a world perceived as a "thou."

18. In *Caring for Souls in a Neoliberal Age* (New York: Palgrave Macmillan, 2016), Bruce Rogers-Vaughn gives an insightful analysis of the ways in which neoliberal commitments and priorities undermine mental health. He makes a powerful case for the reinvigoration of communal modes of being that nurture and support personal life.

19. J. R. McNeill and Peter Engelke, *The Great Acceleration: An Environmental History of the Anthropocene since 1945* (Cambridge, MA: Belknap Press of Harvard University Press, 2014).

20. In *Social Acceleration: A New Theory of Modernity* (New York: Columbia University Press, 2013), Hartmut Rosa argues that the increased speed of life is not simply about how individual people experience and inhabit time but more fundamentally about how economic, social, work, technological, and infrastructure developments compel people to live differently in time.

21. Purdy argues that a commonwealth politics is a robustly democratic politics because people must come together to decide the terms of their shared life and to assess what true wealth is. It is also a hopeful politics, I would argue, because "in a commonwealth economy, we should root ourselves in helping the world, human and natural, to go on being" (*This Land Is Our Land: The Struggle for a New Commonwealth* [Princeton, NJ: Princeton University Press, 2019], 148). "It will take great acts of democratic will to say what is valuable for us, what we want to orient our entire built world toward cultivating and preserving: the unbroken flow of life and caregiving, human and nonhuman. In a commonwealth—which we might also call a democratic Anthropocene— value will lie in work that does what is necessary and sustains its own conditions of possibility, in rest that contemplates a broken but still wondrous world, in play that keeps joy vivid among monuments and ruins and helps ensure that new life will grow there. No one can choose these values alone because they depend on the shared commitments of others and on the shape and terms of a built and shared world. The heroic work of building that world must clear the space for living humbly. We need extraordinary acts to serve the most common things. It will seem less heroic, more ordinary, if it is the work of many hands, and that is the only way it will truly come" (150).

SCRIPTURE INDEX

GENERAL INDEX

abuse, 14, 24, 105, 142, 167, 169, 188,
205n43, 208n18
  bodies, 45
  creatures, 73, 77
  as dead end, 79
  land, 188
  See also violence
Adamson, Glenn, on material intelligence, 16–17
African American farmers, 24
Age of Loneliness. *See* Eremocene
agrarian
  Black agrarians, 25–26
  defined, 15, 21, 45, 57
  Jesus as, 57–58
agrarianism, xiii, 14
agriculture, 12
  abusive, 205n43
  industrial, 182, 187
  regenerative, 160
Amish, 160–61, 227n7
Anaxagoras, 89
Anthropocene, xi, 12, 23, 36–37, 45,
179, 193, 201nn12–13,
234n21
Apostles' Creed, 57
apprentice/apprenticeship, 18, 75, 122,
125–26, 220n28. *See also*
correspondence

Aristotle, 22
  and Chrétien, 142
  on place, 38
  on prayer, 62, 207n1
art, 16, 64–65
askesis
  of Christian living, 94–95, 104–6
  of competition, 91
  defined, 89
  husbandry as, 101–2
  See also *ethos*; *theoria*
attention
  ecologies of, 67–68 (*see also* Citton,
Yves)
  exhaustion, 69 (*see also* economy)
  to history, 124
  and humility, 223n18
  and Jesus, 70–75
  to land, 184–85
  and making, 19
  to others, 158
  to place, 140
  practice of, 63–70, 207n9
  and prayer, 85–86, 101, 119
  and rituals, 171, 173
Augustine, Saint, 33–34, 200n6,
218n17
  and Berry, 220n34
autonomy, 133

NORMAN WIRZBA is the Gilbert T. Rowe Distinguished Professor of Christian Theology at Duke Divinity School and senior fellow at the Kenan Institute for Ethics at Duke University. He is the author and editor of sixteen books, including *This Sacred Life: Humanity's Place in a Wounded World*.

Milton Keynes UK
Ingram Content Group UK Ltd.
UKHW010237080224
437347UK00022B/259